TO STEPHANIE

AND THE NEW ARRIVALS, TED AND ARTHUR

Wrath of God

ALSO BY EDWARD PAICE

Lost Lion of Empire: The Life of 'Cape-to-Cairo' Grogan

Tip & Run: The Untold Tragedy of the Great War in Africa

Wrath of God

The Great Lisbon Earthquake of 1755

EDWARD PAICE

Quercus

First published in Great Britain in 2008 by
Quercus
21 Bloomsbury Square
London WC1A 2NS

Copyright © 2008 by Edward Paice

A CIP catalogue record for this book is available from the British Library

ISBN 978 1 84724 623 3

10 9 8 7 6 5 4 3 2 1

Picture acknowledgements are reproduced on p. 269

Contents

List of Illustrations

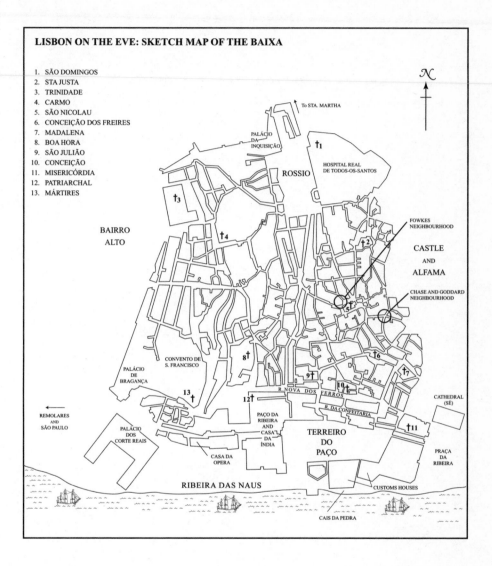

LISBON ON THE EVE: SKETCH MAP OF THE BAIXA

1. SÃO DOMINGOS
2. STA JUSTA
3. TRINIDADE
4. CARMO
5. SÃO NICOLAU
6. CONCEIÇÃO DOS FREIRES
7. MADALENA
8. BOA HORA
9. SÃO JULIÃO
10. CONCEIÇÃO
11. MISERICÓRDIA
12. PATRIARCHAL
13. MÁRTIRES

To STA. MARTHA

PALÁCIO DA INQUISIÇÃO

ROSSIO

HOSPITAL REAL DE TODOS-OS-SANTOS

BAIRRO ALTO

FOWKES NEIGHBOURHOOD

CASTLE AND ALFAMA

CHASE AND GODDARD NEIGHBOURHOOD

CONVENTO DE S. FRANCISCO

PALÁCIO DE BRAGANÇA

R. NOVA DOS FERROS

CATHEDRAL (SÉ)

R. DA CONFEITARIA

REMOLARES AND SÃO PAULO

PALÁCIO DOS CORTE REAIS

PAÇO DA RIBEIRA AND CASA DA ÍNDIA

TERREIRO DO PAÇO

PRAÇA DA RIBEIRA

CASA DA OPERA

RIBEIRA DAS NAUS

CUSTOMS HOUSES

CAIS DA PEDRA

Acknowledgements

I WOULD LIKE TO THANK THE FOLLOWING for answering queries, providing me with interesting leads, or extending some other kindness: Professor Miguel Telles Antunes (Director of the Museum at the Academia das Ciências de Lisboa, for showing me around the excavations of the recently discovered mass grave), Ana Catarina Almeida (at the Faculdade de Letras da Universidade de Lisboa), Professor Alison Blakely, GMD Booth (Senior Archivist at Warwickshire County Council, the repository of John Dobson's papers), Ann Branton (at *The Southern Quarterly*), Max Edelson (at the University of Illinois at Urbana-Champaign, for letting me see his paper 'All May Fall: The Commercial Impact of the Lisbon Earthquake of 1755 on the British Atlantic World' presented to the 2006 Annual Meeting of the Social Science History Association in Minneapolis), David Edmunds (proprietor of John Drury Rare Books, for letting me read, and quote from, Benjamin Farmer's manuscript 'Some Account of Timothy Quidnunc the author by the editor'), Lynn Finn (at the Centre for Kentish Studies, the repository of a copy of the Thomas Chase manuscript), Maria Alexandre Lousada (at the Centro de Estudos Geográficos, Universidade de Lisboa), Dr Paulo Lowndes Marques, OBE, and the British Historical Society of Portugal, Bill

Monaghan (at the Norfolk Record Office, the repository of Henry Hobart's papers), Oliver Nicholson, David Powell (at the Congregational Library, the repository of *Lisbon's voice to England, particularly to London*, attributed to Samuel Hayward), Emma Rainforth (at the History of Earth Sciences Society), Henry F. Scammell and Kristin Fowler (at the Boston Public Library), and Dr José Vicente Serrão (at the Instituto Superior de Ciências do Trabalho e da Empresa). The staff of the Biblioteca Nacional in Lisbon, the British Library, the National Archives, and the Royal Society Library were also extremely helpful.

Alexandra Markl, at Lisbon's Museu Nacional de Arte Antiga, and Esmeralda Lamas and Rosário Dantas, at the Museu da Cidade, gave a great deal of their time and expertise in helping me to select pictures.

Special thanks go to Anthony Cheetham, Richard Milbank, Slav Todorov, Georgina Difford and everyone else at Quercus for their belief in, and enthusiasm for, this project; to Linden Lawson and cartographer David Hoxley; Álvaro Nóbrega in Lisbon; Georgina Capel for her wise counsel; and, as ever, to Terry Barringer for helping in countless ways.

Earthquake? What Earthquake?

IN NOVEMBER 2005 THE 250TH ANNIVERSARY of the Lisbon earthquake was marked by numerous academic conferences and a plethora of
scholarly articles penned by seismologists, philosophers and historians.
Falling less than a year after the huge loss of life caused by the tsunamis
triggered by the Sumatra-Andaman earthquake, not to mention five
weeks after the destruction of New Orleans by Hurricane Katrina and
less than a month after the Kashmir earthquake, the event was imbued
with added poignancy. The Lisbon and Sumatra-Andaman quakes were
both of exceptional duration, magnitude and intensity; both unleashed
tsunamis; both involved colossal loss of life. In the case of Lisbon fire
also raged through the city for more than a week after the shock, destroying a larger area and more buildings than the Great Fire of London in
1666, and making the capital of the Portuguese empire the victim of a
unique triple disaster.

The scale of devastation wrought on Lisbon is not in question. A
century later John Murray's *Handbook For Travellers In Portugal* could
describe it as 'the most fearful catastrophe that history records'[1] without
being accused of undue hyperbole. A hundred and fifty years later the
American geophysicist Harry Fielding Reid affirmed, in the wake of the

1906 San Francisco earthquake, that the Lisbon quake 'still remains the most notable earthquake in history';[2] and the author of an article in *Geographical Journal* about the same disaster wrote that 'we may anticipate, with confidence, that the earthquake of April 18 will take a place in the annals of seismology second only to the Lisbon earthquake of 1755'.[3] On the bicentenary of the quake Charles Boxer, Camões Professor of Portuguese Studies at King's College, London, called it 'a disaster which affected contemporary Europe in a way comparable to that which the explosion of the Atomic Bomb at Hiroshima has had on the world recently'.[4] At the close of the twentieth century eminent scientists still referred to the 1755 'event' as being 'possibly the largest historical earthquake ever described';[5] as 'probably the greatest seismic disaster to have struck western Europe';[6] and as 'one of the most devastating [natural disasters] ever to strike a population centre in the Western world'.[7]

Yet beyond the corridors of academe, and beyond the borders of Portugal, what happened to Lisbon on All Saints' Day 1755 has not left an imprint on the popular imagination comparable, for example, to that of the destruction of Pompeii in AD 79 – even though its effects were visible or sensible right across western Europe. Nine out of ten well-educated, well-travelled Europeans are still unaware of it. 'It is a source of great puzzlement', remarked the great geographer Peter Gould, 'that this devastating environmental event, right at the centre of the century of the Enlightenment, so often leaves hardly a trace in many standard works by biographers and historians . . . If Voltaire had not written his celebrated *Poème sur le désastre de Lisbonne*, one wonders whether the event might have disappeared from human memory altogether.'[8]

It is indeed a source of 'great puzzlement', given the impact at the time. 'Earthquakes had happened before, and whole cities had been destroyed in them, but none of these disasters had a repercussion comparable to that of the tragedy at Lisbon', wrote Charles Boxer. This was an event, he continued, that 'really made men think'[9] and would lead to a revolution in European thought of a magnitude that Goethe deemed comparable to that of the French Revolution. In other words Lisbon was without doubt 'a turning point in human history',[10] 'the first modern disaster',[11] and it has even been said that in the late eighteenth century the word 'Lisbon' acquired connotations of evil 'much as we use the word Auschwitz today'.[12] It was also 'remarkable as the first [earthquake] to be investigated on modern scientific lines'.[13]

In many a weighty historical tome concerning European history in the eighteenth century, which one thinks must surely feature the Lisbon earthquake, it is often inexplicably absent, or barely mentioned;[14] others contain surprising factual errors and even, in the case of one otherwise superb prize-winning book published in 2006, date the disaster to the wrong year.[15] Perhaps the explanation for such oversights can be found in Fernando Pessoa's lament in the 1920s that 'for the average Britisher, and indeed, for the average everything (except Spaniard) outside Portugal, Portugal is a vague small country somewhere in Europe, sometimes supposed to be part of Spain'.[16] Perhaps there is no lasting impression left on the popular imagination by any but a handful of natural disasters. Perhaps the absence of any secular literary output – novels, diaries and so forth – in mid-eighteenth-century Portugal, attributable in part to rigorous state and religious censorship, caused the memory of that country's greatest tragedy to dim. In his vast opus *Depois do terremoto*, Gustavo de Matos Sequeira remarked that with one or two exceptions, Portuguese sources amounted to nothing more than 'a vast series of useless documents'.[17]

Whatever the explanation, it is fortunate that many foreigners – mostly English merchants resident in Lisbon – left eye-witness accounts written in clear, expressive language of a sort which still conveys to a contemporary reader the horror of what happened. Some of those used have been frequently quoted, or gathered in collections such as the excellent one produced by The British Historical Society of Portugal, *The Lisbon earthquake of 1755: British accounts*. Others appear in print here for the first time, and if any claim of originality can be made for this tome it is to be found in the way that the accounts are spliced together to reconstruct the terrible events of All Saints' Day 1755 and their aftermath.

IN 2004 A MASS GRAVE WAS UNCOVERED at Lisbon's Academy of Sciences Museum. Tombs beneath the courtyard of the former Franciscan Convento de Nossa Senhora de Jesus had been opened and filled to the brim with the bodies, or rather body parts, of at least 3,000 men, women and children together with an assortment of personal possessions. Ashes and a lot of burnt wood were also found among the bones.

These were not people who had been buried with any ceremony, a striking anomaly in a deeply religious country. They had simply been scooped up hurriedly and dumped beneath the monastery, probably some while after the time of death. Other peculiarities started to emerge as the process of examining the body parts began. Many skulls had been crushed, others had 'exploded' due to contact with a source of extreme heat. Sand particles had fused with many of the bones, a reaction requiring a temperature in excess of 1,000° Centigrade. The chlorination of some items of silver suggests contact with sea water.

Those who died quickly in what Professor Miguel Telles Antunes, co-ordinator of the excavations, calls 'some singular, calamitous event', were fortunate. In a vast number of cases, perhaps a majority, the dead had been subjected to violent trauma inflicted by the hand of man during a period of total, terrifying lawlessness which ensued. There are skulls pierced by lead shot, and a huge number of bones show signs of cut marks. The knife marks on a thigh bone imply the possibility of cannibalism. The numerous shallow cuts on the skull of a two-year-old child suggest that before dying it was used to extort something from a parent: valuables, or what would have been the most coveted possession of all – food.

It is impossible that the Convento de Nossa Senhora de Jesus was the only site chosen for a mass grave in 1755, posing the chilling question: just how many more lie beneath the city?

PART ONE

A GILT-EDGED EMPIRE

'The Earth trembled and quaked: the very foundations

also of the hills shook, and were removed,

because he was wroth'

Psalms xviii 7

~ ONE ~

Quem nunca viu Lisboa não viu coisa boa:

He who has not seen Lisbon has seen nothing

FOR THE INTREPID ENGLISH TRAVELLERS who set a course for Lisbon in the middle of the eighteenth century, the moment the Falmouth packet boat reached the mouth of the River Tagus was cause for celebration. These 150-ton square-sailed brigs, of which four plied the Falmouth– Lisbon route with mail and a few passengers, measured just eighty feet by twenty-three and were built for speed, not comfort. They could complete a good run – a *very* good run – in as little as eighty hours. A more normal passage took eight or nine days, and the violent storms often encountered in the Bay of Biscay caused terrible seasickness. After passing 'the Groyne', the Galician port of La Coruña, and Cape Finisterre, the seas were usually calmer; but being becalmed in the thick fog which often clung to the Portuguese coast was equally unpleasant – and made lethal hazards of otherwise useful landmarks like 'the Burlings', the Berlenga islands.

Hostile privateers were another danger, even in peacetime; and an encounter with 'Sallymen' – marauding Barbary corsairs who infested the Portuguese coast and were not always familiar with, or respectful of,

I

the latest treaties or terms which their sultan may have agreed with the English Crown – was perhaps the most dreaded fate of all. In 1749 neither the White Ensign flown by the *Prince Frederick*, nor the fact that the packet was named after the heir to the throne, had been sufficient protection for Captain Williston and his crew, who were carried off to Algiers and relieved of their cargo of forty-one parcels of silver, seventy of gold, and two of diamonds. On that occasion the political furore which ensued secured the swift release of the crew and passengers, sparing them a future in slavery or the sultan's army. Many others captured by Sallymen were not so fortunate.

The sight of Cabo da Roca, the 'Rock of Lisbon', was the first indication that journey's end was near. The cliffs, rising 500 feet above the waters of the Atlantic, marked the westernmost point of Europe, and were crowned with a small hermitage said to be the residence for many years of a former English seacaptain who had renounced a life of sin. In the distance lay the wooded slopes of the Sintra mountains, fast earning an Elysian reputation among the handful of foreigners to have visited them. A few miles further south the packet passed Cabo Raso and here, if wind and tide were favourable, skippers could turn east for the run-in to Lisbon.

After this change of course the packet followed the coastline past the citadel at the little fishing port of Cascais towards the gap between the huge seventeenth-century, ninety-four-gun fortress of São Julião da Barra on a barren headland at Oeiras, and a second fort, São Lourenço de Bugio or 'the Bugio', which was built on a sandbar midstream. It was here that the Tagus reached the sea after its 650-mile journey from the Albarracín mountains in Spain and, storms and Sallymen apart, the river bar was the most hazardous part of the entire passage. The Cachopo do Sul,* the shoal on which the Bugio was built, and the Cachopo do Norte – or the south and north 'Ketchips' to English sailors

---

* A *cachopo* is also a type of Asturian sandwich.

– created two channels through which all ships were 'funnelled': a perilously narrow and shallow northern one, and the southern 'carreira da Alcáçova', which was difficult to navigate before the prevailing north-westerlies.

With its swirling currents and minimal leeway for error 'the Bar' had long proved a graveyard for unwary or unlucky friend and foe alike, most notably one of Portugal's own Indiamen, the *Nossa Senhora dos Mártires*, which had been wrecked against the walls of São Julião fortress 150 years earlier and sank with her cargo of Chinese ceramics, pepper and other treasures. All vessels took on a local pilot, therefore, to navigate a hazard which was a rather more effective defence than all the cannon of the two forts. This was usually a visitor's first sight of a Portuguese man, an event which, in the words of one young Englishman, 'made his appearance the greater entertainment'. 'The pilot', he continued, 'wore his long cloak thrown a second time over his left shoulder, which, added to a large perpendicularly cocked hat, and a pair of Falstaff's boots, rendered him altogether a humorous *caricature* . . . With much state did he parade up and down the deck, eating salt meat given him by the sailors, who were offended at his paring off the fat and throwing it away in the sea, which caused execrations against his *Portuguese stomach*'.[1]

Once safely past the Bar a succession of forts in varying states of disrepair were dotted along the north shore of the Tagus. Passing the huge Moorish one of São João das Maias, then that of São Bruno, at the point where the River Barcarena flowed into the Tagus, the gateway to Lisbon hove into view: Belém or, to the English, 'Bellisle'. Here, a few hundred feet offshore stood the handsome and unusual sight of the Torre de Belém with its seventeen cannon portals carved in bastion walls eleven feet thick. Commissioned by Manuel I in the early sixteenth century, the fort's appearance and intricate ornamentation – armillary spheres (symbols of navigation), stone ropework (symbol of maritime skills), Portuguese vessels under sails bearing the cross of

St George (symbols of evangelical endeavour), and 'pepper-pot' cupolas to the corner sentry posts – combined Moorish, Oriental, and Gothic features* and thereby served to remind new arrivals that Portugal was neither part of northern Europe nor the Mediterranean world, and that the Tagus was a frontier between North and South, Europe and Africa, European and Moor.

But first and foremost the Torre de Belém was a monument to the great 'Age of Discoveries'. It was from this spot that Vasco da Gama and his fleet of four ships had set out in 1497, returning two years later having discovered the sea route to India; that Pedro Álvares Cabral had departed for India in 1500 and on the way become the first European to set foot on the coast of Brazil; that Afonso de Albuquerque had left to consolidate Portuguese gains on the East Coast of Africa, in the Persian Gulf and in India; and that a diplomatic mission had been despatched to Abyssinia, reaching its highlands in 1520. As one eighteenth-century traveller remarked, 'at a time when the other nations of Europe were sunk in sloth and ignorance, [the Portuguese] were employed in propagating Christianity, in extirpating Infidelity, and enlarging our knowledge of the sphere'.[2] This was the maritime heritage that the tower presented to all new arrivals, as well as reminding them that it was the capital of a far-flung empire and the most important port on the Atlantic Ocean that they were seeking permission to access.

All vessels were hailed from the fort and required to anchor at Belém while they were subjected to scrutiny by the health inspector. Any that sought to evade this process by hugging the southern shore of the Tagus fell under the guns of the Torre Velha, a little over a mile distant at Caparica. Falmouth packets and warships excepted, all ships were also searched for contraband. With almost a thousand ships arriving each year deadly epidemics were dreaded by the city authorities, and the

---

* One succinct description of the distinctive style of Manueline architecture called it 'a sort of super-decorated, subter-decadent Gothic' (Young, p. 23).

'plague'* of 1723 which began in the neighbourhood of Lisbon's cathedral had killed as many as six thousand residents. In addition to disease, heretical literature and any items which contravened one of the many royal monopolies – even sailors' personal stashes of tobacco and snuff – were deemed contraband by the customs officers; and the zeal with which they undertook their task was usually accompanied by considerable joshing and displays of contempt on the part of English tars convinced that the process was principally aimed at eliciting bribes (or outright theft).

The time spent anchored did, however, afford new arrivals the opportunity to take stock of their surroundings and in particular the colossal 'Gothick' limestone façade, 330 yards long, of the Jerónimos monastery. This 'polygon of petrified pergolas',³ as it was described many centuries later, had also been commissioned by Manuel I to commemorate Vasco da Gama's feats and to attend to the spiritual needs of sailors and explorers departing the Tagus; and it too had been largely paid for by the immense profits from Portugal's monopoly trade with the East. Beyond the monastery stood a testament to more recently earned riches: in the 1720s João V had acquired a small palace and several parcels of land here and then set about creating a new 'royal town'. Thirty years later this magnificent royal complex, complete with its own Opera House in which Italian opera was performed for the first time in Portugal, was considered the Portuguese equivalent of Kensington.

After leaving Belém the packet boat captains often proceeded so close to the shore that it was possible to discern the faces of those making their way by *sège, chaise* or carriage along the Rua de Junqueira to and from the city. The royal carriages, the grandest and most elaborately decorated in Europe, might even be seen rattling along the shore. If by chance the whole Court was on the move there would be a convoy of

---

* This 'plague' was probably one of 'putrid bilious fever', or yellow fever, rather than – as was feared – the arrival of the bubonic plague from Marseilles which killed as many as 100,000 people.

hundreds; and if it was crossing the Tagus or heading upriver to the hunting grounds at the palace at Salvaterra as many as 300 barges and other vessels would bring all river traffic to a respectful standstill. This final stretch of the journey afforded a magnificent view of a succession of noble mansions and *quintas* – Palácio de Ribeira Grande, Palácio dos Patriarcas and Palácio Sabugosa of the César de Menezes family, Palácio das Águias of Secretary of State Diogo de Mendonça Corte-Real, and Palácio da Ega – interspersed with the green-shuttered white houses of lesser mortals and windmills galore. Roses seemed to thrive even in winter alongside less familiar and ubiquitous bowers of bougainvillaea.

A mile and a half from Bélem another royal estate came into view, comprising a palace and *quinta*, the Flamengas monastery founded for Flemish monks fleeing persecution in the sixteenth century, and behind it a *tapada*, or royal hunting ground. Across the new bridge over the Alcântara river, which joined the Tagus at a dock for the King's masts, were the monastery of Monte Calvário and Alcântara fort on the waterfront. A little upstream of the bridge stood the new royal gunpowder factory. The air, every visitor remarked, seemed exhilaratingly pure and wholesome, 'so soft . . . that it is quite delicious'.[4]

Alcântara gate, one of forty-three in the city walls, marked the western extremity of the city itself and once past it yet another royal palace became visible, the Palácio das Necessidades, set a little way back from the waterfront on a small rise. This had also been built by João V in the 1740s. The King's brothers, António and Manuel, lived in the palace itself, while adjoined to it were a convent and chapel for the Oratorians, complete with a library of 30,000 books which were said to have cost 120,000 *cruzados* (£15,000 at the time). A little further on, right on the shore in front of the hill named Lapa, or 'Buenos Ayres' to the English, was the palace of Francisco de Assis de Távora, 3rd Conde de Alvor, patriarch of one of the most powerful families in the land. Five hundred yards further east was the equally magnificent palace of the Marquês de Abrantes at Santos, behind which plumes of smoke rose from fires burning in Madragoa, or 'Mocambo', home to the largest concentration of Africans in Europe; on another hill, to the north-east, stood the massive Convento de São Bento.

Behind 'Packet Boat Stairs', by a knoll on the waterfront known as the Rocha Conde de Obidos, rose the hill of Santa Catarina and beyond it the Convento de São Francisco, charred from a great conflagration which swept through it in 1741, loomed into view. On the waterfront below was the solid, squat edifice of the new Mint, the church of São Paulo, and an area well-known to all sailors – the Remolares, home to many French Huguenots and even more Irishmen and seafaring folk. To the right of this was something else familiar to sailors – the Tronco, the jail into which they were thrown if their onshore antics ran out of control; and by the waterfront stood the Palácio dos Corte Reais. This imposing edifice measured sixty yards square with distinctive pointed turrets at each corner, and had been the palace of Pedro II in the previous century. But after a great fire swept through it in 1750 it was a somewhat forlorn sight, its 185 rooms and eighteen royal salons set around an Italianate garden which reached right to the river's edge all but abandoned.

Three miles from Bélem and nine miles from the ocean, after the royal shipyards and docks known as Ribeira das Naus, stood the commercial and political heart of Lisbon, the Terreiro do Paço, or 'Palace Square'. The Palace itself, on the left side, dominated the open space. Like so many of the city's most distinctive landmarks this too dated from the reign of Manuel I, but it had undergone significant alteration and extension in the intervening years, most notably during the Spanish 'occupation' when its immense quadrangular riverside tower, the *torreão*, was built on the orders of Felipe II. Designed by the Italian architect Terzi, this housed an arsenal on the ground floor; the royal library, a long gallery known as the Sala dos Tudescos in which people assembled before royal audiences, and the Queen's quarters on the first floor; and the Hall of Ambassadors and King's apartments on the upper floor. Newcomers were told that it was from one of the tower's balconies that the Spanish Governor had been hurled headlong into the Tagus when the Portuguese uprising began in 1640. A century later it was also said, perhaps with a greater degree of veracity, that João V had spent prodigious sums of money on this, his 'town palace', and that all its apartments were 'remarkable for the grandeur and variety, [their] costly tapestry and rich moveables'.[5] The Paço da Ribeira, as the waterfront Palace was officially known, had also been extended to incorporate a new Casa da Índia, where all the business of foreign trade was overseen, an Opera House considered by some to be 'one of the most superb buildings in Europe',[6] and a sumptuous new Patriarchal church.

From the Paço da Ribeira the King could look out over the reassuring sight of hundreds and hundreds of vessels in the Mar da Palha, the 'Straw Sea', one of the most capacious and spectacular anchorages in the world, and know that all of them were in some way augmenting the riches of the royal coffers. Plying their way in between the larger ships were countless small craft: *catraieiros* (longshoremen) ferrying passengers across the Tagus in their speedy two-masted *faluas* or *bulletas* (known as 'bean cods' to English sailors after the scimitar curve of their hulls); *muletas* fishing for sardines; flat-bottomed vessels bringing Lisbon's firewood from the forest on the southern shore; gaudily decorated straw boats laden so high that they looked in danger of capsizing; and larger *fragatas* transporting diverse cargoes this way and that.

The Mar da Palha, as its name implied, was effectively an inland sea and its great extent meant that ferocious storms could blow up in a trice. Within living memory the storm of November 1724 was one of the worst – a hundred or more ships were said to have run aground or sunk – and even squalls might be accompanied by thunder of such violence it could be felt in the bowels of a ship of the line and lightning 'so prodigious', in the words of an English vicar who witnessed one of these, 'that the

Heavens seemed to be all on a flame'. 'I confess', the vicar's account continued, 'I was not a little affected with it as seeming to represent something of the terrors and powers of the Almighty.'

Clear blue skies were a more usual welcome for new arrivals, and it was often possible to see as far south as the Arrábida hills, over twenty miles away. The *luminosidade*, Lisbon's beautiful light, enhanced the beauty of the scene still further by day, while at dusk the air was filled with the sound of the boatmen chanting Vespers and at night the river shimmered as if it were 'full of brilliant diamonds'.[7] Legend had it that the city had been founded by Ulysses after the destruction of Troy, hence its ancient name of Ulyssipo; and the locals said that it was built, like Rome, on seven hills. Whether the tales were true or not no one could deny that viewed from the river, Lisbon was 'one of the most opulent, populous, and . . . most magnificent cities in Europe',[8] or even 'one of the most beautiful sights in the world'[9] and 'the work of some benevolent Necromancer'.[10] It was small wonder that at any opportunity *alfacinhas*,* the city's residents, were wont to declare proudly 'quem nunca viu Lisboa não viu coisa boa' – 'he who has not seen Lisbon has seen nothing'.

While the view from the Tagus was indisputably fine, the first impression of the city of those who clambered ashore on unsteady legs was that 'the interior part did by no means correspond with its external magnificence'.[11] Even more surprising to anyone from northern Europe was the realization that Lisbon was so different as to be barely recognizable as a city on the same continent. The very large number of slaves and freedmen from Africa and Brazil was immediately striking. Some eighteenth-century travellers estimated that as much as one fifth of the city's population of a little over 200,000 souls were 'Tawnies, Blacks and Browns'.[12] Galley slaves could be seen everywhere, performing menial jobs for the King or the municipal authorities, and many of the street-cleaners, washerwomen, mussel-vendors, stallholders, whitewashers and bodyguards

* Literally 'little lettuces'; the etymology of the name is unclear.

of merchants and nobles were black. They had their own distinctive patois; their own dances, which shocked the uninitiated with their 'lasciviousness'; and they indulged their great love of music by playing mandolins, tambourines and guitars on street corners.

Equally surprising to outsiders were the hordes of priests, monks and friars who were more numerous than soldiers in Berlin. It was widely believed that as many as one in six of Lisbon's adult population was a *religioso* of some description, and many streets seemed clogged with black-robed Jesuits, purple-robed Augustinians and the white tunics and scapulars and black cloaks and hoods of Dominicans and Jeronimites – to name but a few of the orders. With more than 500 monasteries and convents and countless churches, the Portugal of this era came to be memorably described as 'more priest-ridden than any other country in the world, with the possible exception of Tibet'.[13] There was hardly a day of the year without some procession traipsing through the city, or the public celebration of a saint's day; and at dusk, no matter where they were or what they were doing, everyone would stop and pray when the bells rang.

The Moorish swarthiness of the *saloios*, the country-folk who plied their various trades on the streets, was something else unfamiliar; as were the large number of *ciganos*, the gypsies, and *saludores*, the folk-healers, who promised cures for everything from a broken heart to sickness among animals to sexual dysfunctions, and fortune-tellers. Witchcraft, superstition and magic seemed to seep from the very walls of the narrow, twisting streets and alleys. Then there were the hordes of *meninos desamparados*, destitute children, the swarms of beggars, and legions of blind men selling the texts of plays attached to a stick by pieces of string. Poverty was more evident than in any other capital in Europe, and violence endemic. All men carried swords or daggers under their long black capes; there were ancient feuds between different parishes, and by night robbers reigned unchecked by any police force. Gangs of young nobles, the equivalent of Elizabethan London's 'roaring boys', also took advantage of the unlit streets to indulge in a traditional rite of passage by attacking taverns, brothels, and each other. 'Murthers', wrote one English visitor, 'are so common that there is little notice taken of them, and if you see them happen under your window you have nothing to do but retire.'[14]

Women were a rare sight except among the *saloio* and slave populations; a popular saying had it that they only left their houses to be christened, to marry and to be buried. In summer the heat was suffocating and the 'moscardas' bothersome, and when it rained it did so with extreme violence – a great relief in the opinion of the many who considered the city to be the dirtiest and most unsanitary they had ever seen. At low tide the Baixa, the low-lying heart of the city stretching north from the Terreiro do Paço, was pervaded by the stink of the Tagus mud; and all sewage was deposited out of windows onto the street and the heads of any passers-by unfortunate enough not to respond quickly to a cry from above of 'água vai!'. There were no clubs and few entertainments of the type that were all the rage in London, and for those coming from a city with 6,000 beer houses, 9,000 brandy shops and an average consumption among the population – adults and children – of two pints of gin a week, Lisbon appeared to the average Englishman be almost dry. And then there were the dogs, tens and tens of thousands of mangy curs stalking the streets by day and howling by night.

On the other hand, for those willing to unshackle themselves from their preconceptions and prejudices, and to remember the slums of St Giles, the filth, smog, traffic congestion, pigs and mud of London, the streets were pure theatre. At ground level there was the constant hum of *zum-zum* (gossip) and *murmuração* (whispering), the distinctive cries of the street-vendors, the sound of unfamiliar instruments and songs, the sight of women sitting cross-legged on cork and rush mats, and of footmen smoking cheroots and playing cards while waiting for their masters; while up above ladies on their balconies carried on an animated 'digito-telegraphic intercourse'[15] in their own unique sign language. Some thought that the beauty of Portuguese women, with their striking white teeth, their eyes 'black as the sloe or of clear chestnut or of deep hazel blue',[16] and their luxuriant thick locks, 'surpassed all Europe':[17] even the Reverend John Swinton permitted himself to eulogize their 'graceful fine shape, their delicate features, their charming air and address, their vivacity and poignant wit . . . their attractive winning behaviour', and to pronounce them 'the finest women in the world'.[18] The tens of thousands of 'Gallegos', Galicians who ferried water around the city in barrels or worked as street-porters until they had saved enough to return to their homeland to the north, were an equally fine-looking, and industrious, tribe.

There was an invigorating swagger to street life: it was *'bamboleantes e barulhantes'*,[19] a scene of expectoration and gesticulation, and quaint customs abounded. Gentlemen curtsied to ladies in greeting as if standing before a Madonna, and they kissed each other's left shoulders; a gentleman would always leave a room first in order to show his guest that he was trustworthy, and not about to stab him from behind. Even two muleteers who met in the street would doff their hats to greet each other with the solemnity of nobles; and it was said that most among the 'lower sort' would 'sooner starve than enter into a gentleman's service'.[20] To some such pride and manners may have seemed absurd, to belong to a bygone era; but to others they were curious and endearing.

There was also exoticism in the air – chocolate drink routinely served with spices which cost a king's ransom elsewhere in Europe, the smell of rosemary wafting from charcoal braziers, and the astonishing array of unfamiliar puddings, cakes and buns sweetened with Brazilian sugar in the shops of the Rua da Confeitaria. As one tourist of the time remarked, 'every object has some difference from what our eyes have been accustomed to';[21] and for those who could accept this difference the city undoubtedly possessed 'a peculiar quality of crazy beauty'.[22]

The Terreiro do Paço was the location for great royal entertainments, bullfights, and *autos-da-fé* (at which those sentenced by the Inquisition would receive their incendiary, or other, less final, punishment). Here too, under the arches or on the splendid new quay called the Cais da Pedra, merchants were wont to meet in the late afternoon to discuss business and the arrival of the next fleet bearing riches from Brazil. On the north side of the square the meat market peddled vast quantities of tender (and not so tender) *cabrito*, pork from Lamego, and Irish beef. On the east side stood various substantial customs houses and ware-houses, and the corn market; and beyond these lay another square, the Praça da Ribeira, whose fish-market was 'esteemed for plenty and variety the finest in the world'.[23] The cries of the *regateira*, the fish-wives, with their colourful clothing and gold jewellery, filled the air, enticing people to buy sardines or whiting cooked on little stoves for a quick meal, *bacalhau* – salted cod – from Newfoundland, or mullet from the Tagus large enough to feed a dozen. There were vendors of the best roast chest-nuts in the world, *medideiras* selling wheat, *catraieiro* harpooners who fished on the river by night and Ilhavo fishermen from up the coast selling their catches, and the *borda d'água*, riverine folk who sported large clasp-knives and were said to be 'respected amongst one another in proportion to the number of times they have stabbed people'.[24] Other stalls were laden with *queijadas*, little goat's cheeses from Sintra, or fruit and vegetables twice the size of those that reached northern Europe; and some, like melons, which were never seen at all there. Parrots and monkeys could even be bought.

At the back of the Praça da Ribeira was the curious sight of the studded façade of the Casa dos Bicos, built by the son of the great Afonso de Albuquerque, and behind it rose the two Romanesque towers of the cathedral, whose forty-four-ton principal bell was the heaviest in Europe. Above that the labyrinthine alleys and stairways of the Alfama, the oldest part of Lisbon, snaked their way up past the Limoeiro prison to the castle of São Jorge. East of the square the waterfront continued past the palace of the Conde de Coculim, past the new public fountain, the Chafariz d'el Rei, past the old Mint and the Arsenal to the slaves' *bagnio* at the city limits. The distance from Alcântara to the *bagnio*, the area of waterfront enclosed within the city walls, was, according to a meticulous Scottish visitor, a walk of one hour and twenty-seven minutes at a steady pace of three miles per hour.

Heading north from the Terreiro do Paço through the Baixa maintaining a 'steady pace' would have been out of the question. Although this was the city centre, once one passed the Rua Nova dos Ferros, the grand commercial street, many thoroughfares were so narrow that they could not accommodate a horse and cart let alone one of the thousands of *chaises* which were the city's most common form of transportation; and above ground level occupants of plenty of the mostly dilapidated four- and five-storey houses could reach out from their balconies and shake hands with neighbours across the street. Such dwellings were a stark contrast to the mansions and palaces of Junqueira and Belém, or the houses of the well-to-do up on the Bairro Alto to the west; and for any visitor foolish enough to risk being lost for days by walking north through the Baixa it was something of a relief to emerge at the city's second great square, the Rossio.

If the Terreiro do Paço was the preserve of royalty and merchants, the Rossio was the square of the people. It was here that *alfacinhas* met to exchange news, to make demands, to lament their woes, to watch parades and processions and bullfights put on by the municipality rather than the Crown, and to attend fairs and the great Tuesday markets. Here too, from the palace of the Inquisition on the north side, the unfortunate victims of *autos-da-fé* were led out to confess their sins in front of the people; while on the east side stood the Hospital Real de Todos-os-Santos, one of the largest and best-endowed hospitals in Europe. From the east the square was overlooked by the castle and from the west by the towering arches of the great Carmelite convent, the Carmo.

This, then, was the city of which Lord Tyrawley, for many years of the first half of the century the English Envoy Extraordinary, proclaimed: 'it excites one's curiosity more than any other . . . as being the least known, and quite out of the old John Trott beaten, pack horse road of all travellers'; and which would make those intrepid enough to visit it 'as famous to latest Posterity, as Dampier, Sir John Mandeville, Hacklyut, or Fernand Mendez Pinto'.[25]

~ TWO ~

At the Court of King John

FOR THE FIRST HALF OF THE EIGHTEENTH CENTURY Lisbon to all intents and purposes belonged to João V, whose achievements in that time were nothing if not idiosyncratic. In the seventeenth century Portugal had endured sixty years of being a Spanish province, another three decades of fighting to throw off that yoke, English and Dutch incursions into its empire in the Far East, Dutch attacks on the colony of Brazil, and the collapse of the lucrative Brazilian sugar trade; and when João came to the throne in 1706 his country's fortunes looked no brighter: the country was embroiled, rather reluctantly and at considerable cost, in the thirteen-year War of the Spanish Succession, the contest between the Habsburgs and Bourbons for the Crown of Spain which followed the death without an heir of 'bewitched' Carlos II. But thereafter João had single-mindedly set out to restore Portuguese prestige and power while keeping his country out of any further conflicts. The latter he achieved largely by counting on the alliance with England to bring the Royal Navy or troops to his aid whenever required; and the former he was able to pursue thanks to a stroke of extraordinary luck.

After two decades of recession in Portugal and falling sugar revenues from Brazil, alluvial gold was discovered in an area of south-eastern

Brazil which came to be known as the Minas Gerais, or General Mines. By the 1720s it was clear that Portugal's 'goose' in the Americas was one of staggering proportions, yielding greater quantities of gold than had been mined in the entire world in the previous three centuries. The boom was accentuated by a substantial recovery in Brazil's sugar industry and growth in income from tobacco, hides and brazilwood; and it was sustained by the shipment of vast numbers of slaves from Portuguese territories in Africa. By the end of João's reign up to £2 million of gold, a sum equivalent to half of Britain's annual defence budget, was officially being shipped from Brazil to Lisbon each year; and a huge contraband trade brought in a third as much again. The royal *quinto*, a tax of one fifth on all gold, and the royal monopolies in many other products conferred on João the reputation of being the richest monarch in Europe.

Armed with such wealth, João's ambitions were pharaonic, and none more so than his desire to build a palace-church-convent complex on a windswept plateau overlooking the Atlantic twenty-five miles north of Lisbon. The scheme started out as a monastery for thirteen Franciscan friars but a dozen years later, with the revenues gushing in from Brazil, it was obvious that a match for the Spanish kings' Escorial or even Versailles was under construction. It was managed by a Swabian goldsmith by the name of Ludovice, under the constant supervision of the King himself, and in September 1730, two months before its consecration, Lord Tyrawley reported that 45,000 men were working at Mafra day and night under the watch of 6,000 soldiers. The effect, he lamented, was to drain 'the whole country of their labourers' and leave 'half the land . . . untilled this year'. New taxes were also raised on all the necessities of life, in some cases by as much as fifty per cent, and this greatly exacerbated 'the oppression, the hurry, the confusion' being suffered 'upon account of this church'.[1]

The main façade of Mafra measured over a thousand feet across with great towers a hundred palms high at either end not dissimilar to those of the *torreão* of the Paço da Ribeira, the Royal Palace in Lisbon's main square. The north side was the King's palace, the south the Queen's quarters, and in between a basilica intended to be a replica of St Peter's was planned. The whole complex covered almost half a million square feet, or ten acres. Inside there were 870 rooms, including space for a library measuring ninety yards by ten, and fifty-eight statues were ordered from Rome to occupy niches in the façade and basilica – the largest group of Italian statuary of its kind to be found anywhere in Europe. It was said that there was enough room on the roof terrace to conduct a review of 10,000 troops; and the hunting grounds surrounding it were enclosed by walls nine miles long and twelve feet high and stocked with huge numbers of deer, wild boar, hares, rabbits, partridge and other quarry. At the ceremony to consecrate the basilica to the Virgin and St Anthony on his forty-first birthday in October 1730, João spent several hours on his knees as the carillons were blessed, 9,000 spectators were fed, and a week of extraordinary celebrations began. Tyrawley dismissed it all as a 'farce'.

Outsiders could only guess at the cost. A Swiss physician and naturalist who worked in the Lisbon Mint was 'certain that three-quarters of the King's Treasure and the Gold brought by the fleets from Brazil have been metamorphosed into stone'.[2] He may have been right. The carillons hanging in the towers of the basilica, made by Nicolas Levache and Willem Witlocks of Antwerp, alone cost two million *cruzados* (£285,000), equal to three-quarters of the sum soon to be expended constructing London's magnificent Westminster Bridge. But the expense mattered not a jot to João. Mafra had been built for the glory of God, a monument to Portugal's, and his own, piety; and as such the King had pursued its completion, to Tyrawley's astonishment, 'as if the fate of Portugal depended upon it'. Besides, after diamonds were also discovered in Brazil in the 1720s there appeared to be no reason for João to curb his profligacy. The English Envoy Extraordinary in the later years of his reign, who knew the King's Treasurer particularly well, was told by him that it had 'never been possible to come at an exact amount of [the King's revenue]',[3] but that twenty to twenty-four million *cruzados* (£2.5 million –£3 million) per annum was a fair estimate.

After João had secured Lisbon's elevation to the status of a Patriarchal See from the Pope he also decided that, 'to give relief to his kingdom',[4] it needed a fitting new Patriarchal church with the best-kept and best-dressed clergy in Europe. The first plan was so colossal that even João's normally docile advisers warned him that it might be a little *too* much. For once he took the advice, more because of his doubts as to whether the project could be completed in his lifetime than any concern about the impression it might create at home or abroad, and started extending and embellishing the Royal Chapel attached to the Palace in the Terreiro do Paço instead. When this was complete it included among its adornments a silver cross designed by the great Italian silversmith Antonio Arrighi at a cost of 300,000 *cruzados*, and a vast collection of relics acquired from all over Europe; its annual endowment was set at well over a million *cruzados*.

After suffering a stroke in 1742 which left him paralysed João's pursuit of grand projects in Lisbon became almost manic. Even more sumptuous than the Patriarchal church was the chapel he commissioned for the Jesuit church of São Roque in the Bairro Alto. This was built in Rome to a design by Luigi Vanvitelli, architect to St Peter's, and Nicola Salvi, architect of the Trevi fountain, and transported to Lisbon where it was reassembled. Featuring a pair of candelabra of gilded bronze almost thirteen feet tall and each weighing three-quarters of a ton, eighteen types of marble, intricate designs of lapis lazuli, amethysts and jade, and what would be regarded as 'the finest collection of Italian silversmith's work of the eighteenth century',[5] the chapel of São João Baptista was blessed by Benedict XIV in 1747 and cost over 1.75 million *cruzados* (£225,000). When João recovered partially from his stroke he celebrated by commissioning the construction of the magnificent church, palace and hospice of Nossa Senhora das Necessidades for the Oratorians; and fortunes were spent in his final years on a host of other ecclesiastical projects. João's was truly an era of grandeur and vanity.[6]

The only major undertaking in the half-century of any practical, rather than spiritual, value to the people of Lisbon was the construction of a new aqueduct, the Águas Livres, to bring much-needed water to the city from Caneças; and the thirteen million *cruzados* ($£$1.7 million) cost of that was raised by a succession of taxes on wine, salt, meat, straw and every other staple rather than the Royal Treasury. Nothing more clearly demonstrates João's, or his subjects', conception of his royal duties: his epithet '*O Magnânimo*' was earned for his magnanimity in doing everything in his power for their spiritual welfare, not for improving their temporal lot. Work began on the aqueduct in the early 1730s under the supervision of the Italian architect Antonio Canevari and continued under Manuel da Maia and José Custódio Viera until, in 1747, eleven miles had been completed from springs at Caneças to Amoreiras in the north of the city. Thirty-five arches, the tallest of them over two hundred feet high, supported the structure for a thousand yards as it crossed the Alcântara valley, and eventually the network would be thirty-six miles in length. It was considered, in the opinion of the Irish architect James Murphy and everyone else who saw it, to be 'one of the most magnificent monuments of modern construction in Europe; and in point of magnitude . . . not inferior, perhaps, to any aqueduct the ancients have left us'.[7]

João may not have seen it as his role to enhance the infrastructure of his country, but he was ever keen to augment his own collections of artistic treasures. In the 1720s he bought seventy-five European masters in a single transaction with the Parisian art dealer Mariette, including three paintings by Rubens, three by Van Dyck, and a Rembrandt, as well as 106 volumes of prints; he thought nothing of purchasing a silver service weighing one and a half tons from the great Parisian silversmith François-Thomas Germain; and a little gift for his mistress Madre Paula Teresa da Silva at Odivelas convent consisted of a solid silver bath weighing over a third of a ton made by Paul Crespin, a Huguenot silversmith in London.

He collected people as well, when necessary, to compensate for a shortage of home-grown talent among his small population. The Neapolitan composer Domenico Scarlatti was the musical director of the Royal Chapel for almost a decade; when João wanted the finest opera singers that money could buy he imported the Paghettis at a cost of 20,000 *cruzados* (£2,600) each, five times Tyrawley's annual stipend as the English Ambassador; and military engineers from all over Europe were employed for their entire lifetimes to work on the King's monumental schemes. Writers were not encouraged – literature and books of a secular type familiar to readers in France or England simply did not exist; and even Portugal's best scientists, like the physicians Jacob de Castro Sarmento and António Nunes Ribeiro Sanches, mostly lived in exile. In the case of these two men their status as *conversos* – Jewish converts – was as influential in deciding to leave Portugal as the lure of intellectual freedom: both had suffered persecution at the hands of the Inquisition.

Tyrawley remarked at the time of Mafra's consecration that João's rule was 'the most arbitrary and absolute under the Sun',[8] and no foreign visitor to Lisbon in the first half of the eighteenth century disagreed. João was so rich that not once did he need to assemble the Cortes, the 'Parliament of the Three Estates', during his entire reign; and he was proud to proclaim 'my grandfather feared and owed; my father owed; I neither fear nor owe'. Confident that Britain would always assist in the event of any external threat, and having married his son and daughter to members of the Spanish royal family, he did not bother to fill vacancies in the army after 1736. As a result the army, and the navy, had shrunk

to such insignificance by the end of his reign that one of Tyrawley's suc-
cessors reported there was 'no such thing as a regular fleet' and doubted
whether this once formidable maritime nation could even 'gather a
squadron of ten in an emergency'.[9]

Internally João ruled his excessively inter-married and debt-ridden
nobility with such an iron fist that some were, on occasion, whipped or
beaten in front of him by slaves; the Church was entirely under his
control; and when the populace occasionally rioted, as was the case with
shipwrights whom he had not paid for over a year when the construction of Mafra was reaching its conclusion, he had no reason to worry
that this was any sign of deep-rooted discontent. His subjects seemed
genuinely pleased with, and proud of, their extraordinary king. Besides,
there was an old saying which was well-observed: '*com Elrei e com a
Inquisição – chitão*' ('about King and Inquisition – mouth shut!'). The
Church, rather than an army or police force, could be relied upon to
keep João safe at night.

João appeared not to care in the slightest about his reputation abroad
except in emergencies, and he never left his country. Tyrawley found
this extraordinary, however good his relations with the King, and sometimes downright offensive. When João refused to deal with any diplomatic business for weeks on end while he was busy at Mafra, Tyrawley
considered it a direct insult to George II, whom he naturally regarded
as 'so much in every respect above' the King of Portugal; and when João
proved singularly ungrateful for the twenty-two-month presence of Sir
John Norris's fleet as a deterrent to a possible Spanish invasion in the
1730s – the £1 million cost of which was borne by England – Tyrawley
only continued to refer to him in his despatches as 'thoroughly agreeable' and 'so great a man' because he was trying to persuade his superiors
in London to approve his own scheme to invade Spain. João was also
not above cutting off relations with the Vatican when his requests were
refused, but successive popes found his wealth sufficiently alluring to

put up with countless wrangles over status and make the Patriarch of Lisbon a cardinal, as well as eventually to confer on João the title of '*Rei Fidelíssimo*' – 'Most Faithful King'.

The majority of travellers left Portugal either bemused by, or deeply critical of, João's rule and even the judgements of some of his fellow sovereigns were not always respectful: Frederick the Great is believed to have said of him that 'priestly functions were his amusements, convents his buildings, monks his armies and nuns his mistresses'. It was certainly true that João's was a 'golden age' and some of his achievements, most notably in his patronage of music and the arts, and in maintaining Portuguese neutrality, were laudable. But with a little scratching the gold appeared to be only gilt and the Portuguese monarch seemed to have occupied himself, and spent his windfall, trying to recast his kingdom in the image of the France of a century earlier, or even the Portugal of the Age of Discoveries eulogized in Camões's *Lusiads*, rather than haul the country into the modern world. It was as if, in the words of one observer of the time, 'church and state [were] uniformly of one accord in keeping the nation in that abject state of slavery, ignorance and poverty on which their own conservation and security depend'.[10]

Other factors conspired to keep Portugal isolated, and in a time-warp. The country was in the grip of what Portuguese Liberals of the next century would describe as an 'almost cretinous form of Roman Catholicism'.[11] When the leading Methodist Reverend George Whitefield visited Lisbon on his way to America in the spring of 1754 he was appalled by the sight of people 'beating their breasts, and clapping their cheeks, and weeping heartily' at the 'Dumb Shews' during Lent; at the processions of barefoot penitents with chains fastened to their ankles carrying crosses on their backs; and at the spectacle of such ubiquitous self-flagellation and so many 'little boys with wings strapped on'.[12] When he left the city he consoled himself with the thought that there must be 'a season approaching when the Lord God of Elijah will himself come, and destroy this and every other species of Antichrist by the breath of his mouth and the brightness of his spirit'.[13] Protestant visitors used phrases like 'priest-ridden' and 'infested with friars' to describe the streets, while visitors from other Catholic countries were no less astounded and typically held that the Portuguese 'carry superstition to a greater length than any other nation'.[14] The Spanish thought of their neighbours as simply *pocos y locos* – few and mad. Furthermore, corruption and immorality were endemic in the higher echelons of the Church. Among the Patriarchal dignitaries in the 1730s one 'kept a gambling house', another 'collected pornography and snuff-boxes with pictures of naked women on them', a third kept several mistresses and ended up in prison while a fourth was imprisoned after trying to run away with an Irish prostitute.[15]

The influence of other religious bodies on all aspects of Portuguese life was equally immense. The Inquisition's two-hundred-year, relent-less quest for (or manufacture of) bigamists, witches, Jews, sodomites and other 'malefactors' had created a paralysing atmosphere of fear and sus-picion among a populace encouraged to spy on itself and stifled economic progress and enterprise; and the Jesuits, thanks to their royal patron-age, had secured huge economic benefits in Portugal, the Estado da Índia and Brazil and operated almost as a state within a state. They also controlled such education as João allowed, steadfastly blocking the infil-tration of new and 'pernicious' ideas from outside: in 1746 the Jesuit rector of the Colégio das Artes in Coimbra not only forbade reference to 'new ideas, poorly accepted or useless for the study of the higher sciences, such as those of Descartes, Gassendi, Newton, and others' but also banned 'any conclusion whatsoever opposing the system of Aristotle'.

In the commercial sphere, Brazil's gold enabled Portugal to 'make a respectable figure in Europe', to 'be secure', and in the case of the more fortunate in society to 'enjoy not only the comforts but elegancies of life'. That was the view of the author of *Letters on Portugal and its Commerce*, published in London in 1754, by which time gold production had reached record levels. But little of the wealth trickled down, and to some it seemed as though the riches '[tended] only to encourage idleness, and retard the progress of industry'.[16]

The failure to develop domestic manufacturing industries with the new-found wealth certainly had dramatic consequences. At the beginning of the eighteenth century the Methuen Treaties agreed among other things that England was allowed free access to Portugal for her textiles in return for similar privileges for Portuguese wines exported to England. The year after the treaties were signed Portugal exported £331,000 of goods to England, and England £781,000 of goods to Portugal. At the end of João's reign, however, almost fifty years later, Portugal's exports remained the same while England's had exceeded £1 million per annum for the previous twenty years. Demand for Portugal's wines, salt, fruit, cork and other products simply did not grow as fast as that for the luxury goods, textiles, and foodstuffs fuelled by Brazil's success, and there were almost no domestically manufactured goods suitable for export with which to mitigate the effects of the boom in imports. Indeed England even supplied Portugal's toys, watches, chandlery, arms, and shot; and tooth picks made in Coimbra or the rush mats of Alcácer do Sal were never going to redress the balance. The result was that as much as three-quarters of Portuguese gold left Lisbon in the holds of English warships and packet boats as fast as it arrived to pay other European countries, principally England, for all the things the country could not – or would not – produce itself. A French visitor summed up this state of affairs by claiming that 'one can apply to the Portuguese what M de Montesquieu says of certain African peoples! They are without industry, they have no arts, they have an abundance of precious metals which they pluck hastily from the hand of nature'.[17]

As Portugal's trade deficit became a trade chasm the country experienced another negative effect of the gold rush. It encouraged such a wave of emigration – half a million people left for Brazil in the eighteenth century – that to some outsiders it seemed as though the Portuguese had exported their spirit of enterprise in the same way as they had driven out so much of their mercantile expertise by the persecution of Jews and then the 'New Christians' (as those forcibly converted from Judaism were known).

The prevailing view in Portugal of the state of its trade with England took no account of the advantages of having the Royal Navy as the guarantor of Portuguese independence: there was a widespread belief that the country was being economically exploited by England, and that its ally coveted its American territories. This assessment of the Anglo-Portuguese relationship was, unsurprisingly, shared by the French. France's mercantile supremacy in Portugal had begun to decline after the War of the Spanish Succession and its dominance in the English market for wine had been usurped by the reciprocal trade agreements between England and Portugal. As a result Portugal was rather jealously regarded by France as little more than a colony of a country which had secured 'the privilege of supplying [her] with almost all the articles of luxury, of utility, and even of necessity'.[18] But there were some enlightened Portuguese who recognized the structural flaws in the Portuguese economy and society and could see that unless radical reforms were implemented matters were only likely to get worse.

One such man was Sebastião José de Carvalho e Melo, who served as the Portuguese Envoy in London and Vienna during the 1740s, and who wrote to one of João's Secretaries of State that he considered it 'one of [his] most interesting duties' to have to report to the King 'why he found Portugal in such great decline, while England and other nations were booming'. Carvalho's study of the causes of this anomaly was exhaustive. He read every tract about commerce, science and politics that he could lay his hands on, and talked to anyone who might advance his understanding of particular issues. One of his main conclusions was that the countries of northern Europe were prospering 'by means of reciprocal imitation', that 'each one observes carefully the actions of others so all nations benefit by using the information of ministers about the useful inventions of others'.[19] This practice, he well knew, was alien to peripheral and insular Portugal; and it would be difficult to introduce in the face of Portuguese *brio nacional,* its national pride, and the vested interests of the Church, the Jesuits and the nobility. But he also knew that if his country did not embrace 'imitation' and recapture a spirit of enterprise it risked being left behind altogether, the most backward backwater in western Europe.

This was a painful admission for an educated man whose country had, in the words of one historian, 'introduced engraving to Japan, nunneries to India, oxen to Brazil and maize to West Africa'[20] in times gone by, even though Carvalho knew that his views were echoed by others who had, unlike the King and many of his advisers, seen something of the workings of the rest of Europe. Another 'reformer' was Luís António Verney, an Oratorian priest and theologian who lived in Rome and whose *True Method of Study,* a seminal analysis of the defects of education in Portugal and its consequences commissioned by João and published abroad in 1746, contained a severe criticism of Aristotelian physics (and was therefore rejected by João on the recommendation of his Jesuit advisers). In a similar vein the eminent diplomat Luís da Cunha, a mentor of Carvalho, criticized the stagnant state of industry in Portugal, its censorship, and above all the pernicious influence of the Inquisition in his *Testamento Político.* Da Cunha even suggested that the capital of the Portuguese empire should be moved to Brazil to facilitate a process of reinvigoration and eliminate the perpetual fear of invasion in Portugal.

The *estrangeirados* had one thing in common other than their intelligence, their opinion that their country appeared to lack any form of intellectual curiosity, and their dismay that it was so mired in superstition and tradition of the most stifling sort: as their name suggested, they were all resident abroad. Indeed some, like Manuel Teles da Silva, who was created Duke of Silva-Tarouca by Charles VI and became a confidant of Empress Maria Theresa, were so estranged that they chose to serve other dynasties, in his case that of the Habsburgs. João was prepared to listen to advice from his diplomats, even when it implied the desirability of mild 'corrections' being applied to the prevailing state of affairs in Portugal; and occasionally he acted on it. But for the most part his conduct embodied the 'national prejudice' that he had always fostered among his subjects – the firm conviction that Portugal was the finest country in Europe and that criticism of anything Portuguese was an outrage not to be tolerated. Any Portuguese subject who overstepped the mark at home or abroad found themselves suddenly exiled or in a dungeon.

After a forty-six-year reign João died on 31 July 1750, a day marked with a slight earthquake in Lisbon. For at least a year before his death the kingdom had been largely ruled by João's confessor and a Jesuit priest. But one year later his thirty-five-year-old son José had, in the opinion of Abraham Castres, the English Envoy Extraordinary, 'shewn more instances of justice and humanity . . . than his late father has done during the whole course of his reign'. José had also, on his mother's recommendation, made Sebastião José de Carvalho e Melo Secretary of State for Foreign Affairs and War, to guide him 'in the despatch of business',[21] an appointment which made Castres distinctly nervous about the future of England's Lisbon trade.

~ THREE ~

Terra Incognita

LISBON MERITED A PALTRY FOUR PAGES of Thomas Nugent's 1749 *Handbook for the Grand Tour*. Travelling for pleasure was still in its infancy; and for the young, mostly male, mostly aristocratic Englishmen keen to sample life on the other side of the Channel the emphasis was usually on pleasure with a little bit of learning thrown in for good measure. Venice offered carnival (and the certainty of sexual adventure with the most costly and fabulous courtesans in Europe); Florence and Rome offered art, architecture, and antiquities (and the Italian states were collectively reputed to be 'the mother and nurse of sodomy'); Paris offered fashion and luxury (and the opportunity to consort with anyone of either gender). By comparison the capital of 'Kingdoms of Portugal and the Algarves' offered . . . no one really knew what – although the publication that same year of Udal ap Rhys's *Account of the most remarkable places and curiosities in Spain and Portugal* marked a considerable improvement in the available information.

When Nugent's and Rhys's books were published less had been written in the English language about Portugal in the previous fifty years than about Africa. Aside from new editions of John Dryden's enduringly popular tragedy *Don Sebastian* and reprints of Abbé de Vertot's

History of the Portuguese Revolutions – both concerning the Portugal of yore – there was the odd item of interest only to merchants and, in keeping with the anti-Catholic spirit of the age, a number of grisly tales about the activities of the infamous Portuguese Inquisition and the perils for a Protestant of visiting a country regarded as the bastion of unreformed Catholicism.

There was little even in the way of oral commendation. Istanbul received more English visitors than Lisbon; almost the only Portuguese in London were 2,000 Sephardic Jews who had fled the attentions of the Inquisition, and who formed an insular community not overly minded to sing the praises of its former home; and as the roads were fewer and worse in Portugal than in the Ottoman empire Lisbon was really a cul-de-sac that was seldom combined with touring other better-known European cities. The Portuguese interior was reputed to be dangerous *terra incognita*, and 'the kingdom of the Algarves' was a different world altogether whose 100,000 inhabitants were more closely linked to (and raided from) 'barbarian' North Africa than Europe. If Lisbon was on the way to anywhere it was to the East, or Africa, or Brazil – places where no sane tourist would venture; and if there was any picture of the city in the English mind's eye it was that painted by Samuel Pepys and his contemporaries a century earlier, namely that it was 'a very poor and dirty place',[1] old and decayed.

In his new guidebook Udal ap Rhys sought to counter the fact that 'many are too apt to conclude that there is too little in [Portugal] worth knowing'. The prevalence of such a dismissive view was in many ways surprising: although Portugal had a population of just two and a quarter million, barely two-thirds that of Ireland, the country had a long and illustrious history and in the early sixteenth century had indisputably been 'a hero nation'[2] – the heartland of the richest empire in the world, with the largest and most cosmopolitan capital city. Furthermore, England had for long periods been the most prominent foreign player on Portugal's stage. She had assisted in the birth of this 'small nation with a great history'[3] by sending crusaders to help Afonso I capture Lisbon from the Moors in 1147; and one of those crusaders, Gilbert of Hastings, was consecrated the first bishop of Lisbon.

Two centuries later various commercial treaties between the two nations led, in 1386, to the signing of the Treaty of Windsor which formally established an enduring alliance. This alliance even survived sixty years of 'suspension' during Portugal's 'Babylonian Captivity' at the hands of Spain, which involved the participation of the Portuguese fleet in the 'Invincible Armada' in 1588; and after the Portuguese nobles began their uprising in 1640 it was swiftly resurrected. In 1654 English military aid was exchanged for commercial concessions; and eight years later Charles II took a Portuguese bride, Catherine of Braganza, who brought with her the richest dowry in recorded history – it included Bombay, Tangier and two million *cruzados* in gold (about £400,000). The early eighteenth century had seen the signing of the Methuen Treaties, establishing reciprocal trading privileges for Portuguese wines and English textiles; English troops were stationed in Portugal during the War of the Spanish Succession at the beginning of the century; and a fleet of English warships was anchored in the Tagus for twenty-two months to counter the threat of a new war with Spain in the mid-1730s.

Despite the dearth of tourists' tales and history books circulating among the educated classes, the English public was not entirely unfamiliar with Portugal, even at a time when it was held that there were only two real nations – England and France – and *any* foreigner in London was likely to be assailed on the streets with the cry of 'French dog'. It may have been the 'Age of Gin', but everyone among the drinking public knew Lisbon and Port wines, of which colossal quantities were imbibed each year: indeed three-quarters of all the wine consumed in England came from Portugal. The spending public were equally familiar with Portugal because Portuguese gold coins – especially the 'Jo', named after João V – were common currency, and at certain times in certain parts of the country, the only currency available.

Some people with an interest in such things were dimly aware that an ancient alliance existed between England and Portugal; and anyone over the age of fifty might well have remembered that Charles II's queen had been imported from Portugal. Furthermore, much of the cloth produced in the textile towns of England was destined for the Portuguese empire, and tales of Lisbon circulated freely in every port in the land. It was a well-known hideaway for sailors seeking to escape press gangs or to jump ship after being pressed; it was legendary for the brawls caused by tars mocking the symbols of Catholicism; and the experiences of those pursuing one of the city's best entertainments – visiting a monastery and pretending to be 'whitewashed', or feigning acceptance of conversion to secure gifts of money and clothing – were legendary.

Among seafaring folk there was more than a passing familiarity with the vast extent of the Portuguese trading network. Salts knew that huge quantities of goods were shipped to Lisbon for onward freight to Brazil; that hundreds of thousands of English guns and large cargoes of tobacco were regularly despatched to Portuguese settlements in Africa; and that English slave ships, of which Liverpool and Bristol had almost 150, were always needed to ship human cargoes from Africa to Brazil for Portuguese traders. The whole area around Falmouth grew rich on the packet boat service to Lisbon in the eighteenth century, and the English fleets fishing the Newfoundland banks sold most of their cod in Portuguese and Spanish ports.

In the City of London as well there was considerable interest in 'the Lisbon trade' even if few financiers had ever set foot on Portuguese soil. By the middle of the century over £25 million of Portuguese gold had been imported into England in payment for textiles and other goods – a sum three times larger than the total amount of gold currency in circulation in the country at the beginning of the century – and this inflow formed the bedrock of the growth of the credit market and the issuing of securities, thereby establishing London as the world's foremost financial market and laying the foundations for England's industrial development.

The 'Portugal Walk' in the Royal Exchange could be found in its south-east corner, between Jews Walk and Armenian Walk, and huge shipments of England's 'staple' – wool – and other goods were financed and traded there. Indeed a fifth of all woollen exports, and between a fifth and a third of all grain exports, went to Lisbon, making it sufficiently familiar to City merchants for a member of a family of Birmingham gun-makers to write at this time that Portugal's capital was 'so well known for the advantageous commerce there carried on by the greater part of Europe, particularly the English, that to describe it here is unnecessary'. To him and his kind Lisbon was still regarded as 'one of the richest and best situated cities in the world',[4] and in Garraway's, Tom's, Jonathan's and the other coffee houses near the Royal Exchange what was being discussed in the Portugal coffeehouse in Swithin's Alley was essential knowledge. Merchants and financiers also knew that if they needed to contact a man by the name of Alvarez, Fonseca, Dias, da Costa or Silva – Jewish refugees from the Inquisition – they should begin by enquiring after them in their enclaves in Devonshire Square or Bury Street.

Among the very few Englishmen to have set eyes on contemporary Lisbon and left a written record of their adventures and observations none were as fond of the city as Captain Augustus Hervey. His first visit, in 1737, was as a thirteen-year-old midshipman in the fleet of Sir John 'Foul Weather Jack' Norris, sent to deter a Spanish invasion of Portugal. Three years later, while a lieutenant on HMS *Superb*, he had been seduced by the famous Italian operatic beauty, Elena Paghetti; and on arrival in 1748, better-off to the tune of £6,850 in prize money from his escapades in the Mediterranean during the War of the Austrian Succession, he found that Signora Paghetti was not only 'still very handsome' but keen to renew their intimacy. At her house in Junqueira, to the west of the city, Hervey happily 'passed most of [his] evenings and many of [his] nights'.

His charm was considerable but it was his pedigree that was equally important in ensuring ease of access to Court society in Lisbon. Hervey's father, Baron Hervey of Ickworth, had been a courtier, politician, favourite of Queen Caroline and trusted adviser to Prime Minister Robert Walpole, and such 'qualifications' enabled Augustus to become a firm friend of Dom João da Bemposta, an illegitimate son of João V's brother, and the young Duque de Baños, a 'lively Spanish grandee'. He could not have wished for more obliging *facilitateurs* in the Portuguese capital. Dom João was as hospitable as his late father, the Duque de Beja, had been cruel: from a balcony overlooking the River Tagus the duke had on occasion used passing sailors and boatmen for live target practice, whereas his son placed at Hervey's disposal the magnificent Palácio da Bemposta, the former home of Catherine of Braganza, Queen of England and long-suffering wife of Charles II.

The Duque de Baños, for his part, introduced the English aristocrat to one of the more unconventional pastimes of the Portuguese nobility – visiting the convent grate. The *grade de doces*, or 'sweet grate', was meant to be a genteel meeting between nuns and visitors strictly separated by a grille through which delicacies might be served and polite conversation exchanged. Of the nuns in genuine convents one English visitor wrote that 'no person but a desperado would attempt to debauch 'em even tho' they themselves consented',[5] not least because consorting with nuns was a capital offence. But many of Portugal's convents were rather different institutions whose residents, or inmates, were a mixture of nuns who had taken vows, ladies who had been committed to the cloister by husbands absent in distant lands of the empire, young girls whose fathers were awaiting an eligible suitor for their daughters (or who sought to prevent the dissipation of family wealth through the giving of a dowry), as well as penniless widows, girls sent for a musical education, discarded mistresses and girls deemed guilty of – or showing signs of interest in committing – some moral transgression.

At such institutions the grate often proved permeable and, once inside, the activities could extend well beyond conversation, musical recitals and harmless flirtation. One rather outspoken French visitor of the time accused the 'nuns' of some houses of being 'little better than cloistered prostitutes;'[6] another remarked that 'the grills have an air of indecency and theatricality about them such as in French comedies . . . [the nuns] wear rouge and powder like women of the world and wear corsets which show their assets to the best advantage'.[7] In the early years of the century one convent, the Convento de Sant'Ana in the northern town of Viana do Castelo, had caused a notable scandal when its inmates were discovered using outbuildings intended for cookery practice for amorous assignations and the conduct of a lively trade in contraband tobacco.

In Lisbon no convent of this type was more famous than the one at Odivelas, five miles north of the city, and it was here that Hervey was taken by the Duque de Baños. *This* house had royal patronage: in the early years of his reign at least two of the inmates were mistresses to João V – Madalena Máxima de Miranda and Madre Paula Teresa da Silva – to add to one he kept at the Convento de Santos, Luísa Clara de Portugal. All three bore him children, as did other mistresses, and his illegitimate sons became known as the *Meninos de Palhavã*, the 'Palhavã boys', after the palace in which they were later housed. As their existence was common knowledge, and a source of considerable pride among his subjects, João V was given the soubriquet '*O Freirático*' – 'the lover of nuns' – to add to those of '*O Magnânimo*' ('The Magnanimous') and '*Sua Majestade Fidelíssima*' ('Most Faithful Majesty'). For João's Queen, Mariana Josefa of Austria, being married to a Portuguese royal was little different to the experience of his aunt Catherine when married to a serially unfaithful English monarch, and his infidelities were not regarded as being at odds with his piety. It was said that he even took his ever-present confessor with him on his romantic assignations, 'that he may have their assistance in case of emergency'.[8]

Augustus Hervey left no detailed account of his first visit to the *seraglio* at Odivelas. But he did record many of the other entertainments he enjoyed in Lisbon: hosting dinners on board HMS *Phoenix* for Dom João da Bemposta, his other new friends and the French ambassador; attending functions given in his honour by the leading English merchants in the city; and going to a 'great ball' thrown by one of them at which the star attraction was the singing of the 'very pretty' Francisca Brezio (whom he later 'attacked in the Portuguese manner by going in [his] great Portuguese cloak constantly under her window').[9] Hervey was also a regular visitor to the country house of Messrs Mayne and Burn, the Palácio do Braço de Prata, to discuss how much Portuguese gold the English merchants wished him to take on board *Phoenix* as cargo for London.

Before he left he enjoyed one last memorable adventure. In what he described as a single 'morning's work', Hervey, the Duque de Baños and the Comte de Vergennes, a nephew of the French Ambassador, donned long Portuguese *capotas* to hide their identities and visited 'upwards of thirty ladies houses'.[10] When Hervey, later dubbed 'the English Casanova', sailed for home he took with him not only happy memories but a cargo in gold bullion worth £110,000 on which his commission was one per cent. All in all his earnings for eighteen months' work amounted to £9,000 – a small fortune even after deducting the third due to his commanding officer, and one which could have bought him one of the palatial new houses in London's Grosvenor Square. War, and Lisbon freights, were decidedly good business for eighteenth-century Royal Navy captains.

It was war that had also first brought James O'Hara, another man to leave a glimpse of life in João's capital, to Iberia. His first experience was nearly the end of him. The son of the Commander-in-Chief of troops in Ireland, O'Hara had been sent to Spain with his father's regiment to fight alongside Portuguese troops in the War of the Spanish Succession. He was wounded at the disastrous rout of Almansa in 1707, an unusual battle in that the Bourbon troops were commanded by the English Duke of Berwick and the Anglo-Portuguese force by the French Earl of Galway. Twenty-one years later he returned to the peninsula when he was appointed Envoy Extraordinary to Lisbon. In the meantime he had inherited the title of Lord Tyrawley and the Colonelcy of the Royal Fusiliers, earned a reputation for his wit and wickedness, and had accumulated debts during a dozen years posted in Ireland of sufficient magnitude to make a spell in the diplomatic service, and even its modest stipend, rather welcome. Tyrawley also needed to flee a wife whom he had married in secret for her money but whose father had discovered his plan, and a fifteen-year-old lover who was carrying his child.

A political scandal had created the vacancy filled by Tyrawley. His predecessor in Lisbon, Major-General James Dormer, had been recalled in disgrace for attempting to have his own consul assassinated. Tyrawley assumed that after repairing any damage to English prestige this incident had incurred he would be able to rejoin his regiment or move on to some other diplomatic task. But a long period of relative peace conspired to prevent the former and, despite continual complaints about the 'abominable dearness of all conveniences of life'[11] in Lisbon, his pleas to be transferred elsewhere fell on deaf ears. In the end Tyrawley's tenure in the Portuguese capital lasted thirteen years, during which the irascible peer's despatches matched the forthright tone of those penned during the building of Mafra and the threatened invasion by Spain in the 1730s.

His 'natural temper' was, in the words of his friend Horace Walpole, 'imperiously blunt, haughty and contemptuous, with an undaunted portion of spirit': over the years he variously described his Portuguese hosts as 'not to be trusted longer than the rod is held over them' and possessed of a 'small stock of wits'; their country as 'wholly in a state of neglect'; and the parlous state of their agriculture as likely to lead 'in any one year after an interruption of their trade with us'[12] to mass starvation. But fortunately for Anglo-Portuguese relations Tyrawley also displayed 'a great deal of humour and occasional good breeding'.[13] His rapport with João V, a man he held in 'the utmost regard and high esteem' most of the time, was close; and he was on excellent terms with the leading personalities at a Court he described as 'a lady we have always had much deference for'.[14] By the time he was finally recalled in 1742 he was considered, in England if not in Portugal, 'almost a Portuguese, almost naturalised amongst them, and beloved there'.[15] According to Horace Walpole he departed for home accompanied by 'three wives and fourteen children'.[16]

In 1752 Hervey and Tyrawley returned to Lisbon together. Hervey had been charged with delivering the former ambassador as well as the current incumbent, Abraham Castres, who was returning from leave. Tyrawley's mission, as a well-connected 'expert' on matters Portuguese, was to settle an acrimonious dispute that had arisen in Castres's absence relating to the seizure and confiscation of some gold as it was being conveyed to an English ship. In João's time the clash would most likely have been resolved without a fuss. But two years into José's reign Castres's concerns that his new Secretary of State, Sebastião José de Carvalho e Melo, might attempt to loosen the stranglehold which the English merchants seemed to have over Portuguese commerce, and to implement widespread reforms of the country's economy, appeared to have been justified.

There was no intention on José's part of seeking to renege on the ancient tradition which allowed English warships to export Portuguese bullion without hindrance: after all, his country's trade deficits with its European trading partners had to be settled, and as England was the strongest maritime power and an old ally her ships were the obvious choice for the task of distributing Portuguese bullion in Europe. Carvalho also readily acknowledged the reasons for the status quo. English merchants had skills, and credit, which Portuguese merchants lacked; a traditional, and rather paradoxical, Portuguese disdain for mercantile pursuits, not least due to a perceived association of commerce with Jews and 'New Christians', had allowed foreign merchants to corner their own markets; and the virtual absence of a professional bourgeoisie or middle class in Portugal was a handicap largely of its own making. But he was determined in the long run to tackle all this and revolutionize the way Portugal managed her commercial affairs. In the meantime the grievance caused by the English merchants' blatant conduct of a trade in both legal and contraband gold was an opportunity to fire a warning shot across their bows.

Tyrawley had considerable sympathy with the Portuguese stance. He had never been greatly enamoured of the English 'Factory' (the collective name given to the merchants who with their families formed a substantial part of an English and Irish population in Lisbon numbering 2,000 or more), on account of his distaste for 'commerce' in general; and on more than one occasion he had described its members, who between them handled as much as three-quarters of the trade of the port, as 'a parcel of the greatest jackanapes I have ever met with: fops, beaux, drunkards, gamesters and prodigiously ignorant even in their own business'.[17] This was characteristic bombast on Tyrawley's part; but it was true that just at the time Carvalho was considering how best to set about rescuing Portugal from a state of economic dependency on outsiders, a faction of 'Grumbletonians', young hotheads, were making their presence felt among the English merchant community and conjuring up grievances against their Portuguese hosts at every opportunity. When he discussed 'the state of affairs' with Hervey, Tyrawley 'condemned the Factory as a set of dissatisfied, restless, proud and extravagant fellows', and 'abused them all' for making 'very unreasonable . . . demands'.[18]

On this occasion all parties were reconciled, and Tyrawley left for home unconvinced that the dispute might be a sign of a deliberate Portuguese scheme to curtail the trading activities of English merchants who 'waxed fat and kicked'[19] on the edges of legality, and thought the whole trip had been a monstrous waste of his time. But radical changes were, as Castres suspected, under way at Court. Carvalho had already shown his mettle by persuading the King the previous year to publish a decree subjecting all sentences of the Inquisition to ratification by the Crown, a measure described by one biographer a century later as 'perhaps one of the boldest acts of any minister, in any day, in any country';[20] and it was increasingly obvious to all foreign envoys that after a promising start to his reign José seemed far keener on hunting, opera and assignations with Mariana Bernarda de Távora (whose husband and father-in-law he had for good measure despatched to govern Portuguese India) than on the business of ruling Portugal, of which his tyrannical father had given him no experience whatsoever.

When another dispute arose the following year, after Carvalho banned the export of corn to Spain in an effort to avert a famine, and English merchants used to making fortunes in this trade protested vehemently, it was clear that a new era of greatly increased tension had been ushered in with the arrival of the new King and his new Minister; and the year after that Hervey would be summoned to a meeting with Carvalho at which he made it plain that the frequent 'representations and shicanneries' of some of the English merchants would not be tolerated any longer. A decade earlier Benjamin Keene, the English Ambassador in Madrid, said of Carvalho, 'a little genius who has a mind to be a great one in a little country, is a very uneasy animal'.[21] Now, championed at

Court by the Dowager Queen until her death in 1754, Carvalho's advancement seemed inexorable.

The tensions creeping into Anglo-Portuguese trading relations had no discernible effect on the export of Brazilian gold to England. Indeed record quantities were shipped during the first years of José's reign and Augustus Hervey was a regular beneficiary of the need for the freight services of the Royal Navy. After each visit he left Lisbon with considerable regret, given 'the great attentions that had been shewn me there, and my intimacy with several Portuguese families, which are not easy for strangers to obtain here'.[22] His 'dear friend' Dom João da Bemposta, had been formally recognized by João V as his nephew just before his death and made *Capitão General* of the Royal Flotilla, and he was now a 'firm favourite' of José. This, in addition to being given the run of the Palácio da Bemposta and its *equipages*, gave Hervey an ease of access to Court society which was not enjoyed by any of the English merchants or even Abraham Castres, who in Hervey's aristocratic estimation 'lived in a very niggardly manner'. The King and Queen were always 'very gracious' to him: on one occasion they accorded him the honour of escorting *Phoenix* downriver on their yachts as Hervey left for the Mediterranean, and on another he was even invited to join the Royal Family on their annual hunting trip to the palace at Salvaterra – a month's sport involving the whole Court which was said to cost a staggering £150,000.

At a 'great gala' on the King's birthday in 1752 the Queen told Hervey that she had heard he was having a very 'diverting' time. This was certainly true: Hervey found Portuguese ladies to be 'very amorous' and 'very intent at never losing an opportunity of amusing themselves, their husbands being very jealous and very watchful of them'.[23] On one occasion he was even kidnapped off the street by the servants of the widowed Duquesa de Cadaval and taken to her estate, where she 'fired [him] all over'; on another he had 'as much joy as I ever remember' with fifteen-year-old Felliciana de Silveyra; and he consorted with Maria Anna Leopoldine, Princess of Holstein, a 'very fine woman, but very fat' who was married to the captain of the Queen's Guard. There was 'making love in the *freratica* way' to the 'beautiful nuns' at Odivelas and other convents, and attending Masses at the Trinidade church in the Bairro Alto in order to inspect the ladies and arrange assignations with the 'most lovely piece'. These were halcyon days, freer and more joyous than the last decade of João's reign, and it was impossible to imagine that a city which outwardly seemed so full of riches could be trapped in an economic vortex.

During one stay, in September 1753, Hervey received an invitation from the Court Chamberlain to visit the Royal Treasury in the Palácio de Bragança and was astonished at its contents. He was particularly impressed with the gold toilette given to the Queen on her marriage to José and commented that 'the Brussels lace that covers it all and the bed is beyond whatever could be seen of that kind [anywhere]'. There were scores of priceless pictures, presents from 'the Emperor of Chinay' which filled room after room, and many other 'odd kinds of things that have cost great sums and are of no kind of use'.[24]

In the autumn of the following year, in which a forty-four-ship fleet arrived from the sugar-producing province of Pernambuco, one described by the *Gazeta de Lisboa* as being 'as rich a fleet as has arrived from thence for some years',[25] Hervey also went to inspect the project that best captured the spirit of the age. At a cost of £200,000 or so José was constructing a new Opera House next to the Paço da Ribeira whose 'magnificence and taste', Hervey was certain, would 'exceed any in Europe'.[26]

An increasingly numerous type of English visitor did not come to Lisbon in pursuit of pleasures such as those experienced by Hervey. In the middle of the century the city suddenly became a destination for those suffering the agonies of 'scorbutic acrimony', or venereal infection.

The new 'Lisbon diet-drink' being actively marketed by Mr Leake of Half Moon Street, Piccadilly, caused quite a stir: it was said to provide a cure not only for 'scorbutic acrimony' but for scurvy and a variety of other afflictions too. Leake assured potential purchasers of his potion that nothing could match its efficacy and that 'of late years Montpelier has not been more famous than Lisbon', where it was known as the *German* diet-drink, 'for the means of repairing those constitutions which had suffered from venereal complaints'.[27] Leake's use of the name of the Portuguese capital was shrewd. Lisbon had become the winter destination of choice, the *dernier resort*, for the very sick. Its weather, the first subject of conversation for Englishman as Dr Johnson remarked, was deemed near-perfect – particularly for those with pulmonary and lung complaints who might not survive another English winter; and its air had acquired a reputation for being wonderfully pure and wholesome.

For some a visit prolonged their lives a little, for others it ended in a grave in the English cemetery in Estrela. Among the aristocratic and famous, Charles Mordaunt, 3rd Earl Peterborough, had died in Lisbon in 1735; Alexander Ogilvy, 6th Lord Banff, in 1746; Arthur Mohun St Leger, 3rd Viscount Doneraile and Lord of the Bedchamber to the Prince of Wales, in October 1750; and that same month Philip Doddridge, the great Nonconformist minister and writer of hymns, had arrived after the hot wells at Bristol failed to stop his terrible coughing fits. He died less than two weeks later.

It was in their wake that Henry Fielding – novelist, playwright, magistrate and founder of the Bow Street Runners – set out for Lisbon in June 1754. The late winter in England had been a vicious one, greatly adding to his agonies at the hands of a 'complication of disorders', and his wife had died. Fielding had tried the 'Duke of Portland's medicine', Joshua 'Spot' Ward's purgative Pill and Drops, and dosings of 'tar-water'. But none of these had cured him of his 'distemper of the dropsy', fluid build-up and retention probably caused by cirrhosis of the liver, let alone eased the discomfort caused by jaundice, gout and asthma. As he was beyond being a 'Bath case', and his diseases were now 'uniting their forces in the destruction of a body so entirely emaciated that it had lost all its muscular flesh',[28] Fielding, in desperation, decided to seek the Lisbon air.

Fielding's customary delight in life was considerably diminished by his dreadful suffering. Almost forty quarts of fluid had been drawn from his belly in the spring and summer; he no longer had teeth worth the name; his face 'contained marks of a most diseased state, if not of death itself'; and as he no longer had 'use of his limbs' he had to be 'hoisted . . . with pullies' on board the ship in the Thames to the accompaniment of 'all manner of insults and jests on my misery' from 'rows of sailors and watermen'.[29] Once on board a further ten quarts were drained from him and ahead lay a nightmare voyage lasting, due to contrary winds and other misfortunes, not the six days of a usual packet run, but six weeks.

Fielding had drawn 'brave, good-natured' Captain Rich Veale and the *Queen of Portugal* for his passage. A former privateer, Veale possessed 'a voice capable of drowning all others' and wore 'a sword of no ordinary length by his side, with which he swaggered in his cabin, among the wretches his passengers, whom he had stowed in cupboards on each side'.[30] Veale knew more than most about the dangers of encountering Sallymen on the high seas: in 1746 his ship *Inspector* had been wrecked in Tangier Bay with the loss of ninety-six hands and the imprisonment of most of the rest of the crew (the last of whom was not ransomed until five years later). But it was his six weeks on board, not piracy, which made the voyage so dismal for Fielding and by the time the *Queen of Portugal* finally reached the Tagus in early August he was in no mood to appreciate the view. It was also the hottest time of a fourth year in a row of drought: the soil, he wrote, '[resembled] an old brick kill, or a field where the green-sward is pared up and set a-burning'.

He immediately missed the verdure of home, and before long he would also be missing parsnips, Cheshire cheese and Stilton; he found the attentions of the customs officers and magistrates of health tiresome, though he was amused by the 'contempt and hatred' shown them by the tars; and his observation that the Jerónimos monastery was 'one of the most beautiful piles of building in all Portugal' was more dutiful reportage than opinion. In his dispirited and exhausted state he was even disappointed that although the white buildings on the shoreline looked 'so very beautiful at a distance', at close range 'all idea of beauty [vanished]'. On 7 August Fielding was deposited on shore by Captain Veale, a moment recorded in his *Journal Of A Voyage To Lisbon* as follows:

> About seven in the evening I got into a chaise on shore, and was driven through the nastiest city in the world, tho' at the same time one of the most populous, to a kind of coffee-house, which is very pleasantly situated on the brow of a hill, about a mile from the city, and hath a very fine prospect of the river Tajo from Lisbon to the sea. Here we regaled ourselves with a good supper, for which we were as well charged, as if the bill had been made on the Bath road, between Newbury and London. [31]

The very next day two ships with valuable cargoes bound for Lisbon from Porto were seized by Barbary corsairs and carried off to North Africa.

Quite apart from his propitious escape from slavery in North Africa, and the season, Fielding's arrival was not timed well for another reason. The following week the Austrian Dowager Queen Mariana Josefa died and the whole city went into mourning, displaying what Fielding described as its 'pomp of bigotry'[32] in all its glory. To add to his misery of ill-health his new wife – the maid of the previous Mrs Fielding – was desperately homesick; he became embarrassed by his daughter's governess's attempts to woo the Reverend John Williamson, the English Factory Chaplain whom he considered 'in every way the cleverest fellow I ever saw and who is my chief companion'; and he was horrified to find that he had seemingly landed 'in the dearest city in the world and in the dearest house in that city'.[33] Furthermore there appeared to be 'no such thing as a pen to be bought in all Lisbon'.

After a while, however, Fielding began to feel a little better and his spirits were bolstered by finding a 'kintor' at Junqueira with the help of the English corn merchant John Stubbs. He was able to take on two slaves, man and wife, as the rent was only £6 for a year and he had discovered that it was actually possible to 'make a figure for almost nothing' in Lisbon. He bought a parrot for his daughter and another to send home to his sister, received a visit from 'a Portuguese nobleman', and pronounced himself ready 'to be visited by all as soon as my kintor is in order'. He also felt well enough to consider starting work on a book about Portugal.

The observations of a man with such an intimate knowledge of street life and crime in London, and who was fascinated by the sight and sounds 'of seamen, watermen, fish-women, oyster-women, and of all the vociferous inhabitants of both shores'[34] at Wapping, and by the workings of bawdy-houses, gaming-houses, and all other forms of entertainment, would have given a unique insight into Lisbon life. But on 8 October 1754, just sixty-two days after his arrival, Henry Fielding died. Seventeen years later, among the advertisements for the fourth edition of his collected works which listed his many achievements and accolades, there was one which also mentioned that Fielding had been 'accused by Samuel Johnson of causing earthquakes with his bawdy writings'.

~ FOUR ~

The Gathering Storm

1755 WAS THE 500TH ANNIVERSARY of Lisbon's official elevation to capital city. It began with the traditional New Year and Magos Reis festivals at which all the foreign ambassadors, nobility, senior officials and religious leaders gathered to kiss the royal hand; and after that José removed the Court, as was customary, to the palace and hunting grounds at Salvaterra. The Hon. Edward Hay, the affable and capable son of the Earl of Kinnoull who had recently moved from Cádiz to take up the post of English Consul, reported in early January that the city and the affairs of the British merchants were 'in the utmost tranquillity', and a month later that 'all is pretty quiet at present'.

The fourteen merchantmen making up the fleet for Pernambuco and the twenty-nine vessels of the Rio fleet departed in early January, and the Bahia ships set off in early March. In the meantime small convoys and single ships left for other parts of the Portuguese empire – Paraíba, Maranhão, and Pará in Brazil, Cape Verde and Angola. The Tagus remained as busy as ever: there were seldom fewer than 150 ships from northern Europe and the Mediterranean moored in the river, two-thirds of them English; cargoes of wheat, rye, barley, butter, meat, cheese, bread, salt cod, linen, tar, coal, timber and iron were unloaded and wine, salt, fruit, tobacco, sugar and brazilwood left for foreign ports.

The numerous Lenten processions took place as usual; on São José's day there was a magnificent *serenata de instrumentos* in the Terreiro do Paço; and Easter was celebrated joyously at the end of March. At much the same time the warship *Nossa Senhora da Natividade* arrived from Rio after a ninety-six-day trip with a cargo of two and a half milllion *cruzados* (£325,000) for the royal coffers and one and a half million *cruzados* (£195,000) that was owed to Lisbon's merchants for goods they had shipped to Brazil; another vessel brought more than half a million pounds' worth of diamonds. To the great relief of the *alfacinhas,* plentiful spring rains also meant an end to the drought of the previous five years, and in early April the confident tenor of Edward Hay's despatches to London had changed little: 'there is no manner of news in any department that is worth your notice', he told Sir Thomas Robinson, Secretary of State for the Southern Department, 'everything in the publick way being upon a very quiet footing'.[1]

The greatest excitement at Court was generated by the opening of the magnificent new Opera House adjacent to the Paço da Ribeira on the Queen's birthday at the end of March. Designed by the Italian architect Giovanni Carlo Bibiena, it measured more than sixty yards long by thirty-five wide and many of the best artists in Europe, including the composer Antonio Mazzoni and *castrato* 'Caffarello', had been lured to Lisbon by the promise of payments in excess of ten times the annual salary of Abraham Castres, the English Envoy, plus daily expenses twenty times the wage of a master carpenter. The opening performance of *Alessandro nell' Indie* even included an appearance on stage by the great *toureiro* Carlos António Ferreira at the head of a column of twenty-five horsemen. Word of the scale of the new productions and of scenery unsurpassed in all Europe spread fast: just days later Castres's old friend Sir Benjamin Keene wrote to him from the Spanish Court: 'I am longing for your account of the maidenhead of your new theatre. We, I fear, must *baisser pavillon* before you. We will not throw our money out of the window; you seem neither to mind windows nor doors into the bargain.'[2]

One of the first visitors to see a performance at the new Opera was Augustus Hervey, who returned to Lisbon towards the end of April and described it as 'the most magnificent theatre I ever saw, and everything in it truly royal'. He was also invited by Dom João to a concert at the palace at Belém, at which the King and the twenty-one-year-old Princess of Brazil pulled his leg about his romantic assignations with the married Madame Brignole in Genoa. He then spent the next two months making the most of his time in his usual way. There were visits to Odivelas and the other convents; dinners with the Spanish Ambassador, the Conde de Perelada, with the Papal Nuncio, Filippo Acciaiuoli, and even some of the leading British merchants; discussions on various topics with Carvalho; and he often entertained his friends among the Portuguese nobility on board the *Phoenix*, 'with musick the whole evening on the river and a ball and supper'. His affair with Madame Brignole was no brake on his amorous activities: relations with fifteen-year-old Dona Felliciana, and others, continued 'very well'.

Hervey's social rounds were a source of valuable intelligence as well as entertainment, and at the opera on José's birthday in June he noticed that the King and the young Marquesa de Távora 'did nothing but eye each other as much as they dared in the Queen's presence'.[3] Hervey was probably even better-informed than 'Old Castres', as he referred to him, but soon it was more bellicose matters than Lisbon's social life that began to preoccupy both men. An undeclared conflict between England and France was under way in North America and English ambassadors and naval captains had been made aware that the 'situation of affairs between the two nations had become critical'. Even the Comte de Baschi, the new French Ambassador to Lisbon (and a man whom Castres dismissed as being 'entirely *sans façon* and tho' born a gentleman [possesses] all the turn and language of a downright financier')[4], unguardedly told his English counterpart that in his opinion hostilities closer to home were 'unavoidable'.[5]

A new war in Europe was not something that most Portuguese grandees wished to contemplate. France would try and solicit the support of Spain, which despite appearing more independent of its Bourbon partner than for many a year was still, in Benjamin Keene's opinion, 'bound . . . as a gizzard under the wing of France';[6] and any involvement of Spain would threaten Portugal's security even though the two royal families were closely linked by marriage.* From the English point of view, the ever-increasing influence of Carvalho at Court created equal concern about the extent to which Portugal would support her ally: although Castres judged him to be 'no Frenchman',[7] the new Minister had shown himself to be less malleable than most of his predecessors and the direction of the political current in what the English Envoy called 'this mysterious country'[8] had recently become very unpredictable. On 18 June, just as Augustus Hervey prepared to sail for Gibraltar with a cargo of Portuguese gold coin, the likely conduct of the Court in the event of war was suddenly – and quite unexpectedly – subjected to a dress rehearsal when nine French warships appeared at Cascais and the Comte du Guay, *Commandant de la Marine* at Brest, requested permission to enter the Tagus.

French men-o'-war, far less entire squadrons, did not regularly appear at Lisbon, a port considered to be almost a home from home for the Royal Navy; and given the timing of their appearance there was good reason for Hervey and Castres to fear that the war in Europe might have just begun. Hervey and his friend Dom João rushed for an audience with the King, whom they found 'much displeased' with the situation, and then took a yacht to inspect the French vessels. All were in excellent condition, well-crewed and well-commanded, and before six of them were

* José's Queen, Mariana Vitória, was the daughter of the previous Bourbon King, Felipe V, and his sister was married to Fernando VI.

given permission to anchor off the Terreiro do Paço Hervey had already slipped out of port and was on the way to report what he had seen to his commanding officer in the Mediterranean squadron. Whether the visit of the French fleet was intended, as one of its young marines wrote, to 'throw a bit of powder in English eyes',[9] or to enhance French prestige in Portugal and Spain ahead of the outbreak of the *'guerre générale'*, or to cause the diversion of English ships which might be bound for the other side of the Atlantic to blockade French trade and any further deployment of French troops in North America; or even to provoke an attack, Hervey had no way of knowing.

After the French ships of the line had anchored before the Palace José, whatever his private thoughts on their presence, extended a courteous welcome to his visitors. The Comte du Guay was granted a royal audience, a gala dinner was given on board the *Formidable* for Portuguese dignitaries (which neither the King nor Carvalho attended), and a special performance of Metastasio's *La Clemenza di Tito* was laid on at the new Opera House on the last Sunday in June. Some French officers and marines were invited to visit Mafra, the royal palace and hunting grounds at Salvaterra, and the magnificent royal riding school at Belém, while others were content to see more of Lisbon.

Among them was Charles-Christian, Chevalier des Courtils, a twenty-year-old marine on the *Palmier*, whose letters to his mother paint a detailed, and with hindsight poignant, picture of Lisbon in the summer of 1755. He found the view of the country estates, convents and villages passed on the way up the Tagus from Belém, and the 'amphitheatre' of the city 'most agreeable'; and he was certain that Lisbon was 'made for being the centre of European commerce, due to its marvellous position'. He also admired many of the buildings, describing the new aqueduct as an 'artistic masterpiece', and finding some merit in the churches of São Vicente, São Roque and São Antao. The Patriarchal church he considered 'beautiful and well-constructed', and his friend the Chevalier de

Beaufremont, who visited Mafra, assured him that it was 'truly noble and imposing . . . with a magnificent church'. As for the new Opera, Courtils was immensely impressed when told that it would cost two million *livres* (more than £80,000) a year to run and readily admitted that there was nothing to match this 'superb', 'majestic' and truly '*pompueux*' spectacle in France.

The young Chevalier, certain in his belief in 'the superiority of the French over all the people of the universe' and his opinion that there was nothing that could compare with the Louvre, that 'most perfect model of architecture . . . in the world', was rather less complimentary about other things he came across. Many local customs he dismissed as 'bizarre'; he found the Court dismal by comparison with that of France; street crime appeared to be of proportions as epidemic as in Spain and Italy; and the Paço da Ribeira he considered to be 'a multitude of buildings without taste, order or architecture' which had only its 'immensity in its favour' and was more a 'vast heap of stone than a palace'. From the exterior the *torreão* struck him as a rather sorry sight, as many windowpanes were broken; and inside its appearance was 'much degraded', although the numerous Gobelins tapestries bought at immense cost in Paris in the 1720s caught his eye.

Courtils's view of the state of the nation he was visiting was as chauvinistic as that of any Englishman. To the French, Portugal was a colony of England, which 'fed and clothed' its people, conducted all its commerce, and in return took '30 millions a year' (£1.25 million). This Courtils found inexplicable. 'I like nations capable of great feats', he wrote, in the knowledge that it was to Portugal that 'we owe the discovery of the New World' and that a century earlier it was this nation which 'so bravely threw off the yoke of Spain, who treated them as a master does his slaves'. But now it seemed to him that its people had become 'softened by long years of peace and idleness'. Indeed the country appeared so feeble that he was sure that six ships of the line could easily sail up the Tagus, as his own squadron had done, and hold it to ransom; or that the same could be achieved by no more than a hundred 'determined Algerines' landing at the fishing village of Ericeira and kidnapping the royal family during one of their stays at nearby Mafra. It was time, Courtils declared, for the Portuguese to 'wake up . . . and show themselves like their ancestors', to take control of their own commerce, and 'not leave it imbecilically to the care of foreigners who fatten themselves on their consumption and enrich themselves by their bad politics'. If Portugal ran its finances properly, he suggested, they could buy fifty ships of the line, hire all the soldiers and sailors they required, and thereby become 'one of the greatest powers in Europe' and even hold 'the balance of power between England and the house of Bourbon'.[10]

On 7 July the French squadron finally left Lisbon for Cádiz and Lisbon reverted to its usual 'state of tranquillity'.[11] Benjamin Keene wrote to Castres from Madrid telling him that he did not think du Guay's ships would attack the Royal Navy's small Mediterranean squadron, although he added, 'God knows what they might do if the 5 or 6 attacks we are making at once in America to recover our *own* prove successful'.[12] British reinforcements led by General Edward Braddock had landed in North America in February, with Hervey's youngest brother William among them, and it was expected that they would move to counter what was perceived as French and Indian 'harassment' of various British outposts. But it was news of a naval action, not a battle on land, which arrived in Europe first and caused the French squadron's activities to assume an even greater importance.

In early June a British fleet of eleven ships of the line under the command of Admiral Boscawen had captured two French troop ships en route to North America, and might well have taken all thirteen ships of two French squadrons as well as the new Governor of France's North American empire, the Marquis de Vaudreuil, had bad weather not separated the vessels. In Lisbon, Castres reported with some satisfaction that the news was greeted by 'the middling and lower rank of people' with an open display of 'their utter dislike to the French'.[13] Had the French squadron still been in port at the time the response might not have been so rapturous. As it was, smaller kingdoms all over Europe 'dreaded the consequences, as foreseeing [that war] must become general and that they would be obliged to take some part or other'.[14] In the meantime Sir Thomas Robinson sent expresses to all English warships warning that an 'open rupture' with France was imminent. Castres reported the Portuguese Court to be observing 'as usual . . . a profound silence upon what passes'.[15]

The appearance of the French squadron was not the only maritime 'inconvenience' for Portugal that summer. In May the men-o'-war *Nossa Senhora da Arrábida* and *Nossa Senhora da Atalaya* were sent out to patrol offshore after it was rumoured that 'the Algerines' were preparing to send 'a great number of vessels' to raid the Portuguese coast. José had already authorized one payment of 8,000 *cruzados* that year to secure the release of Portuguese coastal dwellers taken from their homes and enslaved in Barbary; and he responded to this latest threat by ordering that 'a man of war of 60 guns, three frigates, and two stout chebecks, should be manned and equipped with the utmost expedition'. Portugal's meagre naval resources were being stretched to the limit but in early July a squadron was reported to be at the ready to tackle the corsairs, 'who of late have greatly infested the coasts'.[16]

The protection of the fleets which would begin returning from Brazil in the late summer was even more imperative than safeguarding Portuguese coastal dwellers. An early arrival came from Pernambuco, comprising eleven vessels with 220,000 *cruzados* for the King and 'a very valuable cargo' of sugar, hides and brazilwood; and although it had its own escort of two men-o'-war there was always the chance that a straggler from a subsequent fleet – like the lone vessel which arrived at much the same time from Macau – might be picked off unless the corsairs were made to feel Portugal's naval presence offshore.

After the celebration of a succession of saints' days and three days of tremendous fireworks at the convent of São Francisco in mid-July Edward Hay reported that 'business goes on as usual'[17] despite, or perhaps encouraged by, the threat of war. The only real disturbance of the summer for the merchants of the English Factory was the apprehension of Captain William Clies and four of the crew of the *Expedition* packet by cloaked JPs armed with *spadoes* – long swords – who demanded to search them for prohibited goods. Clies swore in his subsequent deposition that he and his men reacted only in a 'defensive manner'. He also claimed to have been warned that such a search was likely, but had resolved that if it was attempted he would refuse and fight his way to the ship's boat. This was exactly what happened. One or two of the JPs were wounded in the fray and another was dragged into the water and given 'a thorough ducking'. As usually happened in any confrontation with officials, a mob quickly gathered and exhorted the English tars to drown the man, shouting that he and all of his kind 'deserved to be hanged'.[18] The crew did not heed the advice, boarded the ship's boat and made for the *Expedition* with their 20,000 *moidores* in gold and a 'good parcel' of diamonds belonging to Messrs Bristow & Ward.

A protest at the 'violent and unprecedented manner' in which a packet boat captain had been challenged while carrying his – and therefore King George II's – despatches was immediately sent by Castres to Carvalho. He knew that the Portuguese Minister was unlikely to condemn outright the behaviour of the officials because, as Castres himself admitted, it was their job 'to stop the counterbanding which is daily carrying on in this river', and in any other port in Europe Clies would have been prosecuted. What was at issue for the third time in as many years was the 'ticklish branch of commerce' conducted by English skippers, namely the illegal but necessarily tolerated removal of gold and other valuables to settle Portugal's debts to English and other

European merchants. When no attempt was made to interfere with the 'big cargoes'[19] of the next five packets to leave Lisbon, Castres believed the incident had blown over. What he failed to grasp in full was that Carvalho was starting, with the full support of the King, to effect a radical reform of the government of the empire and that this would soon have more dramatic consequences for Anglo-Portuguese trade than occasional searches of packet boat captains and their crews.

Sebastião José de Carvalho e Melo would later be described by his first biographer as being 'remarkably tall, well made, and handsome; his countenance intellectual and expressive; his manner engaging, and his diction easy and flowing';[20] and by many admiring Englishmen as, in the words of one, 'without doubt, a character so far superior to any of his own countrymen'.[21] His time overseas gave him a much greater understanding of the mindset of the foreign ambassadors at the Court, and made him deceptively straightforward to deal with, while adhering to what Castres called the Portuguese tradition of 'concealing their real sentiments which way soever they may happen to be inclined'.[22] By the summer of 1755, having fired his first salvo at the Inquisition four years earlier and begun to reduce the Portuguese bureaucracy and reform the tax system, Carvalho's attention was increasingly focused on putting Brazil's house in order.

Replicating the way that the big English mercantile houses conducted business, he formed a new company with monopoly rights over commerce in the northern provinces of Grão-Pará and Maranhão, ordered an end to the activities of the small itinerant traders who were mostly the agents of foreign 'interlopers', and declared that all indigenous Indians were henceforth freed from the temporal power of any ecclesiastical authorities. The first two measures aimed to regain control over northern Brazil's commercial activities; the third amounted to a declaration of war on Jesuit power in the country. Five years earlier Portugal's claims along the Amazonia basin had been upheld in a treaty signed with Spain, and Carvalho's intention was to remove the Jesuits from their vast, autonomous estates on the borders. In the south armed clashes had already begun in the Jesuits' 'Uruguayan' territories. In the north, Carvalho's step-brother Francisco Xavier de Mendonça Furtado was installed as Governor to begin a similar campaign. Carvalho's attempt to 're-nationalize' Portugal's colonial trade and to bring the Jesuits to heel had begun in earnest, and at home he announced the creation in August of a new Board of Commerce – the Junta do Comércio – aimed at concentrating, and increasing, the power of local Portuguese merchants.

In early September, just as news reached Europe of the death of General Braddock and the lucky escape of his aide George Washington after the routing of their force by French and Indian troops on 9 July as it marched on Fort Duquesne, * the Brazil fleets started to arrive in Lisbon. The first, comprising ships from Rio, Pernambuco and Macau, brought a staggering twenty million *cruzados* (£2.6 million) of gold, nine-tenths of which was destined for 'commerce' – Lisbon's merchants – and the rest for the King. Other valuable items among the cargoes included 1,400 'elephant's teeth', a thousand chests of sugar and 41,500 hides. A few weeks later nineteen ships from Bahia and two from Goa reached port with two million *cruzados*, 6,000 chests of sugar, 10,000 rolls of tobacco and 43,500 half-hides aboard. The takings of the English merchants from these fleets were so substantial that Castres and Edward Hay had to request the assistance of HMS *Unicorn*: the packet service was unable to deal unaided with the quantity of gold being shipped to England. War may have become a near-certainty, the more so after the Royal Navy declared French merchant shipping to be fair game and seized the first of what by Christmas would become 300 vessels with cargoes worth over a million pounds; but England's 'Lisbon trade' was thriving as never before.

Before the end of the summer a number of English visitors arrived in

* Pittsburgh.

Lisbon whose names were among those destined to achieve a certain fame in the light of what would happen in the autumn. There was Charles Douglas, the twenty-nine-year-old son of the Duke of Queensbury, an amiable and kind man who had inherited the title of Lord Drumlanrig when his elder brother, who was of a 'melancholy temperament', had been killed in a shooting accident just three months after marrying. Tragedy seemed to have long stalked his family, and in the previous two years Drumlanrig's uncle had died in a hunting accident in Paris and his grandfather, the Earl of Clarendon, had died heirless nine months later.* The cause of Drumlanrig's appearance in Lisbon was no happier. He had not come to sample the delights of Lisbon with which Augustus Hervey, whom he knew from a season they had both spent in Paris in 1749–50, was so familiar: he was suffering from consumption and had given up his seat in Parliament in the hope that the city's air might help him.

Then there was the businessman Benjamin Farmer, who arrived armed with a letter of introduction to Castres from Sir Thomas Robinson, secured on the back of the reputation of the great Birmingham gun-makers Farmer & Galton, who supplied the government as well as the burgeoning markets of India and slave traders, both black and white, in Africa. It had not been a good summer for the family. Benjamin had had a schooner confiscated by the Portuguese in the Cape Verde islands which he sought to reclaim; and his cousin James Farmer, the gun-maker, was desperately trying to remain solvent after a foreign partner in Lisbon had caused him such huge losses that he had secretly remort-gaged an estate that was already in lien to his partner Samuel Galton.

The commercial acumen of the Farmers' fathers, Thomas and Joseph,

---

* Drumlanrig's uncle was the 'idiot' elder son of the 'Iron Duke' of Queensbury who had been instrumental in bringing about the Union of the Parliaments of England and Scotland. On the day of the enactment of the Union he had escaped from his quarters in Queensbury House in Edinburgh while most of the servants were watching the rioting outside, seized a kitchen boy and roasted him on a spit. When the other servants returned he had started to eat the kitchen boy.

had seemingly not been replicated in the next generation, which was widely considered 'a little mad'; and Benjamin himself even admitted that his friends were wont to say that he possessed 'all sense but common sense'. On arrival in Lisbon, he moved into the house of a fellow English merchant on one side of a courtyard overlooked by the apartment of a 'poor lieutenant of the Green regiment' whose eldest daughter liked to gaze 'very smirkingly' at him;[23] and from there he set about soliciting the assistance of his influential cousin, David Barclay, Farmer & Galton's Lisbon agent, the banker Sam Montaigut, and Abraham Castres in the hope of securing redress at the Portuguese Court.

A third new arrival was a close friend of Sir Thomas Robinson, and one of the 'bright particular stars of Massachusetts Society',[24] Sir Harry Frankland. The reason why Frankland had left his lucrative position as Collector of the Port of Boston had nothing to do with the war in North America. The previous year he had had to return to England to deal with a lawsuit concerning his uncle's will, and then in April 1755 he had started to take the 'Lisbon diet drink' and a purgative known as 'sacred bitters'. Sir Harry may or may not have been syphilitic, as that was the principal malady the diet drink was designed to combat. His youth had certainly been colourful. Fourteen years earlier he had left England for the colonies under something of a cloud, having fathered a child through a below-stairs liaison; and soon after arriving in Massachusetts he had plucked sixteen-year-old Agnes Suriage from scrubbing floors at the Fountainhead inn in Marblehead and later installed her on his beautiful 480-acre estate at Hopkinton.

But at thirty-nine his youth was behind him, and Frankland was a sensitive, somewhat tortured soul: his diary, alongside a meticulous account of all he spent and did in Lisbon, is full of little admonitions such as 'terrify not thy soul with vain fears; neither let thy heart sink within thee from the phantoms of the imagination' and 'cheerful, but not gay; serious but not grave, he drinketh the joys and sorrows of life with steadiness and serenity'.[25] Furthermore, Sir Harry was devoted to his illegitimate son, named Harry Cromwell after Frankland's Puritan forebear, and by the time they arrived in Lisbon Agnes had been accepted in North America, if not by the Frankland family in England, as the *de facto* Lady Frankland.

Having been delayed for three frustrating weeks by contrary winds, the Reverend Richard Goddard also arrived to stay with his brother Ambrose in the last weeks of October 1755. The Goddards were a leading Wiltshire family – it was said that the history of Swindon was the history of the Goddard family – and Ambrose was in business with Benjamin Branfill, the nephew of William Braund, a leading merchant in the City of London, and John Jackson, the son of Philip Jackson, a director of the South Sea Company. Richard Goddard found his brother 'very well' and 'his situation . . . such as could be wished in every respect'.[26] On his first day he rode out with Benjamin Branfill and became certain that his decision to spend 'a most agreeable winter'[27] in Lisbon had been an excellent one, and that it would serve its purpose of ridding him of a recent bout of ill-health.

One of the late summer events attended by many of the English community and their guests was a great bullfight in the Rossio. Among them was a young English merchant named Thomas Chase who, having lived all his life in Lisbon, spoke Portuguese and noticed that all the talk in the crowd was of an old prophecy of great mischief happening to Lisbon in a year with two fives in it. But on 20 October Abraham Castres reported 'we have nothing stirring here'.[28]

~ PART TWO ~

AN AXIS OF ELEMENTS

'Imagine only to yourselves (if any imagination can paint such a scene of horrors) imagine you see a wealthy and flourishing city, abounding with all the blessings which an extensive commerce can collect from all quarters of the habitable earth: a city that (for all its immense Riches drawn from her gold and silver mines, both at home and in India) might justly be called The Treasure-House of Europe; a city at peace to enjoy unmolested (ah! 'tis to be feared too securely indulging) the treacherous delights of affluence and ease; no enemy without, no faction within, to disturb its repose, or alarm its fears: imagine this populous and renowned city full of natives and foreigners, apprehending no more danger than we that are here present at the moment . . .'

Sermon by Thomas Nowell, 1756

~ FIVE ~

All Saints' Day

ON THE LAST DAY OF OCTOBER 1755 Mr Stoqueler, the Consul of Hamburg, was visiting the beautiful wine-growing district of Colares, on the west-facing slopes of the Serra de Sintra. The weather was 'clear, and uncommonly warm for the season' and at four o'clock in the afternoon he was surprised, because it was usually a summer phenomenon, to see a fog coming in from the sea. A little later the wind changed direction and the fog was driven back out to sea, becoming as thick as he had ever known. As it receded he heard, or thought he heard, the sea 'rise with a prodigious roaring'.[1] At much the same time a fountain in Colares village almost ran dry and all along the Portuguese coast people began to realize that the evening tide was two hours late. At Ericeira, fifteen miles up the coast from Colares, the fishermen pulled their boats higher up the beach: late tides normally indicated that something untoward was in the offing.

In Lisbon the physician João Mendes Saccheti Barbosa thought that the atmosphere that afternoon 'had the appearance of clouds and notable offuscation'.[2] For several days people had been complaining that there was an abnormal taste to the water, and now dogs, mules and birds in cages all seemed strangely agitated. Elsewhere in the country rabbits and other animals were seen leaving their burrows and worms were observed crawling to the surface en masse. In Evora a well suddenly dried up completely. In Aveiro there was a sulphurous smell in the air. Throughout Spain similar phenomena would later be recalled, and all over the Iberian peninsula fountains ran very muddy, or dried up altogether, or began to gush forth water at an unusually prodigious rate.

At five in the morning on Saturday, 1 November, the skipper of an English merchant vessel rose and made ready to sail from Belém to the city. It was three days before the new moon, and throughout the early hours 'luminous effects', possibly the traces of a meteorite or comet, had been visible in the night sky. But after sunrise, at about seven o'clock, the morning was as fine and clear as the weather of the previous ten days. A very slight breeze blew from the north-east, and by nine the skipper had anchored his vessel before the warehouses by the Ribeira das Naus, the dockyard to the west of the Paço da Ribeira. As he did so, the sun seemed to dim a little but it remained as warm as a July morning in England.

All the way upriver, and now from every quarter of the city, the crew's ears were assailed by the sound of church bells. It was All Saints' Day, a red-letter day which in the opinion of most foreigners was one of the most dismal festivals in the year. The 'lugubrious knells' seemed to 'diffuse melancholy through every bosom',[3] and most chose to stay in their houses or leave for the countryside until the rituals were over. By 9.30 a.m. many Lisboetas were already attending Mass, others were visiting relatives before a later service, and some were doing business on the street, as Sir Harry Frankland's *chaise* clattered its way from Belém past the house of his friend Francisco de Ribeiro. Everything about Lisbon was still new and of interest to him and he was making for the city, in full Court dress, with the unusual intention of witnessing a traditional Portuguese Mass. He had been reliably informed that anyone bold enough to attend such a thing would be treated to a spectacle he would never witness at home in Boston: *alfacinhas* talked, laughed, flirted and even ate and drank in church.

Those English merchants who had not left the city prepared for work or to visit friends. The Wiltshire woollens merchant Ambrose Goddard was on his way to call on Portuguese customers and his brother, the Reverend Richard, was taking a stroll up to the castle before morning service at the chapel in the Envoy's house in Santa Martha which was due to start at 10.30 a. m. He was enjoying himself so much that, after checking the time, he thought he would linger another few minutes before making his way down again. In the same street as the Goddard house, Rua das Pedras Negras, in the home in which he had been born exactly twenty-seven years earlier, Thomas Chase was just opening the bureau in his bedroom on the fourth floor when he felt the whole building start to tremble and the glass in the windows rattled. Like all the buildings in this street a few hundred yards north of the Terreiro do Paço, his was old and rickety and any passing carriage 'made it shake all over'. Up in the castle Richard Goddard also noticed the 'noise of several coaches', and Harry Frankland thought that the King's coach must have just passed him. But those, like Thomas Chase, who had grown up in Lisbon knew instinctively that what was happening could not be attributed to carriages, no matter how grand.

Just a few streets to the west of the Rua das Pedras Negras Lawrence Fowkes, a wine merchant who originally hailed from Cork, had finished breakfast and was with two Portuguese friends in his counting-house in the Beco das Mudas, a little enclave of English and Irish families a stone's throw west of the church of São Nicolau, when he too heard 'a great noise like a coach and six driving by'. To the west, in the Bairro Alto, Charles Douglas, Lord Drumlanrig, was sitting down in his physician's house to write a letter to his parents, the Duke and Duchess of Queensbury, when he was simultaneously 'astonished with a violent shaking of the room' and felt the whole house start to 'swing from side

to side'.[4] Less than a mile to the west of the Terreiro do Paço, in the parish
of Santa Catarina, a merchant by the name of Braddock was also writing
a letter in his first-floor apartment when he noticed his table begin 'to
tremble with a gentle motion'. Then 'the whole house began to shake
from the very foundation'. It often did this when several coaches together
passed by on the way from Belém to the city at that time of day. But
Braddock was immediately 'undeceived' when he recognized the 'strange,
frightful kind of noise underground, resembling the hollow, distant
rumbling of thunder'. He had been on Madeira in 1748 and, like Thomas
Chase, knew from experience what was now happening in Lisbon.

The English skipper who had moored off the Ribeira das Naus less
than an hour earlier was surprised when he felt 'an uncommon motion'
run through the ship, as if she had just run aground. That he knew to
be impossible: she was moored in many fathoms of water. As the motion
grew more pronounced his concern, and puzzlement, increased; then he
turned to the shore and was 'immediately acquainted with the direful
cause'. All along the waterfront from São Paulo to his left up to the Bairro
Alto, and east as far as he could see, and due north all the way towards the
Rossio, every edifice seemed to be 'tumbling down with great cracks
and noise'.[5] Stupefied ships' crews looked on as crowds started to flee
down to the river, crying out for assistance from the watermen, fathers
and mothers screaming the names of their children while behind them
the whole city seemed 'to wave backwards and forwards like the sea
when the wind first begins to rise'. Then the anchors of even the largest
ships 'were propelled all the way to the surface',[6] and sailors and boatmen
had to turn their backs on the turmoil onshore to re-secure their
moorings. Before doing so, some had noticed that in places cracks in
the ground were spewing out water and sand, 'flung up as if it had been
done with shovels'.[7]

Richard Goddard's view from the castle should have been as
panoramic as that from the river, but he was too busy trying to stay on his

feet to inspect what was happening down in the Baixa. All around him people were shrieking and throwing themselves on the ground. Goddard grabbed hold of a flagstaff, and just as he did so he saw the upper parts of the castle begin to fall, and the houses round it start 'to share the same fate'.[8] In his house directly below the castle Thomas Chase rushed out of his bedroom and up the stairs to the *eirado*, the rooftop conservatory which commanded a view of the part of the city between the Terreiro do Paço and the castle. He hoped to see just how much of it was being 'agitated with the like violence', and the sight that greeted him was 'a prospect the most horrid that imagination can form'. He could not fix his gaze on the dreadful scene for more than an instant: his own house was now swaying beneath him with a 'tumbling sort of motion . . . like the waves of the sea', and Chase was so unsteady on his feet that he was forced to lean out of one of the *eirado*'s windows in an effort to prop himself up against the wall of the Goddard house opposite. The sound of all the houses 'grinding . . . one against another' had become 'the most dreadful jumbling noise', and as he tried to brace himself against the exterior wall of Ambrose Goddard's room it suddenly gave way. Chase pulled himself back just before the whole of the upper part of the Goddard house collapsed – and, so it appeared, the walls of every other house between him and the castle. In the *eirado* the two stone pillars supporting the roof suddenly bent until they almost met, and Chase felt himself tumbling downwards.

In the Beco das Mudas, Lawrence Fowkes quickly ushered José and Francisco Alvez out of his counting-house, believing that their best hope of safety was beneath a stone arch near his brother's home. Fowkes led the way, wearing only his nightshirt and a pair of slippers and dodging falling tiles and masonry dislodged by the street 'seemingly dancing' beneath their feet. When he reached the arch he turned to see José close behind him and over his shoulder glimpsed his brother's house, and those belonging to Mr Joyce and Mr Major, crash to the ground, enveloping them in great clouds of suffocating dust. Of Francisco Alvez there was no sign, and to their horror Fowkes and José Alvez realized that he must have 'perished in the way'.[9]

Up in the Bairro Alto, to the west of the Baixa, Lord Drumlanrig had rushed into the next room where he met one of his servants. As the motion of the house increased they grabbed onto each other and 'reeled' to the stairs for protection. While huddled there, beneath stone arches which they hoped would prove their saviour, Drumlanrig's room simply 'fell in'. This terrified them so much that they 'determined to sally out' into the open. The first sight of what lay outside was bewildering. The neighbourhood was 'so totally in ruins that it was not possible for strangers to know where one street had been from another',[10] and within seconds of stepping outside Dr Richard Scrafton's house it collapsed behind them. All over the city, amid the din of the 'grinding of the houses, the fall of the churches, the lamentable cries of the people', everyone was certain that this was 'the last moment of their lives', that they were already 'in the bowels of the earth'.[11]

As soon as Mr Braddock had realized what was happening he jumped to his feet, put down his pen and for a brief moment pondered whether to go out onto the street. His state of undress – he was still clad in just a gown and slippers – decided him against it, and his experience in Madeira a few years earlier made him think that the commotion was probably over. A 'most horrible crash' disabused him of this idea: it was a crash so loud that it sounded as if 'every edifice in the city had tumbled down at once'. Braddock was barely able to stay on his feet as the house 'shook with such violence' and the walls '[rocked] to and fro in the frightfulest manner', cracking open as they did so. The rafters were sprung from the ceiling and as the floors above him could be heard collapsing Braddock was certain that he was about to be buried. At that precise moment 'an Egyptian darkness' descended on the city, a darkness *such as might be felt*.[12] Not far away from him Sir Harry Frankland had dived out of his *chaise* and taken shelter under the gateway of a house and as he looked back he saw the building opposite collapse on the *chaise* and his servants. The arch under which he had sought shelter then fell as well, and he lost consciousness.

Three miles upriver Mr Latham, a wine merchant, had been taking a customer to a village when their boat had suddenly 'made a noise as if on shore or landing'. The two men had looked back towards the city and watched in horror as houses came 'tumbling down . . . on both sides of the river' and 'a convent on a high hill fronting the river' also collapsed. It looked from a distance as though some people were even pitched 'neck and heels' straight into the Tagus while others, those who could, streamed like so many disturbed and confused ants from the ruins and into the river 'up to their middle and necks'.[13] Latham's view had then been obscured as an avalanche of dust billowed out over the river, so thick that the sun was blotted out and Latham could hardly even make out his friend just a few feet away.

'God bless us, it is an earthquake!' exclaimed Latham's companion.

~ SIX ~

A City Laid in Ruins

THE PEOPLE OF LISBON WERE USED to disasters. The great earthquake of 1531 belonged to a different age but within living memory, in 1724, the city had been severely shaken and the same year a storm hit the Mar da Palha with such ferocity that more than a hundred ships sank or ran aground. In 1750 there had been a quake on the very day that João V died, a fire that ravaged the Hospital Real de Todos-os-Santos in the Rossio, and another that gutted the Palácio dos Corte-Reais by the waterside. But nothing could compare with the impact of what would later be recognized as the greatest seismic 'event' in the recorded history of western Europe. Its duration in Lisbon, between seven and ten minutes, was so exceptional that it has rarely been equalled.*

There were three distinct tremors, each separated by a pause of no more than a minute. The second of these was the greatest. On these facts nearly all eye-witnesses were agreed, although opinions differed slightly on the exact time of the first tremor. The earthquake was later assigned a magnitude of 8.75–9 on the Richter Scale, and assessed on the Modified Mercalli Scale as having an intensity of IX–XI, indicating a

---

* The duration of the Sumatra-Andaman submarine earthquake on Boxing Day 2004 is estimated at 8.3–10 minutes.

'disastrous' or 'very disastrous event. * In just fifteen minutes one of the largest cities in Europe was, in the words of Edward Hay, the English Consul, 'laid in ruins'.[1]

Benjamin Farmer, the merchant who had recently arrived in Lisbon to press his claim for a ship impounded in the Cape Verde islands, had stayed close to the staircase of his house, hoping, as did many, that it might afford him some protection. When he stepped outside into the courtyard he found it 'full of rubbish' and while he was surveying the destruction he heard a voice calling his name. Looking up he saw his neighbour, the 'lieutenant of the Green regiment', and some of his family 'hanging as it were in the air' in a first-floor room of a house that now had no exterior walls. The lieutenant's daughter, whose 'smirking looks' in his direction had rather enlivened Farmer's days since his arrival, was frantically pointing at the debris and shouting something in Portuguese he could not make out. But then he heard a 'shrill child's note' from in front of him, and realized what had happened: one of the children had either been buried while playing in the courtyard or had fallen from the first floor when the walls collapsed.

Farmer made his way towards the sound and began to clear the ground near the crying as best he could. The child's father and brother also appeared – how they had managed to descend to the ground Farmer knew not – and together they scrabbled in the ruins until Farmer felt his hand touch a small face. A slight tremor, strong enough to bring more tiles and stonework tumbling into the courtyard, made them all run but as soon as it stopped they began work again and at last the little girl was pulled free. She appeared to be quite unharmed, and as Farmer would later recall, 'no words, or pencil, can describe the countenance of the father when he got his child in his arms, and the confused sound of his voice is altogether indescribable'.[2] As for the father, he would

* The Mercalli Scale calibrates intensity on a range of I–XII based on eye-witness accounts, the movement of objects and damage to buildings.

forget every detail of what had occurred that morning before the rescue of his daughter.

Up in the castle the Reverend Richard Goddard's predicament was an unenviable one. He was alone, a complete stranger in the city, and gripped by a terrible anxiety; later he would write 'I will not affect to have been a calm and unmov'd spectator while all was horror and confusion around me'. When the dust cleared and he looked down at the streets of the Baixa he was convinced that there was not a chance that his brother Ambrose and his friends could possibly have escaped 'the general destruction'. There seemed nothing for it but to go and look, however, and he started to make his way down through the winding alleyways of the Alfama, the old Moorish quarter of the city flanking the castle. 'Heaps of ruins' lay everywhere along his route, and he was 'struck with the many miserable objects' sprawled on the streets. Everyone seemed to be in a terrible hurry, 'tho' without knowing where to fly for greater security'. Some were scrambling over the rubble up to the castle while others, like he, were making their way towards the Baixa or the waterfront. Many were 'maimed and covered in blood'. All wore the same look – 'a most perfect representation of horror and distraction'.[3]

Several minutes after the quake had subsided and the dust slowly began to settle, Lawrence Fowkes cautiously stepped away from the arch under which he and José Alvez had sought sanctuary, and peered through the gloom. The neighbourhood was utterly unrecognizable, and Fowkes was uncertain if he would even be able to determine which set of skeletal remains among the vast heap of 'rubbage' had been his brother Joseph's house. Then he noticed a lady struggling down a broken and exposed staircase with her children and, seeing that it was his sister-in-law, Anne, he rushed to help them. After they had embraced the Fowkeses 'scrambled along' through the ruins towards Lawrence's own house, gathering up friends along the way.

Moving anywhere about the city, for those who were able, was now like living a nightmare. Every step was over debris under which neighbours or passers-by were probably crushed. Here and there limbs, and even bloody heads, of the living and the dead protruded.[4] The experience turned people's minds as much as the quake had stunned them, and so traumatized was Anne Fowkes that only when she was nearing Lawrence's house did she realize that not all her children were with her: three-year-old Harry had been playing on a veranda when the quake struck, and no one had seen him since. Two neighbours immediately volunteered to retrace their steps, calling out for Harry as they went until they heard a little voice cry out from beneath the rubble that 'he had fallen in the dirt'. The child had been completely buried up to his head, he had wounds on his legs and bruises all over his face and body, but no bones were broken.

Lawrence Fowkes's house was still standing, but when he climbed up on the remains of what had been a neighbour's house and called out to his wife there was no answer. Four times he shouted in all, and only then did a servant answer from within that all was well. Fowkes then looked around him and realized that, with the exception of his building, the street, the little English and Irish enclave in the heart of the city that had been like one big family home, no longer existed. With each passing minute, however, coughing and hoarse voices began to be heard above the creaks and crashes of houses falling or about to fall. The Joyces appeared, then the Majors, then Mrs Buckley, then Andrew Morrogh and his son Frank, all with 'pale and dirty faces'. Everyone embraced, tearful and joyous at each other's survival. Then it became apparent that Mary Morrogh and her other son were not among the gathering.

Not far away, in the direction of the castle hill, Thomas Chase, his mind a jumble of 'confused ideas', started to regain consciousness. His last thought as he had begun to fall from his *urada* had been that the whole city must be 'sinking into the earth'; in fact he had fallen the full height of his house in the Rua das Pedras Negras, and survived. His first sensation was that his mouth was 'stuffed full of something' which he quickly sought to clear so that he could breathe properly. He then wriggled until his head was clear of the debris strewn about him, and was 'astonished to the last degree' by his surroundings. He lay in a space measuring just ten feet by two. Above him were four fifty-foot walls, seemingly without doors or windows, and it was some time before his mind was able to recall that there was just such a cavity between his own house and the one next door. Chase pondered his situation for a while, and slowly took in the fact that there was no chance of being spied from above nor, it seemed at first glance, of escape to the side. He was trapped, and was certain that he would starve to death. A little to the west of the Terreiro do Paço Harry Frankland was in a similar predicament. He regained consciousness to find that he was buried next to a lady who in her death-throes was biting clean through his broadcloth coat and into his arm.

In the parish of Santa Catarina, also to the west of the Terreiro do Paço, Mr Braddock was 'almost choked' by the 'prodigious clouds of dust and lime' which engulfed his room for ten minutes after the quake; and when it became possible to see again he was astonished to find that there was a woman sitting on his floor cradling an infant which was 'all covered with dust, pale, and trembling'. The woman was desperate for something to quench the thirst caused by all the dust, but Braddock's water jar had shattered so he could not offer her any relief. She was also quite unable to say how she had arrived in Braddock's apartment and repeatedly asked him, 'in the utmost agony [if] the world was at an end'. While Braddock contemplated this question he suddenly realized that he was only wearing his gown and slippers. This was not the state in which he would have wished to meet his unexpected visitor. But he was greatly relieved by the thought that if he had been dressed and ready to visit a friend in the Baixa for breakfast, as he had planned, he would have run out into the street with the first shock, as did everyone else in his building; and he would have had his 'brains dashed out as every one of them had'. Now, however, he was certain that it was time to leave as fast as possible; so he pulled on his coat and shoes, grabbed hold of the woman, and chivvied her downstairs.

Once out in the street it became obvious that heading straight down to the riverside was not a possibility: in that direction it was blocked by rubble piled as high as the second storeys of the collapsed buildings. So Braddock led the woman to the other end of the street in the hope of getting through to the main thoroughfare leading from Belém to the Terreiro do Paço. Another 'vast pile of rubble' blocked this route as well, but it looked easier to climb over, and Braddock carefully picked his way up and over the debris. Just as he was reaching the thoroughfare the other side he heard a wall collapse behind him and turned to reach for the woman and child, who had been following just a few feet behind him. They were both 'crushed . . . in pieces' beneath a 'vast stone'. Braddock's reaction to the death of the people he had been endeavouring to escort to safety by the river was pragmatic. 'So dismal a spectacle at any other time would have affected me in the highest degree', he later wrote; but, as was true of survivors all over the city, his grief was overcome by his 'dread . . . of sharing the same fate' unless he pressed on. The woman and child were dead. There could be no dwelling on the fact, especially in a place of such obvious danger.

Braddock went on and clambered over the last of the rubble blocking his street and then turned into Rua Direita da Boa Vista, the long narrow street of old four- and five-storey houses which ran parallel to the river towards the Terreiro do Paço. Most buildings had collapsed, and others looked – and sounded – about to do so at any moment. Bodies were strewn about all over the street, as were many survivors 'so bruised and wounded that they could not stir to help themselves'. The dead were the fortunate ones, Braddock thought, and wished that when his own 'unavoidable destruction' came it would be swift: the suffering of the 'poor unhappy wretches' who were mortally wounded was too dreadful to contemplate. He steadied himself and then made his way as fast as was possible to the far end of the street, past the alley leading to the Mint, and into Largo de São Paulo.

The sight of the once sturdy church in the middle of the square, which had collapsed burying as many as a hundred of the congregation, made Braddock pause for a few moments to consider where to make for next. What he sought was somewhere devoid of 'tottering houses' if there were to be another quake, and he decided that the open spaces along the waterfront must be the safest place of all. As he made his way over the rubble on the western side of the square, past the ruins of the new sugar refinery, he was not alone. Many others were intent on reaching the Tagus, and on the waterfront he found 'a prodigious concourse of people of both sexes, and all ranks and conditions', including purple-robed canons from the Patriarchal church, priests in their full vestments, half-dressed ladies and many of the Irishmen and women from the Remolares. All 'were on their knees at prayers', striking their breasts and wailing 'Misericórdia meu Deus!' Mercy, my Lord!'.

Amid the 'tears, bitter sighs and lamentations', Braddock recognized an old priest from São Paulo moving about, endeavouring to comfort the people but also encouraging them to repent of their sins and telling them that 'God was grievously provoked' and that if they 'called upon the Blessed Virgin she would intercede for them'. An Irishman offered Braddock a little statue of St Anthony so that he could join in the prayers; and when he gently turned down the offer the man indignantly asked if he did not believe there was a God. Braddock had no 'inclination to mock at their superstitions', but he wondered how many in the crowd who were brandishing 'useless pieces of wood' of one sort or another had 'left their children to perish'. On the other hand, the distraught state of everyone around him would, he later wrote, 'have touched the most flinty heart'. He knelt down and began to pray 'as fervently as the rest, though to a more proper object'.[5]

In the Rua das Pedras Negras, on the east side of the Baixa beneath the castle, Thomas Chase had remained in a 'state of stupefaction' in his ten-foot by two-foot prison. Showers of broken tiles and debris were still falling on him every now and then, and as time passed he began to think that his end was more likely to come from being buried alive than starvation. But when he moved a little to try and make himself more comfortable he noticed for the first time that there was a small cavity in the wall behind his head. This might, he thought, offer the possibility of escape; but on the other hand if there was another tremor he would certainly be crushed under the weight of the collapsing wall. Still very groggy from his fall, and in increasing pain, Chase considered what he should do and finally, with great difficulty, began to heave himself under what he assumed was the top of a foundation arch supporting the wall above him, and into the cavity.

His decision seemed vindicated: after falling a couple of feet 'into a small dark place', he felt his way down a narrow passage. To his great relief this led to a small room and there, in the gloom, stood a Portuguese man covered in dust who, at the sight of Chase, exclaimed 'Jesus, Maria e José' and began backing away from him, frantically crossing himself as he retreated. Convinced that a malevolent spirit had cornered him, the man cried out 'Who are you? Where do you come from?'. For the first time since his fall, Chase took stock of his appearance. His right shoulder was dislocated, causing his arm, which was clearly broken, to hang limp at his side; his stockings were shredded, revealing legs covered in wounds and a right ankle swollen 'to a prodigious size'; and his left side felt 'as if beat in', making it hard for him to breathe. Blood streamed from of his face, which was swollen and raw, and had cuts above and below his eye. Thomas Chase was in a 'mangled condition'.

The Reverend Richard Goddard was nearing the Rua das Pedras Negras, where his brother's and Thomas Chase's houses had stood, when suddenly a huge 'piece of a building' crashed down into the street just twenty yards in front of him. It was part of the cathedral, which had suffered severe damage to the cloister and the main chapel. This stopped him dead in his tracks. He must be mad, he thought, to have ventured down from the castle, a place to which multitudes were heading for safety, in the hope of finding a brother who was most probably dead and hadn't been at home anyway. So he turned and started to trudge all the way back up to the castle.

Lord Drumlanrig and his retinue of servants and attendants were, like Goddard, complete strangers to the city, and totally disorientated. But they had to move: standing disconsolately in front of the ruins of Dr Scrafton's house waiting for someone to rescue them did not seem a sensible course of action. As they began scrambling over the roofs of collapsed houses they fell in with an English watch-maker who, when he was told Drumlanrig's 'name and quality', promised to guide him through the maze of streets to the Rossio and declared that 'they would live or die together'.[6] The group then picked its way over 'the most terrible ruins', all the while accompanied by the screams and wailing of those buried alive under the rubble, and in an hour they managed to progress a distance that would normally have been covered in a ten-minute stroll. But at last they reached the great square of Rossio whose open space would at least ensure that they were safe from falling masonry.

The sight that confronted Drumlanrig in the Rossio, even by comparison with what he had already seen, was shocking. Thousands and thousands of people had converged on the square, and thousands more were filtering in from the streets which led to it from east, west and south. There were 'old, young, male and female seeking their parents, children, relations and friends, many sick, many maimed and wounded from the fall of the houses, some dead and most part especially women half naked'[7] wrote Thomas Jacomb, a woollens merchant who lived in a house overlooking the scene; and another English merchant described the wailing issuing from those 'in the utmost confusion and distress' as 'the most hideous noise I ever heard'. Many people were 'smiting their breast and beating their faces in a most cruel manner', making them 'swollen to a monstrous size, and so discoloured as to render them quite ghastly'.

This was a scene of religious fervour, or religious fever, such as no outsider would have seen before, and when the merchant saw Drumlanrig being forced to kiss a cross, he advised him to escape the 'mad behaviour'[8] as soon as he had recovered his strength. Drumlanrig, and any other Protestant outsider, had every reason to be terrified. 'Heretics' were an easy target for blame. In Lisbon the populace had turned on the 'New Christian' Jewish converts after the earthquake of 1531, and as recently as the plague of 1723 clerics had blamed the visitation on the greed of merchants (a majority of whom were foreigners or suspected of being New Christians). It was not a city to be in at a time of catastrophe, any more than it had been safe to be a Catholic in London after the Great Fire almost a century earlier.

To the west of the city, the lady who had bitten through Harry Frankland's coat and left teeth marks in his arm had died beside him.

~ SEVEN ~

Shockwaves

SIX HUNDRED MILES SOUTH-WEST OF LISBON on the island of Madeira, first occupied by the Portuguese in 1419 and once the source of all Europe's sugar, the morning had also dawned fine and calm. Thomas Heberden, one of the first physicians to extol the benefits of a sojourn in Funchal for sufferers of chest and bronchial complaints, was indoors when he first heard the 'rumbling noise in the air, like that of empty carriages passing hastily over a stone pavement'; and immediately afterwards the floor of his house began to move 'with a tremulous motion, vibrating very quickly, the windows rattled, and the whole house seemed to shake'. But the shock was of much shorter duration than in Lisbon. After little more than a minute it was all over, 'dying away like a peal of distant thunder', and Charles Chambers, by far the biggest shipper of Madeira wine, recorded the time at which the earthquake struck as 9.38 a.m. Both Chambers and Heberden were relieved that the quake did not appear to be as bad as that of 1748, the one which Mr Braddock had also witnessed: that had destroyed a large part of the palace of the Bishop of Funchal, the Igreja do Monte, and many other buildings.

The earthquake also hit the coast south of Lisbon minutes earlier than the capital and here, unlike Madeira, the effects were equally devastating. At Setúbal, or St Ubes as it was known to the English, a fishing port and site of extensive saltworks on the Sado estuary, almost all churches, convents and houses were ruined and by the end of the day more than a thousand people were dead. At Sagres, on the south-western tip of the country, the fort and all the houses were wrecked, and the damage throughout the 'kingdom of the Algarves', home to 100,000 people, was considerable. At Lagos one in ten of the town's population were killed and nine in every ten houses were destroyed; in Vila do Bispo all houses were destroyed; in Boliqueime more than a hundred perished; and in Faro more than two hundred. Among the important buildings that were ruined were the large Jesuit college and the convent of São Francisco at Portimão; the cathedral, castle walls, town hall, court-house and prison of Silves; a dozen religious institutions in Lagos; and the cathedral, Episcopal palace, Jesuit college, sumptuous church of São Pedro and the convent of the Capuchins in Faro. From there Captain Thomas Bean of the *Bean Blossome* wrote to his father two days later of the 'Dreadfull Vissitation from ye Almighty of a terrebell Earthquack Which I Was in and a Spacktator to'; 'The Lord grant I Neaver May behold Such another', Bean continued, 'So Dreadfull was ye Seen. It is almost impossibell to Discribe it to you, in Less you where Eye Witnesses, the Lord grant you neaver may'. [2]

To the north of Lisbon Portugal's second city, Porto, felt the shock within minutes of the capital. There too the inhabitants noticed a sound 'like thunder, or the rattling of a coach over stones' as the quake first struck, and there too it was said to have lasted about ten minutes. 'We all ran into the street, and everybody seemed frightened out of their senses, as if they thought the world was at an end', wrote one English resident; another would remember the ghastly sensation of watching 'the earth heave . . . just as if it was in labour'; and Tilman Henkel, a Hamburg merchant, later recalled that 'all of us were afraid of being swallowed up'. Two ships bound for Brazil were just approaching the river bar and only narrowly escaped foundering on it; and a number of vessels in the River Douro capsized or lost their moorings. But the damage was insignificant compared to that of the capital and the south, and although a few people, including an Englishman by the name of Webber, died through 'mere fear',[3] the loss of life was negligible.

All over Spain clocks stopped, bells rang out and the water in wells rose or fell as the earthquake swept through the country. It was the worst such visitation ever experienced and only diminished markedly in strength as it reached the north-east. In Madrid, where the shaking lasted five or six minutes, it was later reported that 'every body at first thought, that they were seized with a swimming in their heads', that in the churches 'people trod one another under foot in getting out', and that those who observed what happened to towers throughout the capital were 'very much frightened, thinking, that they were tumbling to the ground'. The trauma was immediate and considerable: 'a great many' were said to be 'indisposed by the fright'.[4] Benjamin Keene, the English Ambassador, was at the Escorial at the time and hastened back to the capital, as did the Royal Family who took up residence in tents in the palace grounds at Buen Retiro, on the outskirts of Madrid.

Fissures, landslides and rockslides were witnessed throughout Spain, but it was in the south-west, in Andalucia, that the damage was worst. In Seville a thick fog had settled over the town before the quake and when it struck the noise was likened to that of a hurricane. It may have lasted as long as eleven minutes here, and an account published in the Gazeta de Lisboa two weeks later recorded how 'all buildings and temples were severely damaged by the great violence. Churches and houses were abandoned and those at confession begged the heavens for mercy.' Forty monasteries and twenty-eight convents collapsed, as did a vast number of houses; and of the twenty-eight parish churches only one was left relatively unscathed. The famous Giralda bell-tower of the cathedral 'crumpled like a sheet of paper',[5] while in Granada the Colegiata

San Salvador and the cathedral both sustained significant damage.

On the coast all the churches were ruined in Ayamonte, where the tremors may have continued for as long as fifteen minutes; and at Cádiz, Spain's principal port, a general panic was only averted by the confidence of the populace in the very strong walls surrounding the island city. All the towers and houses shook and, according to one Englishman resident who was planting out some flowers at the time, everyone experienced 'seasickness, a swimming in the head and qualmishness'.[6] But only the most ramshackle houses experienced any real damage. On 'the Rock' – Gibraltar – the guns of the battery 'were seen some to rise, others to sink' as the earth assumed 'an undulating motion'. It was reported that 'most people were seized with giddiness and sickness, and some fell down', while others 'were stupefied'[7] and a few who were riding or walking at the time were sick even though they felt no motion at all.

In northern Europe the shock was felt in Toulouse, Bordeaux, Brittany and Normandy; in the Alps and parts of northern Italy; in Hamburg and a hundred miles to the east of that city; and in Cork.[8] On the British mainland the earthquake was not 'sensible', but a plethora of extraordinary observations later collated by the Royal Society showed that it was certainly *visible*. The earthquake of 1722 which had struck the Algarves with an intensity of IX on the Mercalli Scale, denoting a 'violent' shock, had caused discernible disturbances on the Scottish lochs, and three decades later the experience was repeated.

It was at about 9.30 a.m. when Angus M'Diarmid, the inn-keeper at Tarbat, noticed a 'strange phaenomena' on Scotland's largest loch, Loch Lomond. To his astonishment the water suddenly 'rose against its banks with great rapidity', and then retired so rapidly that within five minutes it was 'as low . . . as anybody . . . had ever seen it in the time of the greatest summer drought'.[9] Five minutes after that the loch rose again to the previous level, and it continued to rise and fall at five-minute intervals until 10.15 a.m., when a less pronounced ebb and flow commenced, lasting for a further forty-five minutes. When at last the loch was calm again, M'Diarmid measured the high-point to which the loch had risen at two feet four inches above its level before the disturbance.*

At about ten o'clock on Loch Ness, twenty-three miles long and more than 700 feet deep in parts, a brisk wind was blowing from the south-west when a physician by the name of Robert Gardener set out for a morning stroll. He had arrived the night before at Fort Augustus, which just ten years earlier had been captured by Bonnie Prince Charlie's Highlanders during the Jacobite uprising; and he had only just started when several people had approached him, including Mr Lumisden the barrack-master, and said that they had witnessed 'a very extraordinary agitation' of the loch. Gardener paid little attention to their story and returned to his lodgings after taking the air. An hour later, however, his own clerk and the town's brewer rushed in exclaiming that 'a more extraordinary agitation than the former' was taking place and that the brewery, situated at the point where the River Oich flowed into the loch, was in 'some danger'. By the time Gardener reached the brewery the water was calm. But he noticed that the riverbanks were wet above the normal waterline, and onlookers spoke of a wave two or three feet high having run 200 yards up the Oich before breaking on a shallow and returning to the loch. This ebb and flow had continued for about an hour until eleven o'clock when a wave 'higher than any of the rest' had broken 'with so much force . . . as to run upon the grass upwards of thirty feet from the river's bank'. At much the same time at Queen's Ferry, ten miles west of Edinburgh at the narrowest point of the Firth of Forth, the water rose a foot or eighteen inches 'which made the barks and boats then afloat run forwards and backwards on their ropes with great rapidity'. The motion continued for three or four minutes when, after the 'second or third rush of water',[10] it returned to a state of calm.

* The veracity of Angus M'Diarmid's observations has been questioned due to the time he attributed to them. Given that they are plausible and far from unique it seems likely that he simply read his watch incorrectly, or that it was set wrongly.

Similar disturbances were witnessed all over England. A little after
10.30 a.m. an 'extraordinary motion of the waters' occurred at Portsmouth, over 900 miles from Lisbon. HMS *Gosport* had just berthed in
the North Dock, and 'was well-stayed by guys and hawsers', when she
unaccountably ran three feet astern then three feet for'ard, pitching
bow to stern by the same degree. In the basin, enclosed by two pairs of
gates, HMS *Berwick*, HMS *Dover*, and a 600-ton vessel unloading a
cargo of tar were similarly 'disturbed' by an unaccountable swell of nine
inches. Out in the main harbour HMSs *Nassau* and *Duke*, 60- and
90-gun warships respectively, were also 'rocked in the same manner'.[11]
As the weather was fine, and it was completely calm before and after
the motion, what had happened was noted with interest and puzzlement by onlookers.

On Lake Windermere the Reverend John Harrison reported that
two fishermen on the shore had just pulled their boat up when 'on a
sudden the water swelled, floated the boat, heaved it up about its length
farther upon land, and took it back again in the falling back of the
wave'.[12] Here too there was no wind, and the flux and reflux of the water
lasted about ten minutes. At 10.30 a.m., five miles from Durham, a
gardener heard 'a sudden rushing noise, like the fall of water'. He ran
to the pond and 'saw it gradually rise up . . . until it reached a grate,
which stood some inches higher than the common water-level'. The
pond subsided again, and then continued rising and falling for six or
seven minutes. The gardener was 'so alarmed that he ran to the house
to call his fellow servants down to look at it'.[13] At Yarmouth Haven as
well, just before noon, a ship under repair was suddenly shaken by 'an
uncommon motion, and the water was violently agitated'[14] although
there was no wind.

At Peerless Pool, near Old Street in London, two waiters were 'engaged
in some business near the wall' which enclosed the fish pond when
'large waves rolled slowly to and from the bank near them', leaving the

pond dry for several feet. When the water returned it overflowed its usual mark by twelve feet, and the motion continued for five or six minutes. A similar motion disturbed the 'pleasure bath'[15] as well, although there was no disturbance of the 'cold bath' in between the fish pond and the 'pleasure bath'. Not long after this occurence at Peerless Pool Henry Mills was on one of his barges unloading timber at Rotherhithe when he was 'surprised by a sudden heaving up of the barge from a swell of the water, not unlike what happens when a ship is launched from any of the builders yards in the neighbourhood'. The barge rose in this unaccountable fashion 'three or four times'.[16] Detailed observations of seiches were made all over southern England – in Godalming, Midhurst, Guildford, at the Earl of Macclesfield's seat at Shirburn Castle, in Edenbridge and many other places. At Cobham 'an old sensible man' was watering his horse at a pond when the water ran away, leaving the bottom visible, and then returned 'with that impetuosity, which made [him] leap backwards to secure himself'.[17]

In only one place in England was it claimed that the quake was *felt*, as opposed to observed, and that was in the lead mines on Eyam Edge in Derbyshire. There, at eleven o'clock in the morning, Francis Mason, the overseer, 'felt one shock, which very sensibly raised him up in his chair'. One hundred and twenty yards below him a miner was 'so terrified . . . that he immediately quitted his employment, and ran to the west end of the drift to his partner, who was not less terrified than himself'. The two men did not dare to climb up the shaft in case it collapsed and counted five shocks in all, after each of which there was 'a loud rumbling in the bowels of the earth, which continued for about half a minute'.[18] Their horrifying ordeal lasted a total of twenty minutes.*

On the fjords of Norway and southern Scandinavia, the basins of Le

---

* These shocks could have been caused by a small explosion of 'slickenslides', a species of galena commonly found in the mine which could ignite at the touch of a miner's pick and explode with a noise very similar to that of an earthquake. A huge explosion of this type had occurred at Eyam Edge in 1738.

Havre and other ports of northern France, and rivers and ponds throughout northern Europe equally unusual disturbances of the water were observed and noted. At eleven in the morning in The Hague there was 'so violent a motion of the water, that the ships were struck against each other, and broke the cables which fastened them';[19] and in Switzerland many rivers turned muddy and the level of Lake Neuchâtel, 1,000 miles from Lisbon, rose by almost two feet and remained there for 'a few hours'.[20] Lake Lucerne was observed to be 'uncommonly high and rough, placing ships in peril of shipwreck';[21] and even at Töplitz, a famous spa town nine miles from Prague, the spring that fed the thermal baths, and which had flowed at the same rate since the year 762, started to churn out murky and muddy water mid-morning and then stopped flowing altogether. Half and hour later the spring suddenly gushed again with such 'prodigious violence'[22] that the baths overflowed. Furthest of all from Lisbon, the water was disturbed at the port of Åbo (Turku) on Finland's River Aurajoki – 2,200 miles from the epicentral area.*

Out at sea a great many ships' captains recorded extraordinary occurrences. Captain Elliott of the *Bristow Galley* was two days out of Lisbon, sailing at three knots, when he was 'alarmed with a noise which seemed like casks rolling about the ship's decks'. Before he could get up on deck the noise increased to such an extent that he thought his vessel must be 'striking over sunken rocks'. He immediately 'put the helm a-weather and sounded, but found no ground'; then he 'sounded the pumps and found the ship to make no water'. Finally, as the rumbling continued, he 'ordered the lashings of the long-boat to be cut loose, and the tackles to be in readiness in case of necessity'.[23] Five days, and sixty leagues, out of Lisbon bound for America, Captain Johnson noticed an inexplicable 'strong agitation'[24] run through his ship. The skipper of a vessel forty

---

* When Charles Davison compiled his ground-breaking study *Great Earthquakes* in 1936 it was, in his opinion, these 'remarkable' seiches alone that earned the earthquake its place in his catalogue: never before or since had this phenomenon been 'so widely and notably observed' (Davison, Charles, *Great Earthquakes*, Thomas Murby & Co. Ltd, 1936, p.1)

leagues from shore thought he had 'struck upon a rock', but when he threw out the lead he 'could find no bottom'.[25] Closer to shore the captain of the *Nancy*, sailing off Sanlúcar, also 'felt his ship so violently shaken, that he thought she had struck ground'; and he too 'after heaving the lead overboard, found she was in a great depth of water'.[26] Captain Clark on the *Mary* off Dénia, south of Valencia, reported that his ship was 'shaken and strained as if she had struck a rock, so that seams of the deck opened, and the compass was overturned in the benacle';[27] almost all the bottles, china and earthenware in his cargo were smashed. A great many ships even fired their guns in distress.*

A comprehensive catalogue of what occurred in North Africa never emerged. In Morocco the intensity of the quake has been assessed at VII–IX on the Mercalli Scale, but there were substantial discrepancies between 'Arab' and European accounts of what had happened in individual towns and cities. The Governor of Gibraltar, General Fowke, collated what information he could and reported that at Tangier 'the trembling of houses, mosques &c was great', that at Tetuan 'it was feared the whole city would fall down', and that at Fez and Meknes 'vast numbers of houses fell down, and a great many people were buried under the ruins'. It is certain that the Franciscan convent, church and hospital complex in Fez was completely destroyed, but reports that the entire population of one town, numbering '8–10,000 persons, together with their cattle of all sorts, camels, horses, horned cattle &c' were 'swallowed up', and that at 'the Scloges' not far from Fez a mountain was split open 'and a stream issued out as red as blood'[28] were less credible.

The exact location of the epicentre of the 'Lisbon' earthquake is still

---

*There were also plenty of 'seaman's tales' generated: the master of a vessel bound for the West Indies reported seeing the sudden appearance from beneath the waves of the mid-Atlantic of 'three craggy pointed rocks, throwing up water of various colours, resembling liquid fire' (Bevis, p.331).

The *Gazeta de Lisboa* reported on 6 May 1756 that the constable of the fortress of Mazagão was carried off by the tidal wave, only to be returned by an influx moments later through the postern gate. The man was apparently 'given the Sacrament, but after he had vomited sand, whelks, little shells, and some congealed blood, he recovered'.

not known. The most likely area is on the Azores-Gibraltar fault zone, where the Eurasian and African tectonic plates meet, at a distance of 125–175 miles south and west of Lisbon. What would become apparent, after reports from across Europe were collected together and the more fanciful ones cast aside, was that the quake had been sensible at a distance of 1,500 miles and its effects were visible over an area comprising not less than six million square miles – twice the size of Australia. This was, without doubt, in the words of José Manuel Martínez Solares, Director-General of Spain's Instituto Geográfico Nacional, 'one of the most extraordinary earth events [that] ever occurred'.[29]

~ EIGHT ~

Fire and Water

FOR A FULL HOUR AFTER THE EARTHQUAKE the ground beneath
Lisbon continued to tremble and groan. Then – while Mr Braddock was
on his knees in prayer by the river, Harry Frankland regained consciousness to find himself entombed, Thomas Chase took stock of his
'mangled condition' and Drumlanrig resolved to head for the Envoy's
house before he was lynched – a massive aftershock hit the city.
Experiencing it in the confines of a basement, Chase thought the tremor
was 'more threatening'[1] than what had come before, and most people
would later agree that it was only 'a little less violent than the first'.[2]

In the Beco das Mudas the inhabitants of the little Anglo-Irish enclave
were still in a state of shock at the realization that not all of them had
survived, that Andrew Morrogh had lost his wife and a son, and José
Alvez his brother, when this next disaster struck. Lawrence Fowkes's
house swayed 'to and fro like the mast of a ship in a storm' and looked
certain to topple and crush them all beneath it. They 'called on God for
Mercy' and their prayers were answered. The house stood, and when
everyone was once again steady on their feet a Portuguese neighbour,
Senhor Luiz, clambered onto the mountain of debris separating them
from the Largo de São Nicolau to see if he could find a way through to the

square. When he returned he confirmed that it was possible to reach it – but said nothing about the spectacle that had greeted him there. Fowkes gathered together his family, his brother's, and those from the neighbourhood who wanted to move, and followed Senhor Luiz as he retraced his steps back over the ruins. Mr Joyce stayed with Andrew Morrogh and his son Frank on the ruins of their home. It was the last time that Fowkes saw his friend Morrogh alive.

The church of São Nicolau with its imposing façade of smooth masonry, two towers and eleven chapels dated back to the thirteenth century. Two hours earlier it had been one of the richest and most sumptuous of the city's parish churches. Now it was a complete ruin, as were the numerous brotherhoods and infirmaries adjoined to it. Scores of worshippers had been killed, and many others who had sought safety in the open space of the small square had been crushed by collapsing buildings. The bodies of the dead and dying were strewn all over, while the living roamed about behind priests determined that those about to expire should be given the chance to confess their sins and receive final absolution. Everyone was 'shouting to God for Mercy'.

In the confusion caused by this 'shocking spectacle' Fowkes suddenly realized that not everyone was still with him. His son Sam, his sister-in-law and Senhor Luiz had disappeared in the crowd along with a number of neighbours who had accompanied him. There seemed little point in turning back as all of them had still been following him when they reached the square minutes before, so Fowkes decided to strike out for the Rossio in the hope that they had gone on ahead. Having scrambled over the ruins in the square to its north-east corner, he found that the Rua das Arcas, which ran north to the Rossio, appeared to be passable and those still with him pressed on. They passed what had been the Beco do Mezas, the Beco do Pato and the ruins of the comedy theatre, stopping every now and then to offer a hand to people emerging from ruined houses, and eventually reached the great square.

Fowkes, like Drumlanrig, found that even by comparison with what he had witnessed in the Largo de São Nicolau 'the scenes of horror were doubled' in the Rossio. 'I can compare it', he wrote, 'to nothing but the idea I had formed in my youth of miserable sinners at the last day crying to God for Mercy'. 'Numberless objects' lay all about, 'expiring with groans and misery'. The palace of the Inquisition on the north side of the square was ruined, as was the adjacent convent of São Domingos and its church, in which all those condemned by the Inquisition were displayed in effigy. The vast edifice of the Hospital Real de Todos-os-Santos on the east side was also badly damaged, and above the square to the south-west the convents of the Carmo, the Trinidade, and every other building in the lower parts of the Bairro Alto appeared to be in varying states of collapse. Fowkes blundered on through the throng until he reached the middle of the square and then turned to find that now only his wife, his son Neb and a Miss Lester were still with him. So he sent Neb, 'a worthy, courageous, valuable lad',[3] to retrace their steps in search of the others. When he returned with some of them Fowkes was so worried, and so determined to get out of the Rossio and into the countryside, that he decided to press on even though his brother's family and one of his own sons were still missing.

Somewhere nearby Lord Drumlanrig was also preparing to flee the Rossio. He had 'amply rewarded' the kind watch-maker for guiding him to relative safety, and even though he was still weak from his exertions he had no desire to loiter a moment longer amid 'the madness'. With John Morrison, his clerk, Mr Douglas, his factor, Alexander and the rest of his servants he set off up the Rua das Portas de Santo Antão in the direction of Abraham Castres's house at Santa Martha. It was less than a mile away, in the parish of São José, and had substantial grounds in which Drumlanrig hoped his party 'might find some succour and protection.'[4] As they all moved off, the servants were gratified to see him display 'surprising strength'[5] as they made their way over the first heaps of rubble.

Up in the castle the Reverend Richard Goddard was in a state of 'utmost perplexity'. His only consolation, being unable so much as to ask directions of anyone around him, was the appearance of 'a Factory man' with whom he was able to chat. It looked to them as though everything down below – houses, churches, convents and palaces – was now 'composing one undistinguishable heap of ruins'; and, after agreeing that there was a likelihood of further aftershocks, they decided it would be best to stay put even if this course of action was not without its own hazards. Goddard was particularly concerned about the mood of the crowd around him which, to a Protestant parson from Wiltshire, seemed to be increasingly hysterical. Everywhere people were 'engaged in deprecating the vengeance of heaven', and priests were performing the absolution en masse. Goddard in no way doubted 'the sincerity of their devotions', but he was 'scandalized by the large mixture of idolatry and superstition which prevailed in them'.

He and his companion endeavoured to stay well out of the way, but after a while they were spotted and a great crowd descended on them 'in a most violent manner'. Goddard was terrified, believing that 'they were going to throw us from the castle as hereticks who had brought this judgement upon them'. The Factory man, who spoke Portuguese, managed to extricate himself from the mêlée, but Goddard was trapped. Then, to his great relief, everyone seemed to calm down and sought to reassure him 'by the tenderness of their behaviour'. The crowd began their devotions again, gesturing at him to join them, and when they had finished they all embraced him. Goddard thought that he may have been 'baptized' as a Catholic;[6] but as this seemed to have enabled him to slip away he was not unduly perturbed.

Down in the Baixa a new danger was now visible. Plumes of smoke were billowing from the palace of the Marquês de Louriçal in the Largo da Annunciada and from the convent of São Domingos in the Rossio, and before long overturned fires and candles in houses and churches also set light to tapestries and furniture. Fanned by a strong wind which had started to blow from north-east and east, the flames spread rapidly and merged with other blazes deliberately set by looters. Even under normal circumstances putting out the smallest of fires in the maze of narrow streets in the Baixa was a difficult task; now, with all streets blocked and a populace bent only on prayer or flight to the country, no attempt was made to check the advance of the flames. Soon the temperature started to rise in the Rossio, and throughout the Baixa the air became acrid and suffocating.

In the Rua das Pedras Negras, the terrified Portuguese man whom Thomas Chase had encountered in the basement had fled through the door when the ground started to shake again. Chase could hear people screaming out in the street, so rather than follow him he retreated as fast as his injuries would allow back to the arch under which he had escaped. There he stayed until 'the horror abated', when he retraced his steps to the doorway through which the Portuguese man had fled. A narrow staircase led from it which, to his surprise, took him directly into the street. The aftershock had brought down many more buildings, and the air outside was thick with dust and smoke, the light as poor 'as if it had been a very dark day'.[7]

Peering through the gloom Chase was able make out scores of ghostly figures, covered in dust from head to toe, kneeling in prayer. He hoped that his injured leg would support him as far as the river, which was only 500 yards away. But when he could make out the state of the Beco de João das Armas, the very narrow street running downhill from the Largo das Pedras Negras towards the Terreiro do Paço, his hopes of a flight in that direction were dashed. The Rua das Armazens, running uphill, was also blocked, as was the street running towards Santa Maria Madalena and the cathedral. Not knowing what to do, Chase's strength now failed him and he collapsed on the ground. He was dimly aware of his neighbours, Ambrose Goddard and Benjamin Branfill, and some others from the woollen merchants Jackson, Branfill & Goddard talking close by; but he found that he could not speak to tell them he was not just a corpse, and soon he lost consciousness altogether.

For those who instinctively fled to the open spaces along the waterfront after the earthquake, the aftershock was no less terrifying than for those still in the streets of the Baixa or in the Rossio. It simply confirmed that the catastrophe that had begun shortly after 9.30 a.m. was not over, and with this in mind people desperately sought, and fought to get, a passage on a boat across the Tagus. The sight, and din, of people in varying states of undress shrieking at boatmen and screaming to crewmen of the larger ships offshore was pitiful. In front of the ruined church of São Paulo, to the west of the Terreiro do Paço, Mr Braddock had only just managed to stay steady on his knees in prayer during the aftershock. On the rise behind him countless buildings that had been damaged but not ruined in the earthquake came tumbling down, and even though he was almost 500 yards from the church atop the hill of Santa Catarina he could hear the cries of 'Misericórdia!' as it fell, crushing many who had gathered in the square in front of it and mortally wounding others. Minutes later, however, the aftershock ceased to concern those by the water.

At Cascais, less than a dozen miles west of the city, the sea was suddenly observed withdrawing as much as three miles, and at Oeiras, five miles to the west, more than a mile. Then, with a velocity of 400 miles per hour or more, a wall of water surged towards the city. The soldiers in the Bugio, the fort in the middle of the entrance to the Tagus around which the water fell so far that waves broke 'feather white'[8] over the river bar, fired their cannon in distress – and then dashed to the highest point in the tower as the fort was swamped by the forty-foot tidal wave. People fleeing the city towards Belém on foot, horseback and mule turned and ran or galloped towards higher ground. But those in the city, preoccupied with their immediate surroundings or with trying to secure a place on a boat, never saw the wave approaching.

Braddock was still transfixed by the tragedy on Santa Catarina hill when he first heard someone scream 'the sea is coming – we shall all be lost!'. He turned, and saw the most extraordinary occurrence he could ever have imagined. The Tagus was four miles wide from where he stood to Barreiro on the southern shore and the entire surface of the water was 'heaving and swelling in a most unaccountable manner', despite the absence of any wind. Then a twenty-foot wave, which to Braddock looked 'like a mountain', advanced 'roaring and foaming'[9] towards the shore. From the ship that had moored off the Ribeira das Naus that morning the skipper looked on as the water 'overcame and overflowed the lower part of the city', and the 'already dismayed inhabitants . . . ran to and fro with dreadful cries'[10] which he could easily hear on board. Ships on the mud in Bull-Bay, in front of Braddock, were hurled onto land as were great pieces of timber, casks, and barrels from the wharves.

Every soul in Lisbon knew of the terrible sea wave which had followed the earthquake at Lima nine years earlier, and which had completely overwhelmed its port at Callao, killing all but a few hundred of the 25,000 inhabitants. Those on the waterfront who were able, and who reacted quickly enough, turned and ran. But even those who were most fleet of foot found themselves in water up to their waists and hung on grimly to any fixed object they could grab as the water receded with 'equal rapidity'. Braddock clung to a huge beam, which saved him from being sucked into the river by the first tidal wave, but no sooner had the water drained away than he made out a second wall of water heading for the shore. He dashed for 'a small eminence at some distance from the river' but even there, with 'the ruins of several intervening houses to break the force'[11] of the wave, he found himself up to his knees in water. The shore was flooded three times in all, the waves reaching streets, squares and gardens up to 200 yards from the waterfront and leaving a mass of timber and broken boats littered about.

Those who had already managed to secure a place in boats on the river were no safer than those on shore. Many of them, in the words of the skipper of the English vessel, were simply 'tossed on land by the sudden rise of the water',[12] where a few managed to jump out and save themselves by grabbing hold of some fixed object. But most were sucked back out into the river which, in the space of a few minutes, had been transformed from complete calm into a turbulent and 'confused forest of entangled masts, and a horrible cemetery of floating corpses'.[13] From a vantage point on a small rise three miles upriver the wine merchant Mr Latham and his companion had watched in amazement as the wave advanced over the road to Lisbon, 400 yards from the usual low-water mark. Countless small craft were 'dashed to pieces', and even the biggest vessels on the Mar da Palha were 'whirled about',[14] pitching sailors into the river. On the Outra Banda, the southern shore of the Tagus, Latham observed that the cliffs provided some resistance to the waves but in many places they collapsed, sending a huge quantity of dust out over the river.

For about five minutes it was impossible to see anything from the river. But when the dust cleared the English skipper noticed that, in addition to the waterfront being 'overspread with boats, vessels, timber, masts, household goods, casks &c', there was an even more shocking sight. The Cais da Pedra, the splendid new quay running along the river in front of the Customs House on the east side of the Terreiro do Paço, on which hundreds of people had been waiting for boats, had simply disappeared. Those who were close enough for him to make out their expressions, and who had noticed the same thing, looked convinced that the poor souls on the quay had descended straight to Hell and that now 'the dissolution of the world was at hand'.[15]

~ NINE ~

Teletsunami

THE FORCE OF THE TIDAL WAVE WAS SO GREAT as it hit the mouth of the Tagus that boulders weighing as much as twenty-five tons were hurled thirty yards inland. In one place a 200-ton boulder was displaced, and at Cabo Raso an entire 'field' of huge rocks was deposited fifteen to twenty yards above sea level.[1] At Cascais the sea inflicted even greater damage than the earthquake: the fort and barracks were ruined, as were the port's two principal parish churches, the convents of Nossa Senhora da Piedade dos Marianos and St Anthony of the Capuchins, and the palace of the Marquês de Cascais. The sea also completed the destruction of the port of Setúbal. One subsequent report simply stated that there were 'no traces left of this place, the repeated shocks, and vast surf having concurred to swallow it up, people and all'.[2] In these two coastal towns alone more than 1,500 people had perished, while to the north there was extensive damage to the fishing village of Ericeira, and at Peniche more than fifty people were lost to the waves.

On Portugal's south coast the seabed was exposed to a depth of twenty fathoms in some places before the first wave, up to a hundred feet high, hit Sagres. Sturdy forts at Arrifana, Lagos, Portimão and Armação de Pêra were reduced to rubble, and at Armação almost all the fishermens' houses were swept away. Here, at Albufeira, and in many other coastal towns and villages, people perished because they had sought refuge on the beach after the earthquake. The Bishop of the Algarves recorded that in Lagos and Albufeira above all 'the sea rose with such an infernal fury that it swept away the remains of everything that had been ruined by the earthquake';[3] and the historian Damião de Faria e Castro, who was in Faro at the time, claimed that the force of the tidal wave was so great that 'in some parts [it] mounted cliffs ninety fathoms in height'.[4] At Loulé more than a hundred people drowned, at Albufeira nearly two hundred, at Portimão more than fifty and at little Armação between fifty and a hundred. The full death toll caused by the tidal waves on the Algarves would never be known, but it was certainly over a thousand. Among the larger Algarve settlements only Faro, which was afforded a little protection by its offshore islets, and Tavira, on the leeward side of Faro, were relatively unscathed.

When the earthquake had hit the great port of Cádiz, the hub of Spain's trade with its empire in America, Benjamin Bewick, a young merchant from Hallaton Hall near Market Harborough, had observed the water in the town's underground cisterns slosh backwards and forwards 'so as to make a great froth'; and the whole population had dashed about 'in a terrible consternation'. But the city's walls and build-ings were known to be 'excessively strong' and this helped to avert a general panic. A little over an hour later, however, on a morning still as fine as 'the finest summer-day in England', Bewick happened to look out to sea and saw a wave approaching from 'eight miles off, which was at least sixty feet higher than common'. 'Everybody', he remarked, 'began to tremble', and then ran, 'some one way, some another'. Two other English residents also saw the rapid approach from beyond St Sebastian's Point of the 'prodigious large wave of the sea like a mountain'; and they too 'did not think it proper to stand [their] ground'[5] and started to run towards the city centre, expecting that at any moment the water would be at their heels. In the harbour Captain Joseph Hibbert and two other New England skippers were approaching the brigantine *Hannah* when they saw the 'heavy sea, about half a mile distance, coming towards the shore', and only just managed to clamber on board in time. When the wave hit shallower water it broke 'in a heavy manner and very high', and the three men looked on in amazement as it 'destroyed everything without the walls, carried before it a great length of the town walls, dismounted several batteries, and ran over a good deal of the lower part of the city'.[6]

The tidal wave hit the west side of the town between La Caleta and the Santa Catalina castle, and although the rocky shore on that side diminished its force a little it still broke over the sixty-foot parapet of the city wall, flooding the residential quarter of Vigne and carrying 'pieces of eight or ten tun weight, forty and fifty feet'.[7] Inside the walls one of the Englishmen who had fled to the city centre noticed that everyone was so anxious to save themselves that they ignored even their neighbours in the stampede; and he was sure that if so much as two feet of water had swept right through the city it would have been sufficient to drown thousands. Only a handful of people were killed within the walls, but the long and well-constructed causeway which connected Cádiz to the Isla de León and the mainland was 'washed away as if it was nothing', along with 'forty or fifty people', carriages and 'many animals'.[8] If the Governor had not ordered the city gates closed before the wave hit, many more might have perished trying to flee the city.

The official death toll in Cádiz was put at 200, but few believed it was less than 1,000. The first sight of the scene beyond the walls almost defied description. Boats, huts and goods that had been on the mole had all disappeared completely; the whole bay was awash with barrels, timber and other detritus; and a large Swedish ship had sunk in the harbour. By the time the sea returned to normal a little after one o'clock, a total of five tidal waves had battered the city. Don Antonio de Ulloa, the great Spanish general, scientist and mathematician, soon afterwards informed the Royal Society that he was certain that the 'violence' of what had happened to Spain's south-western coast that morning could not have been less than that which had 'swallowed up'[9] Lima and Callao; and an English merchant wrote to a friend at home saying that 'to have seen this disaster and to tell it is a great comfort, but I cannot possibly refrain from tears; we all of us appear as if risen from the dead'.[10] Elsewhere on the Spanish coast at least 400 people drowned at Ayamonte, and at Lepe more than 200.

At much the same time as the tidal wave hit Cádiz Thomas Heberden, the physician who had carefully observed the effects of the earthquake on Madeira earlier in the morning, looked on as the sea '[retired] suddenly some paces, and, arising with a great swell, without the least noise, as suddenly advancing, overflowed the shore, and entered the city'. The water rose fifteen feet above the high-water mark in the first surge and ebbed and flowed four or five times until at last 'it subsided, and the sea remained calm as before this phaenomenon had appeared'.[11] The waves shocked the wine merchant Charles Chalmers 'more than the [quake] itself' and later in the day he wrote to his father, 'God, of his infinite mercy, preserve us from all disasters!'[12] Compared to the east and north of the island Funchal was relatively protected. At Porto da Cruz 200 *pipas* – ninety-two-gallon casks – of wine, several brandy stills and stocks of grain were swept away from the quayside; house doors were smashed down and warehouse walls flattened; and when the water receded 'great quantities' of fish were left flapping in the streets. The same was true of Machico, where the seabed was exposed for over 200 yards during one of the ebbs, and where the weather changed from fine and clear to 'very dull and dark, the sky being entirely overcast with heavy black clouds' until the following day.[13]

There were no reliable accounts of what happened on the Atlantic coast of Morocco. From Salé, home port of the infamous Sallymen, came the news that a 'tidal wave engulfed a caravan heading for Marrakech'; and there were reports of 'much destruction' to Asilah, Santa Cruz (Agadir), Safi, Ceuta and Tetouan. The Governor of Gibraltar heard that at Tangier the sea rose 'up to the very walls, a thing never seen before' and that 'commotions of the sea were repeated eighteen times, and continued till six in the evening'.[14] On the Rock of Gibraltar itself, the sea rose and fell in fifteen-minute cycles until two in the afternoon, sometimes ebbing so far that fish and small boats were left stranded in the bay.

A little after two, just as the Tagus started to become calm again, it was the turn of Cornwall to be struck by 'the most uncommon and violent agitation of the sea ever remembered': the tidal wave had reached British shores. William Borlase, the renowned Cornish naturalist and antiquary, noted that at Mount's Bay the weather was 'remarkably calm' and the barometer as high as at any time in the previous three years when, about half an hour after the ebb tide, the sea began 'to advance suddenly from the eastward'. For ten minutes the water surged higher and higher, and then it retired to the south-west and west 'with a rapidity equal to that of a mill-stream descending to an undershot-wheel', leaving the water level six feet lower than before. This spectacle, like a vastly accelerated spring tide, continued for two hours in its 'full fury' and did not cease altogether for five and a half hours.

Pandemonium followed the first surge. The livelihoods of almost everyone in the bay were dependent in one way or another on the sea – there was a new pilchard factory at the harbour side – and as many as dared took to the water trying to save their boats. But no sooner were people aboard than the second surge began to carry the vessels in towards the pier once again; and then, just as they were made fast, they were pulled straight back out towards the open sea 'with incredible velocity'. The only mercy was that the waves struck in daylight: Borlase was sure that, had it happened at night, 'not one boat out of fifty would have been saved, and consequently many lives lost'.

Three miles to the west, at Penzance, the 'greatest violence' was observed at three o'clock when the water level surged eight feet above the norm. One mile west of that, at Newlyn, the water rushed in like a 'high-crested wave, with a surprising noise' and the first advance, the most violent, was estimated by onlookers to be 'ten feet perpendicular or more' – double the height of the surge at Mount's Pier and two feet higher than that at Penzance. At St Ives it also rose between eight and nine feet, floating off two vessels which had been high and dry; an 'extraordinary boar' occurred at Plymouth, driving 'several ships from their moorings' and 'twirling [all] vessels round in a very odd manner'; and the Creston ferries, a mile to the south-east, were left 'with several persons and some horses quite dry in the mud'[15].

Kinsale, the almost landlocked harbour on the estuary of the River Bandon in Ireland, was affected at a similar time. Major Lewis Nicola, the Huguenot commander of Charles Fort, was astounded when he saw 'a large body of water suddenly pour into [the] harbour'. His account continued: 'the cables of two sloops, each moored with two anchors, broke as were the moorings of several boats lying between Scilly and the town which were carried up, then down, the harbour, with a velocity far exceeding what I ever saw by a ship or boat'. At one quay the water rose five and a half feet, and at the market quay it overflowed altogether and as people tried to flee the market-place they found themselves in an instant in water up to their knees. The worst 'violence' only lasted ten minutes at Kinsale, and the deeper parts of the harbour seemed to have been less disturbed than the shallows, where 'the bottom . . . was much altered'[16] by what had occurred, but between six and seven o'clock there was another surge to keep people in a state of terror.

At Swansea two vessels of over 200 tons which were loading coal broke their moorings when the 'great head of water' rushed in at about 6.45 p.m.; and even the east coast of England was affected. At Sir Thomas L'Estrange's estate at Hunston two gentlemen and a servant were out shooting on the seashore and would have drowned if they had not clambered to safety up the cliffs. Accelerated ebbs and flows continued all round the southern coasts of Britain and Ireland until the following morning, and it would be many days before the tides returned to normal.

By the late afternoon the immense energy unleashed by the earthquake had propelled shockwaves right across the Atlantic. William Hillary, a physician who had lived on Barbados since 1747 to study tropical diseases, witnessed the water level in Carlisle Bay rise to a height two feet above that of the spring tide and sweep through the wharves and streets of Bridgetown. At Antigua Lieutenant Philip Affleck of HMS *Advice* recorded a 'tide' that 'rose twelve feet perpendicular several times and returned almost immediately'.[17] At Martinique and most of the other islands of the French West Indies the sea first retreated as much as a mile and then 'overflowed the low land . . . and into the upper rooms of the houses'; in the Dutch Antilles, at Saba, it rose twenty-one feet, much the same as at Lisbon; and at St Maarten a ship in fifteen feet of water 'was laid dry on her broadside'.[18] Hillary was sure that what had happened must be the result of some cataclysmic event, and every witness throughout the Caribbean islands agreed that they had seen 'such a sea . . . as had not been known in the memory of man'.[19] Three months later Hillary would hear of the Lisbon earthquake and was certain that the tidal waves – the first of only two 'teletsunami' * ever recorded in the Caribbean – were part of the same event.

---

*A tsunami that has travelled over 1,000 kilometres.

~ TEN ~

The Second Aftershock

WHEN LISBON WAS HIT BY A SECOND massive aftershock at noon
Thomas Chase regained consciousness to find himself on a bed. He
dimly remembered being scooped up off the street by a kindly Hamburg
merchant called John Jorge,* but his immediate concern was to shield
his face from falling plaster. This time he was certain that he was about
to be 'released from farther misery', and as the bed became covered in
debris, and he started to choke on the dust, Chase concentrated his last
ounces of strength on heaving himself off to try and escape by the door
beside the head of the bed. The noise he made brought Jorge running into
the room and he persuaded Chase to move into a little room at the side
of the garden if he was afraid where he was. There he ordered a bed to
be made up for 'dear Mr Chase' and told him that he had already sent
for Richard Scrafton, the physician in whose house Lord Drumlanrig
had been staying. No one knew if Scrafton was alive or dead but in the
meantime Jorge and Ambrose Goddard, who had also been invited in
from the street, took it in turns to check on Chase and do their best to

* Chase and other Englishmen commonly spelt his name Jorg, but the parish records show him as
Jorge and record the death in the earthquake of two daughters of a presumably related Agostinho
Jorge in the Rua das Pedras Negras (see Macedo, Luís Pastor de, *O terremoto de 1755*, p.12) and the
existence of an António Jorge in nearby Calçada do Correio.

make him comfortable. Goddard told him of several friends who were known to have perished, including his partner Benjamin Branfill's housekeeper – Mrs Hussey – who for many years had looked after Chase's father. She had been pulled alive from under a pile of rubble but died soon afterwards. Chase contemplated the news, and his own state, and considered Mrs Hussey's fate 'much happier than [his] own'.[1] From his window he saw for the first time that fires had broken out all over the city.

Less than half a mile away, up in the castle, Ambrose Goddard's brother, the Reverend Richard, had fallen in with a group of Factory families after his reluctant 'baptism'. To his immense relief they offered to take him with them to a country house at Marvila, a village on the river a couple of miles north-east of the city. With the fires burning strongly now, and news circulating that the sea had 'backed in' during the morning, putting 'all the lower part of the city under water', Richard Goddard thought that if his brother were still alive he too would surely be trying to escape. So he accepted the offer and was glad to have done so when, before they had gone far, he recognized two of his brother's servants, who assured him that Ambrose and Benjamin Branfill were both alive. He also met Edward Hay and his family in an olive grove just beyond the city walls and heard of their dreadful experience: Mrs Hay had given birth to a daughter ten days earlier and had had to be carried out of their house by the nurse during the quake. Now she was on a makeshift litter covered only in a cloak; the nurse carried the infant and Hay was doing his best to keep Harriott and Polly, their other daughters, happy. The Consul was understandably 'very perplexed';[2] but this did not stop him from offering Goddard shelter at another house in Marvila to which he was heading. Goddard thanked him for this very kind offer but decided to stay with his party rather than lumber Hay with yet more worries.

Among the hordes struggling out of the city Lord Drumlanrig and his party were making reasonable progress towards Abraham Castres' house north of the Rossio. They had passed the Marquês de Louriçal's palace just as it caught fire, but it was a 'very difficult task' making their way past all the other obstacles in their path. Drumlanrig was sure that without the help of Mr Douglas, Alexander and the others, he 'must have sunk'. At last they broke through the rubble and found Bosc de la Calmette, the Dutch Envoy, with his family and their seven or eight servants, who were also 'very bad and tired'[3] and hoping to be taken in by Castres. It took them all three hours from the time they had left the Rossio to complete a journey of less than a mile, but at least they found Castres' house standing; and the elderly Envoy, who had jumped out of a second-floor window during the quake but seemed none the worse for it, was dispensing refreshments to the growing number of refugees in his grounds.

Lawrence Fowkes and his family were up in the Bairro Alto above the Teatro dos Bonecos, the puppet-show-house, when the second aftershock struck, and soon afterwards reached the Largo do Rato. It was only then that Fowkes began to wonder if he had been mistaken to assume that his son and his brother's family were all safe with others from their neighbourhood. He also realized, when considering where to go next, that he had 'not a shilling'[4] on him. So he asked his son, Neb, to run back to their house and fetch some money and he returned with 350 *milreis* he found in his father's desk. This was a mission that few would have undertaken as cheerfully as Neb, but so great was his enthusiasm that Fowkes allowed him to go back again, with two friends, to see if other valuables could be saved. This time there was no way through. By mid-afternoon most of the Baixa was aflame, and Benjamin Farmer, having succeeded in digging out more of those trapped in the little square by his house, decided that it was time to leave. As he plodded north among a stream of disconsolate refugees he looked about him. Everyone's eyes seemed to be 'staring and fixed, attending to no object, their mouths wide open making a most hideous noise, and their hair wild and standing up'. Amid such an atmosphere Farmer soon found himself 'seized with the same horror'.[5]

By about two in the afternoon the dust cloud over the city cleared a little, the sun became more or less clearly visible through the smoke, and boats could once again be seen plying their way across the Tagus. There had been 'some little repose' from violent shocks and in Mr Jorge's house in the Largo das Pedras Negras, where Thomas Chase was in the rooftop garden room, everyone 'began to hope that the worst was over'. Minor tremors continued, each causing 'the same dread and terror' as the one before, but the collection of English, Dutch, Irish and Portuguese people who had taken refuge in the house began to consider that it was now time to think about escaping from 'the ruinous city'. Jorge distributed some fish and with that everyone began to leave. It was clear to Chase that 'all parties were so intent upon their own preservation as not to be at leisure to assist others'; even Goddard, Branfill and 'their people' had departed without offering to take him with them. On the other hand, he did not think he would survive long and that 'very few hours more would relieve me from all farther cares'. Eventually the garden was empty, leaving only Jorge, his elderly uncle and an old lame lady who had been abandoned in a nearby house and fetched by Jorge's servants.

To the west of the city Harry Frankland had struggled for hours after regaining consciousness to shift a stone that was pinning him down next to the lady who had died earlier. At last he wrenched himself free and saw a shard of light towards which he pulled himself and then worked around it until there was an opening large enough for him to squeeze through. Outside he saw Lisbon in ruins and fire at the end of the street. His thigh was badly bruised and he had a couple of wounds in his side, but he was able to stagger as far as the house of his friend Francisco de Ribeiro and was overjoyed to find it still standing. When he was eventually well enough to resume keeping his diary he wrote simply: 'I was buried in ruins . . . Hope my providential escape will have a lasting good effect upon my mind'.[6] Within days he finally made Agnes the official Lady Frankland.

Not far away from Frankland Mr Braddock was unsure 'whither to retire to shelter' after the tidal wave and the second aftershock. With fires blazing in several parts of the city it seemed as if 'the four elements were [now] in league to destroy [it]'.[7] He finally decided that he had as good a chance of survival at the Mint, which he could see had withstood the earthquake, the aftershocks and the battering from the river, as anywhere else and made his way across Largo São Paulo as fast as he could. When he reached the far side of the square he was astonished to find only a single young lieutenant, Bartolomeu de Sousa Meixa, still at his post. All the guards had deserted, in spite of the fact that Braddock knew, as did every other merchant in the city, that the building contained a fortune in gold brought by the Brazil fleets in the autumn. Braddock 'expressed his admiration' for de Sousa Meixa's devotion to duty, and the two men decided that as the ground was still shaking, and the build-ings on either side of the gate were only twenty to thirty feet distant, they would be better off in the courtyard. It was full of water from the tidal wave but they selected a 'hillock of stones and rubbish' that was dry, and settled down on that. Only then did it occur to Braddock that he had not 'broken fast' that day.

Braddock's hunger reminded him that he had been intending to dine with his friend in the Baixa; and as the man lived at the top of a tall building and spoke no Portuguese Braddock became extremely con-cerned for him. In the end, despite feeling very safe chatting to de Sousa Meixa on their hillock in the courtyard of the Mint, he decided he must go and try to find him. Once again he set off over the ruins in the Largo São Paulo to the riverside and then on to Corpo Santo, the Irish Dominican convent and college, which had been shaken to the ground and at which small groups of monks were staring 'with dejected countenances'. He then made his way along the Rua da Corte-Real, but at the far end it was blocked by the ruins of the King's magnificent new Opera House, built, as everyone knew, 'at a prodigious expense' and considered to be one of the most solid and magnificent buildings of its kind in the whole of Europe. It was a tragic sight. That very evening *A Destruição de Troya* – 'The Destruction of Troy' – was to have played.

Opposite, the entrance to a house owned by John Bristow, one of the wealthiest English merchants, was blocked by 'a vast heap of stones, each of several tons weight', and Braddock would later learn that Bristow's partner, Mr Ward, had had one foot over the threshold when the west end of the Opera had fallen and had narrowly escaped being crushed beneath it. Unable to continue towards the Terreiro do Paço by this route, Braddock tried others and eventually found the way through into the square in front of the Patriarchal church. The roof of the church had collapsed, as had part of the façade, and Braddock found the square 'full of coaches, chariots, *chaises*, horses, and mules, deserted by their drivers and attendants, as well as their owners'. They were the transport of all the nobles who had been at Mass when the quake struck and who had fled on foot. It was a strange sight and Braddock was sad at the 'distress of the poor animals'. Some were dead, most were not, and those who were not seemed acutely aware of their likely fate.

Braddock pressed on towards his friend's lodgings, climbing the Rua Nova de Almada and encountering there 'horror [which] exceeded all description'. Groans, wails and sighs were the only sounds to be heard and Braddock found that he could 'hardly take a single step without treading on the dead or dying'. There were more 'coaches, with their masters, horses and riders, *almost* crushed to pieces', 'mothers with infants in their arms', and 'richly dressed ladies, priests, friars, gentle-men, mechanics . . . all in the same condition, or just expiring'. Some of the victims had broken backs or legs or arms, others had great stones on their chests, others still were almost completely buried and cried out feebly to anyone passing. Braddock turned away and strode on towards his friend's lodgings on the edge of the Baixa. But when he reached the correct street he saw that the house and all those near it were no longer standing. As it was late afternoon, and he would soon be needing shelter, Braddock knew he must now head for Morley's public house in Buenos Ayres while he could still see to make his way. It took him almost an hour to cover the half-mile to Morley's, and when he arrived he was relieved to find a huge number from the English community, as well as many Portuguese, even if all of them were 'in the same wretched circumstances'.[8]

For most of the afternoon of his birthday, Thomas Chase was beset by 'the most melancholy reflections'. The aftershocks may have become less frequent, but within his field of vision from Jorge's garden over the Baixa flames appeared to be engulfing the city 'with inexpressible swiftness'. Soon after most of the others who had taken refuge in the house had left for the waterfront Chase had asked his host to try and hire servants to carry him out, but Jorge had said it was impossible, that 'the city was quite deserted', and that he himself meant to stay put because 'venturing out . . . would be only to encounter greater dangers'. By five o'clock, however, flames seemed about to devour the building and Jorge came into the garden room, stared at Chase a while, and then left without saying a word, closing the door behind him. After a few minutes had elapsed and Chase had still heard no noise from the adjacent room he was certain that Jorge, still unable to secure any helpers to move his friend, had been forced to leave without him.

The thought that he had been abandoned terrified Chase, and he determined to get onto the balcony outside his window so that he could throw himself off into the street, and thereby put 'an end at once to all my excessive miseries'. But there was no way out to the balcony from his room so, using two chairs as crutches, he began to make his way towards the door. The agony of moving was so great that he had to rest a while before he even reached the door, certain that he couldn't 'have gone a step farther had the room been on fire'. When he had recovered sufficiently to continue he opened it, and was astonished to see Jorge, the lame old lady and two others sitting in silence in the outer room. Jorge was equally surprised to see Chase and asked him what he was doing. Chase answered that he knew that they were all in mortal danger and that he could not rely on his friend for further assistance; but he 'begged . . . with tears in [his] eyes' that before leaving Jorge would throw him off the balcony 'or any other way despatch me'. It would, he added, be far better than having 'to linger out a few hours . . . in violent agonies' only 'to die a most dreadful death' at the end of it.

Jorge thought his young neighbour must be delirious, and assured him that he had no intention of abandoning him, let alone throwing him off the balcony. If they had no choice but to leave, then he would carry Chase himself and they would 'take [their] chance together'. But, he added, the house was still not completely surrounded by fire and it should be possible to make their way to the Terreiro do Paço if they chose to. Chase was comforted by Jorge's words but, terrified of being alone any longer, he could not return to the garden room. As darkness began to fall Jorge disappeared every half-hour to check on the progress of the fire. By then there was a new danger in the streets: amid the ruins, the smoke and the flames utter lawlessness now prevailed. At 5.30 p.m. another Hamburg merchant watched as a few miserable-looking soldiers appeared in his street and told the groups of *alfacinhas* huddled there that they had a decree from the King to clear it. The answer was forthright: they had no king now and would stay put. The soldiers disappeared without a word.

By mid-afternoon a huge procession had been organized in Seville at which the crowd sang the litany of All Saints and wept, imploring God's mercy; and in Cádiz the same happened, with the Dominicans solemnly parading the statue of Nuestra Señora del Rosario around the city walls, begging for protection. As people throughout southern Spain were goaded into a religious frenzy, and Dominicans, Franciscans, Carmelites and Capuchins went into open competition to hear the confessions of a terrified populace, the question in everybody's minds concerned what they might expect next.

As dusk descended on Lisbon a British surgeon, Richard Wolfall, who had been attending as best he could to the wounded in the Terreiro do Paço since noon, gathered the thoughts which he would later commit to paper:

The shocking sight of the dead bodies, together with the shrieks and cries of those, who were half-buried in the ruins, are only known to those who were eye-witnesses. It far exceeds all description, for the fear and consternation was so great, that the most resolute person durst not stay a moment to remove a few stones off the friend he loved most, though many might have been saved by so doing: but nothing was thought of but self-preservation; getting into open spaces, and into the middle of streets, was the most probable security. Such as were in the upper stories of houses, were in general more fortunate than those, that attempted to escape by the doors; for they were buried under the ruins with the greatest part of the foot-passengers: such as were in equipages escaped best, though their cattle and drivers suffered severely; but those lost in houses and the streets were very unequal in number to those, that were buried in the ruins of churches . . . all the churches in the city were vastly crouded, and the number of churches here exceeds that of both London and Westminster.

Had the misery ended here, it might in some degree admitted

of redress; for though lives could not be restored, yet the immense riches, that were in the ruins, might in some part have been digged out: but the hopes of this are almost gone, for in about two hours after the shock, fires broke out in three different parts of the city, occasioned from the goods and the kitchen-fires being all jumbled together . . . Indeed every element seemed to conspire to our destruction; for soon after the shock, which was near high water the tide rose forty feet higher in an instant than was ever known, and as suddenly subsided. Had it not so done, the whole city must have been laid under water. As soon as we had time for recollection, nothing but death was present in our imaginations. [9]

~ ELEVEN ~

The First Night

AT MORLEY'S PUBLIC HOUSE IN BUENOS AYRES Mr Braddock tried to make himself as comfortable as possible. Soon after nightfall the air became 'sharp and piercing', despite the all-consuming conflagration less than a mile to the east, and only the very fortunate had a cloak or blanket with which to cover themselves. There was certainly no room inside for any but the most sick or wounded. As far as anyone at Morley's knew the city was deserted, abandoned to the flames which so illuminated the night sky that Braddock was able to read by it, and to malefactors. 'Everyone', he recounted, 'had his eyes turned towards the flames, and stood looking on with silent grief, which was only interrupted by the cries and shrieks of women and children'.[1]

There was little to say, and those who did speak exchanged, in hushed tones, stories of miraculous escapes and the tragic deaths of friends. Dear old Mrs Perochon had run out of her house behind her husband, Elias, and been killed beneath falling masonry; Elias, just feet away from her, had survived. Old Daniel Casamajor, doyen of the English merchants, had perished. Giles Vincent, who had been out of the city for months on business and only returned the previous evening, had been crushed to death, as had John Churchill, another young merchant.

Charles Holford, a teenage 'gentleman apprentice', liked by all for his 'modesty and affable behaviour', had been walking past a church when a large stone fell on him smashing both his legs. For ages he had lain in the street, beseeching passers-by to help him until at last a Portuguese man stopped and carried him into the church. In the aftershock the church had largely collapsed, trapping everyone inside, and when the fire took hold Holford and his saviour had been burnt alive. Poor Mrs Sherman had been consumed by the fire because she was 'too lusty to follow her maid servant through a passage'.[2] And then there were the children who had perished, like little John Morrogh and the infant Elizabeth Legay.

All these names were well-known to the survivors in an English community in which everyone knew everyone, and the ways in which the dead had met their fate conformed to no pattern. Some had saved themselves by getting onto the water while others had been drowned by the tidal waves. Some had escaped by being at the tops of houses, others by being in basements. Some who had been trapped beneath ruins, but were unharmed by the tremors, were then roasted alive by the fire. There were plenty of tall stories too – about how the palace of the Inquisition had been the first building to fall while the brothels in the 'Rua Suja' had been spared, how all the soldiers garrisoning the Bugio had drowned, how a 70-gun ship in the docks at Ribeira das Naus had been set alight and then floated out to sea, unmanned, on the tidal wave.

Among the English community there were many who seemed unlikely to live much longer. Thomas Chase was one, and Lord Drumlanrig, who had found refuge at Abraham Castres's house in Santa Martha, was another. His consumptive cough had worsened considerably due to the combination of becoming 'excessively heated' during his escape and the night-time cold. It was a source of mounting concern to his household and everyone else, and ensuring his survival soon became a symbolic act of defiance by the English community against all that had befallen them. A 'grand consultation'[3] took place to decide whether

Drumlanrig would be better-off spending the rest of the night in the warmth of the house (which might collapse during one of the after-shocks which were still reverberating through the city), or in the grounds (where he might die of cold); and it was thought better not to move him outside. Sleep for anyone was impossible, not only on account of the cold and the bright sky. All night tremors continued, the earth never being still for longer than fifteen minutes at a time; and out on the Tagus ships' crews were required to stand to throughout the hours of darkness to beat out the cinders from flames that were now visible forty miles away in Santarém to the north-east and were falling from the sky like a light rain.

For many who were huddled together in Castres's grounds and at Morley's it was only now that they heard for the first time how tidal waves had swept up the Tagus 'in a most wonderful manner' and 'threat-ened to overwhelm the lower parts of the city'. Some said that rocks that had never been seen before were exposed in the river; others that Captain Clies on the *Expedition* packet had considered abandoning ship. A vessel was believed to have foundered on the river bar, and another was grounded; and it was said that the bar was 'so shifted that it will be difficult for ships to come in or go out'. Some debated how and where the fire had first started. Most worrying of all, however, and quite beyond com-prehension, was the complete disappearance of the Cais da Pedra and the people who were on it when it was 'swallowed up'. Some said 100 had perished, others 300, others 900.

Contrary to the belief of those who had fled, the city centre was far from deserted. At about eleven o'clock two servants of Mr Wappäus, John Jorge's nephew, appeared at his house and, as the flames were again encroaching from all sides, Jorge declared that it was 'time to remove'. He went to fetch his hat and cloak, came back with a cap and quilt for Thomas Chase, and asked his nephew and the two servants to carry him to the Terreiro do Paço and then to return for the lame old lady. Chase was carried in a chair by the three men, with someone else leading the way with a torch, and as they stumbled along through a narrow passage that was the only route to the waterfront not blocked by ruins or on fire they were assailed by the cries of 'poor wretches begging for help'. At the church of Nossa Senhora da Conceição the door was open and in the light cast by candles on the high altar Chase could make out the figures of priests busying about 'arrayed in their ecclesiastical habits'. In the porch lay a pile of bodies.

Although there were huge stones lying about in the Rua da Correaria, which led downhill to the church of Santa Maria Madalena, its houses were mostly intact; so too were those of the Rua dos Ourives da Prata, the silversmiths' street, although Chase could see many people 'throwing bundles out of windows' and preparing to flee. When they reached the Largo do Pelourinho at its southern end they found that both ends of the Rua Nova dos Ferros, the grand merchants' street, were on fire, as was the Rua da Confeitaria. It seemed as if they had escaped just before flames completely encircled the whole of the Baixa, a slight wind fanning them 'gently onwards', and even in the Terreiro do Paço the Palace was now smouldering.

The scene in the Palace Square was horrifying. It seemed to Chase as though everyone had decided that this was Judgement Day: some chanted litanies, others 'stood harassing the dying with religious cere-monies', and with each new tremor all fell to their knees again crying 'Misericórdia!'. Such zeal unnerved him, as it had done many others among his countrymen that day. Who was to prevent the crowd suddenly turning on the Protestants in the square and exacting retribution for their misfortunes? There was not a soldier to be seen anywhere, nor any sign of a senior cleric keeping order. His saviours made their way down the side of the Customs House until they came across Mrs Alford, who pointed out her sister, Mrs Graves, and her family sitting nearby on bundles of possessions. Wappäus thought it best to place Chase under cover and out of the wind, alongside others who were badly injured; and at last, fourteen hours after tumbling from the rooftop *eirado*, he found himself 'suddenly relieved from the constant apprehension of falling houses, and dangers of the fire'. 'Extreme despair' gave way to euphoria and despite his agony Chase began to 'indulge a hope that it was yet possible to live . . . and this soothing gleam continued a while, till new terrors rushed in'. A rumour was circulating in the Terreiro do Paço that the square had been undermined by the tidal wave and that further after-shocks might cause it to be 'swallowed up' into the earth.

Two hours later Jorge had assembled his whole family in the Terreiro do Paço at the Graves's little encampment, and Chase was compelled to struggle out from his shelter to join them as the flames came ever closer. Three loud explosions, caused by the fire reaching gunpowder stores along the waterfront to the east, terrified everyone; indeed the only brief respite from the state of dread which gripped the English party was the disappearance of a seemingly 'half-mad' Irish beggar-woman, and her swift reappearance with a bottle of wine from Houston's coffee house for which she would accept no payment. Chase found the liquor 'indeed a most welcome refreshment', and as he surveyed the scene around him he was certain that 'the Inquisition, with all its utmost cruelty, could not have invented half such a variety of tortures for the mind' as he had undergone on his birthday.

Sunday was All Souls' Day, traditionally celebrated in Portugal as *Dia de Finados* – 'the Day of the Dead' – when it was customary to honour the faithful departed. A little before dawn the breeze started blowing from the north-east again, driving the flames which had raged all night in the area around the cathedral towards the Terreiro do Paço 'with the utmost rapidity'. The English encampment which Thomas Chase had joined was forced to move closer to the waterfront on the Customs House side of the square and then, when the heat there became 'scorching', across towards the Palace. Although the fire seemed to have burnt out and the Palace roof had long since collapsed, the walls looked as though they might fall at any moment and everyone was careful not to venture too close to them.

At nine o'clock the sun was shining through the smoke when boats started to arrive at the Terreiro do Paço to rescue those who had spent such a grim night encircled by fire. The son of Chase's housekeeper, who was himself badly injured, suddenly appeared beside him and asked if he wanted to leave with them. But Chase was loath to abandon his saviour Jorge, and he thought that the fire must burn itself out soon, so he declined the kind offer. The scene on the waterfront was chaotic as hundreds of people jostled for the available places on each boat that arrived. As Chase watched his housekeeper's son depart he caught sight of his friend George Barclay being carried towards the river on a mattress, a 'mashed' foot dangling to one side; and although Jorge chivvied those in his care who could move towards the waterside they soon returned when it became clear that there was no chance of them all being able to leave on the same boat. There was another reason to vacate the water-front for the middle of the square: flames had suddenly leapt from the Customs House to stacks of timber by the river and were racing along the south side of the square towards the ruins of the Palace which soon, to Chase's 'great surprise', began to blaze anew. On every side there was now 'a prodigious fire', and Chase pulled his quilt over his face to protect himself from the 'violent' heat and 'showers of ashes'. Moments later the quilt was set on fire by the burning harness of a bolting mule, but it was quickly pulled away and Chase emerged a little blackened but not burnt.

In a state of 'the utmost anxiety' Chase was moved to the north-west corner of the square, which appeared to offer a little shelter from the cinders and had just settled down when a great cry of 'Misericórdia!' went up. All the bundles of people's belongings in the centre of the square had caught fire, creating a giant bonfire from which little could be saved. Flames slanted over Chase's head, and once again he 'lost all [his] spirits', and was certain that he now faced 'the sort of death [he] so much dreaded'.[4] After a few minutes, however, the wind suddenly dropped and as the flames from the bundles started to burn vertically Chase's terror gave way to a ravenous hunger. He had eaten nothing since the previous evening, and had been told that provisions were so scarce that an ounce of bread was now worth a pound of gold, so he almost wept when an Irishwoman appeared at his elbow and, having ascertained that he was the son of old Mr Chase, handed him a large piece of water-melon. A few minutes later his meal became a feast when Jorge also appeared with a piece of bread for him.

At 11.30 a.m. the Fowkes family, who had camped in the open a mile and a half north of the Terreiro do Paço, were surprised by the sudden appearance of Caesar, one of their slaves. He had come from Sacavém, where many of the wine merchants had cellars, and told Fowkes that 'all was well' at his wine cellars there, that 'only the tiles [were] shattered, and the walls a little open in some places'.[5] Fowkes immediately gathered together his family and friends and by one o'clock they had walked the seven miles to Sacavém. On the way they called in at Senhor Luiz's *quinta* and were delighted not only to find that he had survived and was there, but even more so by the news that Luiz had rescued Joe, Fowkes's nephew, and that the lad was now being cared for in another house nearby. There was more good fortune to come. Soon after setting out again Fowkes came across a Portuguese woman with Nancy, his two-year-old niece, in her arms; and at Sacavém he heard that his own son, Sam, his sister-in-law Anne and her four-year-old son Billy had all ended up on board a ship in the Tagus.

In the Terreiro do Paço John Jorge had left Thomas Chase where he lay and taken his uncle and the lame old lady to the waterfront once again in the hope of finding a boat. When they failed to reappear after more than an hour Chase was sure that they must have succeeded,

despite Mr Wappäus's assurances that they would not have abandoned
him, and he was just grateful to Jorge for having looked after him until
'the most imminent dangers' appeared to be over. But Chase knew that
he must find a refuge before the day was out and with the help of John
Houston, the coffee house owner, he finally managed to secure a place
on a boat and was carried to the waterside 'with the greatest joy imaginable'. As the boatman pushed off, the cool temperature on the water was
a wonderful sensation and before dark, having been held to ransom by
the boatman and dumped near the city walls to the east, then carried by
two servants for a mile eastwards, Thomas Chase arrived at the Hake
family's *quinta*. He was almost unconscious and quite unable to make out
the identities of any of the multitude until Joseph Hake's figure emerged
from the gloom. He and the rest of the Hake family, all second-
generation residents like Chase himself, welcomed their friend 'in the
most affectionate manner possible'. In no time he found himself bedded
down in a tent made from carpets strung across a vine walk, plied with
'strong white wine' and fed delicious morsels of bread and butter; and he
was at last able to send his two tenacious 'conductors' back to the city
with eighteen shillings each for their efforts.

Back in the Terreiro do Paço the Graves family and John Houston
were among those who, having decided to wait until they could leave
with what remained of their possessions, endured another terrible ordeal.
After dark the fire suddenly started to burn with such renewed ferocity
that John Houston had to abandon his chest of 'pieces of Holland',[6] and
when he and the Graves family crossed the river the next morning they
did so with nothing but the clothes on their backs.

~ TWELVE ~

Horroroso Deserto

AT ABRAHAM CASTRES'S HOUSE IN SANTA MARTHA, a little to the
north of the city, Lord Drumlanrig continued to put a brave face on living
in a makeshift tent constructed from poles and sailcloth by day, and
inside a building propped up with wooden beams by night. On Tuesday
morning, however, his servants decided that he should be moved to the
Expedition so that he would be among the first to leave for England.
Quite when that would be, nobody seemed to know. An embargo had
been placed on all shipping, preventing any departures from the Tagus;
there was no reliable information about the condition – or position –
of the river bar; and after the tidal wave the tides were so irregular that
reaching the open sea was impossible anyway. But at least Drumlanrig
was ensconced in conditions which he described as 'Paradise'[1] in
comparison with those at Castres's house.

Out at the Hakes' *quinta* Thomas Chase's condition was also of
great concern to his friends. His right arm had been set by the King's
farrier, a celebrated bone-setter, but both the farrier and a barber-surgeon
had failed to notice that Chase's right shoulder was dislocated, which
meant that his whole right side was numb and his left side so painful
that at times he could barely draw breath. When Richard Scrafton

arrived at the *quinta* on Tuesday, having been almost 'pulled to pieces by the people' during a harrowing journey all the way from Belém, the physician bled him, and after the fourth bleeding Chase began to feel a little better.

Drumlanrig, Chase and Harry Frankland, who was recovering at his house in Belém with Agnes and who had also been visited by Scrafton, were exceptionally fortunate in the attention they received. There were only three English physicians in the city, all of whom had lost their instruments and were even without bandages and dressings; and of seventy-five people among the French community who had limbs amputated by their surgeon, Monsieur Dufour, only ten had survived beyond twenty-four hours. The kindness shown to Chase by the Hakes was also remarkable in that they had their own loss to mourn. Elizabeth Hake, the wife of young Christopher and sister of the Governor of New York, had last been seen disappearing under a collapsing building in the city. Her body, 'not at all changed',[2] would not be discovered until weeks later.

For those who had not sustained wounds of any description shock set in. Survival, in Chase's words, 'brought back along with it the cares of life', and many people were in such a state of distress that at times they even envied the dead. The greatest source of worry after the fate of relatives was financial ruin. One of the city's leading bankers, Sam Montaigut, wrote to his uncle in London putting the situation in the starkest terms: 'all who have effects or affairs in this unhappy city must no more think of them – all is lost'.[3] Joseph May, of the house of Coppendale & May, had lost all his cash and stock and had an outstanding loan to his brother of £4,000; Duncan Clerk, a wine and textiles merchant, had saved £700 in goods and £180 in cash, but he was owed £2,000 by debtors, which he knew he would never recover; and the losses of Jackson, Branfill & Goddard were known to be 'uncommonly severe'.[4] Among the largest houses it was rumoured that Bristow &

Ward, holders of the contract for the Brazilian diamond trade, had saved 'not the minutest trifle'[5] of their huge cash holdings; and Gerard Devisme, of the equally substantial house of Purry, Mellish & Devisme, told everyone that after two failed attempts to make his way through the fire which was still burning in the Baixa to their counting-house in the Rua Nova do Almada, he was certain their position was the same.

The news from the other foreign merchant communities was equally disastrous. The Hamburg merchants were mourning the deaths of old Thor-Laden's son, Johann Burmester and Johann Carstens, the son of the President of Lübeck; and few thought they would save anything. Among the thirty or forty French houses Grenier et Perret had lost large quantities of pepper, Pedegache et Blanc had lost money and merchandise to the value of £5,000 or more and held £15,000 in now worthless letters of credit. Indeed the entire French community of five hundred, concentrated in the parishes of São Paulo, Santa Catarina and Encarnação, now had hardly a house between them; and according to Gerard Devisme, the entire Italian community, mostly from Genoa and Florence, had left the city and were on their way home overland.

There was a sense of urgency among the merchants to try and salvage what they could as quickly as possible – even if the fire was still blazing in the centre of the city. A rumour that Barbary corsairs were massing off Cascais, preparing to descend on the city for slaves and treasure, started to circulate; another that the Baixa was soon to be 'cannonaded' in an attempt to stop the fire; and word of a procession that had made its way to Belém to protest to the King that what had happened could be attributed in part to the city's folly in showing 'so much favour to Hereticks' raised the possibility of having to flee the country within days. Some even said that the King was about to abandon Lisbon for the Alentejo.

Fire was not the only danger with which anyone venturing back to the ruins of their former homes had to contend. It was clear, as Lord Drumlanrig related to his parents in a letter written on board the *Expedition*, that 'good order and discipline and security were no more' and for the first few days after the quake 'the Government neither exerted power to protect nor to punish'. The only displays of 'spirit' being shown by anyone, so far as he could tell, were 'in such as were daringly wicked enough to take advantage of the general consternation and put in execution all kinds of villanies which they were at full liberty to do'.[6] Nobody could, or did, disagree with his assessment. Abraham Castres declared the city to be the preserve of 'swarms of Spanish deserters';[7] others spoke of 'mobs of ruffians and demons . . . left uncontrolled to perpetrate every diabolical outrage'.[8] It was also certain, in the opinion of Richard Wolfall and the other physicians, that 'pestilence' would now be rife in the city.

Gerard Devisme was one who, despite all the dangers, made yet another attempt to reach his firm's counting-house. This time he went all the way from Castres' house to Belém and then hired a boat to take him to Boa Vista in the hope that he could find a way through from the river. Once on land he managed to make his way beyond the ruins of the convent of São Francisco, past the smouldering wreck of the convent of Boa Hora in the Rua Nova de Almada, and eventually entered his house by the rear entrance. The building was a charred ruin but the counting-house still stood, giving him hope that his cash chest might be salvageable. Everything was so hot, however, that only when he returned the next day was he able to remove it; and although he was glad to recover the £16,000 it contained, the total capital reclaimed by him and his partners was no more than that with which they had started out in Lisbon twenty years earlier.[9]

Mr Braddock was even less fortunate when he set out from Morley's public house to try and rescue some of his possessions. As he made his way through the ruins past countless bodies – some 'horribly mangled', others 'half-burnt', some 'quite roasted' – and past churches outside which the dead lay 'in vast heaps, piled one upon another', he had to cover his nose and mouth to block out the stench; and when he reached his neighbourhood he wasn't even able to tell where his street had been until he was helped by some Gallegos. He could retrieve nothing, and turned his back on a city which he now described as a 'vast heap of ruins' and trudged disconsolately back to Morley's, to 'the same wretched circumstances' and the same 'inclemency of the night air'[10] he had endured for the last few days. Even seventeen days after the disaster Lawrence Fowkes found that the 'rubbish' of his house was still hot enough to set fire to the baskets in which he endeavoured to remove it while searching for his 'money, plate and jewels'. His two sons, Sam and Neb, set to 'with great resolution and courage' and seemed undaunted by working amidst 'the ruins of old walls and dead bodies'. Just occasionally their father was able to 'perceive a tear of concern stealing from them'.[11]

On Tuesday morning Abraham Castres learnt that the secretary of the Spanish Embassy intended to send a messenger to Badajoz with the tragic news of the death of the Conde de Peralada, the Spanish Ambassador and Castres's greatest friend in the diplomatic community. It was the first opportunity to send anything to the outside world so Castres hastily penned a note to Sir Benjamin Keene, the English Ambassador, telling him of the 'very distressed state' of the English community, and reporting that 'the palace, churches and most of the stately buildings' were ruined and 'flames were still destroying the remains of the city from one extremity to another'. Most merchants, he added, would be embarking for home as they had nowhere to live; and he promised Keene he would send a 'full and particular account of the late deplorable event'[12] to England by sea at the first opportunity. As the English merchants had just requested that the departure of the *Expedition* should be delayed until everyone had had the opportunity to salvage their cash, Castres was uncertain when this would be. There was also no certainty that the messenger would be able to reach the border with Spain, a journey which was arduous and hazardous enough at the best of times; and for all Castres knew Madrid might also have been reduced to rubble. To all intents and purposes Lisbon was cut off from the outside world, and the only news to have arrived so far was from devastated coastal settlements and towns and villages on the Tagus.

Castres was unable to give many details of the situation in Lisbon, not only on account of the hurry to catch the messenger but also because he was suffering from extreme exhaustion and 'great trouble of mind'. Furthermore his information was still limited to that brought in after forays into the city by those for whom he was providing shelter, or by his servants, and much of it was contradictory or based on rumours. He had no idea how many among the English and Irish communities had perished or were wounded, although his impression, his fervent hope, was that the merchants had 'escaped pretty well considering the number of houses we have here'. In addition to these impediments Castres knew that whatever news he conveyed to his masters in Whitehall would almost certainly be redundant by the time it arrived, and his first despatch to Sir Thomas Robinson, written two days after the message he sent to Madrid, began, 'You will, in all likelihood, have heard before this . . .'. But the Envoy did his best to convey something of the magnitude of what had occurred to 'this opulent city, now reduced to a heap of rubbish and ruins by a most tremendous earthquake on the 1st of this month followed by a conflagration which has done ten times more mischief than the earthquake itself'.[13]

Castres knew that there was one duty he had to perform before completing his despatch that was even more important than caring for the crowds of hungry and miserable refugees in his grounds: he had to pay his respects to the King. For the first two days after the quake the possibility of making the journey to Belém was unthinkable. But by

Wednesday he considered his mission could be put off no longer, no matter how arduous it would prove, and he and Bosc de la Calmette, the Dutch Envoy who had sought sanctuary with him, succeeded in reaching the Palace, where they found the entire Royal Family and household camping in the garden. José was reported to have welcomed Castres with the words 'I was four days ago the richest man here, and now you see me poorer than the meanest beggar in all my dominions – I am without a house, in a tent, without servants, without subjects, without bread.'[14] It was also said that the King, fearing they might escape if their cages were damaged by a further quake, had ordered all the animals in the menagerie to be slaughtered 'for the public good' – lions, bears, tigers, leopards and 'a huge number of other rare animals'.[15] In his despatch Castres simply related how José had told the two envoys that he was 'extremely glad to see [them] both safe', and that he 'owed great thanks to Providence' for his own survival. Castres added that 'though the loss his most Faithful Majesty has sustained on this occasion is immense, and his capital city is utterly destroyed, he received us with more serenity than we expected'. The Queen and Princesses also sent a message thanking the envoys for their attendance and excusing themselves from appearing in person because the standard of dress imposed on them by living in tents was 'not fit to appear in'.

Castres gave what news he could of the fate of the merchants, knowing that this intelligence would be subjected to the closest scrutiny in London, and he hoped that the inclusion of news that two of the leading merchant houses – Purry, Mellish & Devisme and Raymond & Burrell – had managed to retrieve their cash chests might be reassuring enough to prevent total panic in the Royal Exchange and in textile businesses throughout England. But he knew that the death of so important a personage as the Conde de Perelada and the 'dismal accounts' of the losses of the nobility, many of whom were 'quite undone', would be regarded as very shocking indeed. As for his own state, Castres did not seek to disguise the considerable strain he was under: providing for the Dutch Envoy and his household, Lord Drumlanrig and his household, a large number of distraught merchants, and a still greater number of 'miserable objects among the lower sort . . . who all fly to me for bread' had, he confessed, 'greatly affected' him.

One of Castres's greatest regrets was that there had been no English or Dutch man-o'-war in the harbour on 1 November, and only three merchant ships of any size. Large vessels could have provided carpenters and deckhands to repair his house, the floors of which threatened to give way every time a new tremor was felt, and to make better shelters in the grounds. Everyone thought heavy rain was now in the offing, and as his home could not 'bear any number of fresh inhabitants' he knew he would have to find some other 'proper method for sheltering the poorer sort'.[16] HMS *Bedford* had been expected for days, but there was still no sign of her, so the only other options were to hire a Portuguese hulk or try and charter one of the larger English vessels. Both options would be very expensive and although he had cash aplenty, for the time being his resources were finite – and he might have to wait months to be reimbursed by the government at home. Furthermore, many of the 'poorer sort' – tailors, shopkeepers, shipwrights, sailors keen to avoid being pressed by the Royal Navy for the as yet undeclared war – had nothing to return to England or Ireland for, and were likely to stay as long as they possibly could, at his expense, in the hope of either recovering what little they had from the ruins or finding some other new means of survival in the city. Despite the strain and trauma that Castres was suffering, he assured Sir Thomas Robinson that he was 'determined to stay within call of the distressed as long as I can remain on shore with the least appearance of serenity'.[17] The sense of charity displayed by the elderly Envoy, who three decades earlier had produced the English translation of Andrea Guevarre's influential 'Ways and Means for Suppressing Beggary and Relieving the Poor, by Erecting

General Hospitals and Charitable Corporations', was little short of heroic under the circumstances confronting him.

By the end of the week some of those who were languishing in Castres's grounds, on ships, or in various places on the outskirts of the city began to write down their thoughts for the first time. Edward Hay, the Consul whose wife had just given birth, scribbled a barely legible and distraught note to his brother, the Bishop of St Asaph, expressing his faith, or hope, that 'God Almighty gives strength upon these occasions';[18] the sickly Reverend Williamson, the chaplain to the English Factory whom Henry Fielding had complimented for being 'the cleverest fellow I ever saw' and who now lived in mortal fear of catching a cold and 'relapsing', told a friend that he had 'lost every single thing that belonged to me';[19] Edward French, whose brother was still missing, was so 'overcome with concern'[20] that he was unable to finish a letter home; and Richard Goddard wrote to his brother Thomas in Wiltshire in a state of great confusion. He had planned to spend 'a most agreeable winter' in Lisbon and the climate had already begun to have a 'most agreeable effect' on his health. Yet now his brother's house was no more and 'poor Brosius' was ruined. There seemed little for it but to 'fly from a country which is one continued scene of desolation'[21] at the first opportunity.

Lord Drumlanrig's dilemma was the worst of all. He tried to reassure his 'Dear Papa and Mama' by telling them that there had been no tremor for twenty-six hours, that Mr Douglas and the servants were all well and had been 'greatly instrumental in preserving' him, and that he was now safe from 'rogues and violences from people who might have been drove to any thing from their distress for want of provisions.'[22] But he was close to death, and he and all his household knew that if he returned in the *Expedition* to England he would not survive the winter. His only hope lay in the possibility of a miraculous appearance by an English warship bound for the Mediterranean. Elsewhere, the Papal Nuncio wrote to Benedict XIV on 4 November 'from the desolate ground which last

Saturday was Lisbon' and told him about 'the *grave flagelo* which God
had seen fit to give the city and its inhabitants' and the 'horror which
we judge never to have been equalled'.[23]

Many of these first letters, written on any scrap of paper a person
could lay their hands on, included such phrases as 'from the place where
Lisbon stood', and 'from the place which *was*, but *is not* Lisbon', or they
asserted that 'Lisbon is entirely destroyed' and that 'Lisbon is no more'.
When such dramatic descriptions were first read in England there were
some who would not, or could not, believe them. But had they stood on
the castle walls at the end of the week after the earthquake, at the place
from which Richard Goddard had observed it, their incredulity would
have vanished immediately. Plumes of smoke still rose from many parts
of the Baixa and small fires were continually being rekindled by scav-
engers or people raking through embers for lost possessions. Below the
castle to the left, on the waterfront, the Terreiro do Paço was unrecognizable. The square itself was filled with the half-burnt piles of abandoned bundles, the bloated and rotting bodies of dead mules and horses,
abandoned coaches, timber and other detritus swept from the waterside by the tidal wave, and the debris cast about by the collapse of all the
surrounding buildings. As Thomas Chase had witnessed at uncom-
fortably close range, the Royal Palace and the Customs House were
charred ruins; the Casa da Índia and its entire record – manuscripts,
maps, charts and inventories – of 250 years of trading with the East, the
Casa dos Seguros, and all other buildings from which all the workings of
Portugal's overseas commerce were overseen, were no more; and the
brand new quay, the Cais da Pedra, had disappeared beneath the waters
of the Tagus.

On the western flank of the square the magnificent Patriarchal church,
Bibiena's new Opera House which had only been open seven months, and
the convent of São Francisco, which had just completed its costly reno-
vation after a great fire in 1741, and which housed a priceless library of

9,000 volumes, were all destroyed. The Ribeira das Naus, the naval shipyard, was burnt out. On the eastern flank of the square the scene was the same. The main cereal and meat markets had burnt down; and all along the riverfront on both sides scorched ground was all that remained of hundreds of warehouses and stores in the waterfront parish of São Julião. No one would ever know how many of these had been filled with goods brought by that autumn's Brazil fleets. The loss of countless records and ledgers, as merchants of all nationalities were discovering, was every bit as traumatic as the loss of physical stock; and São Julião, Lisbon's most populous parish, was without a single home for its 20,000 or so inhabitants.

In the Rossio, the 'people's square' below the castle to the right, the seat of the Inquisition was a ruin; the convent of São Domingos with its two libraries of 10,000 books and 5,600 volumes of rare manuscripts was gone, and as the fire had swept through the huge Hospital Real de Todos-os-Santos – its second conflagration in five years – hundreds of patients unable to flee had died where they lay. All other hospitals in the city had also been shaken or burnt to the ground, as had the prisons: in the Limoeiro, the largest of these, over 400 prisoners had died and most of the rest had taken advantage of their new-found freedom in the ruins, or had fled the city. Three-quarters of Lisbon's principal religious institutions, numbering well over a hundred, had also been destroyed or severely damaged; all offices housing the records of the municipal authorities were gone; and in at least thirty of the forty parishes, the communities which were the very fabric of daily life, there was no longer a parish church. All over the city miserable groups could be seen 'lugging about saints without heads or arms'[24] and as Lisboetas were buried beneath their parish churches and not in cemeteries, the loss of so many was to create an additional problem in the weeks to come.

Directly below the castle nothing at all remained standing in many of the parishes between the Terreiro do Paço and the Rossio. On the morning of the earthquake Lawrence Fowkes and his family had escaped past the ruins of São Nicolau, the hub of Lisbon's second most populous parish, and by the time the fire had finished its passage it was, in the words of the prior, nothing but 'an uninhabitable desert and mountains of ruins'.[25] Even two years later the parish authorities, housed in the chapel of Nossa Senhora da Pureza, not far from Abraham Castres's house to the north of the Rossio, would only be in contact with 1,500 adult parishioners – barely one in six – and they were scattered all over the city and its surrounding districts. In the neighbouring parish of Nossa Senhora da Conceição, between the modern Rua Áurea and Rua Augusta, not a single one of almost 2,500 homes still stood. To that parish's west and south, in Mártires, the site of the convent of São Francisco, the church was also a ruin, as were the palaces of the Bragança and Corte-Real families and those of the Conde da Ribeira Grande, the Conde de Vimiero, the Visconde de Barbacena, the Conde de São Miguel, the Marquês de Távora, and the Conde de Atouguia. Not a single habitable building remained standing in the parish. It had ceased to exist, and even two years later its register would list just seven households with forty-six inhabitants. To the east of Nossa Senhora da Conceição, beneath the castle walls, Thomas Chase's parish of Madalena had prided itself on having one of the richest ecclesiastical estates of any of its 'rivals' in the city. Now it was completely destroyed by fire. To the north of Nossa Senhora da Conceição, towards the Rossio, Santa Justa, home to more than 8,000 adult parishioners, was a wasteland.

The view from the castle of the Bairro Alto, the far side of the Baixa, was no less shocking. Most striking of all was the sight of the charred arches of the great church of the Carmelites. Many monks had died here in what was regarded as 'one of the most sumptuous places of worship in all Lisbon',[26] as had many more – and several hundred among the congregation – in the nearby convent of Santíssima Trinidade. The Trinidade also lost its library, valued at more than

Lisbon, with an English fleet in the Tagus to deter invasion by Spain in 1735.

Lisbon's great aqueduct, constructed in the eighteenth century and universally acclaimed as one of the most magnificent monuments in Europe.

It was to the Terreiro do Paço (top), with the palace on the left and the Customs Houses on the right, that Thomas Chase and many other survivors fled by boat in the hope of escape.

Mr Braddock made his way to the Remolares (bottom): the Mint is the large waterfront building on the left, and a little to the right of it is São Paulo church.

Street scenes from the city of which Augustus Hervey (top right) was so enamoured.

(opposite) A contemporary Dutch engraving depicting the earthquake, tsunami and fire that destroyed Lisbon on All Saints' Day, 1755.

(right) Benjamin Farmer managed to rescue a little girl from beneath the rubble of his neighbour's house.

(below) Many survivors, like these in Largo de Sta Catarina, were forced to flee in a state of undress.

(bottom) When the Fowkes family escaped, through the Largo de São Nicolau, they found its great church in ruins.

The ruins of the Palácio de Bragança (top), whose priceless treasures were seen by Augustus Hervey in 1754, and a depiction of José I directing the rebuilding process (bottom).

After the earthquake Sebastião José de Carvalho e Melo, Marquês de Pombal (top left), soon secured a position of political supremacy by eliminating all opposition. Some members of the nobility were executed for allegedly plotting against the king (top right), while many others were imprisoned as he pursued his mission to rebuild Lisbon and revitalise Portugal. Fifty years after the quake the new Praça do Comércio (bottom) was substantially complete.

A year before the 250th anniversary of the disaster was commemorated with a special mass in the ruins of the church of Lisbon's Convento do Carmo (above) a mass grave containing parts of more than three-thousand victims was unearthed beneath the Academy of Sciences (below left).

However controversial his legacy, it is the Marquês de Pombal (above right) who looks out over the centre of the city, which he did so much to save.

200,000 *cruzados*, and its two famous organs worth 50,000 *cruzados*. In this same neighbourhood of the affluent parish of Sacramento, which encompassed the area between the Jesuit church of São Roque, the Italian church of Loreto in the Chiado, the Rua do Carmo, and the Rua Largo de São Roque, the palace of the Duque de Lafões along with those of the Marquês de Nisa, the Conde de Cocolim, the Conde de Oeiras, the son of the Marquês de Marialva, Dom João de Ataíde (the Governor of Alentejo province), Ilustríssimo Gonçalo José de Alcácova, the scholar Rui da Silva, the Conde de Valadares, and Admiral Dom António da Silveira would all be entered in the parish records as 'reduced to cinders'. The contents of just one such palace near the Loreto church, recently bought by an Italian family from a former Secretary of War, were valued at 500,000 *cruzados*. In all, ninety-four residential buildings containing the homes of four-fifths of the parishioners of Sacramento were destroyed.

Out of sight to the south-west, beyond what the week before would have been the rooftops of the Bairro Alto, Mr Braddock had seen the roof and façade of São Paulo collapse with the loss of scores of lives. He, and all the skippers of vessels in the Tagus, had also seen Santa Catarina church tumble onto the crowd in the square in front of it; and Braddock knew first-hand that all buildings between the Irish monastery of Corpo Santo and the Mint were ruined, robbing a further 7,000 or 8,000 people of their homes. The convents of Bernadas, Inglezinhas and das Trinas do Mocambo in Madragoa were all destroyed or badly damaged, that of Calvário in Alcântara collapsed causing thirty-two deaths, the royal palace at Alcântara was a ruin, and even as far west as Belém the immense edifice of Jerónimos monastery had been so badly shaken that the great arch of the church transept would collapse the following year. To the east of the Baixa, in the Alfama and elsewhere, the damage was also immense. Four hundred people had died when the convent and church of Santa Clara collapsed, the great churches of

Santa Engrácia and São Vicente de Fora were both shattered, and even the heavy bell-tower of the cathedral, Lisbon's most solid edifice, had fallen, as had the high arched passage connecting the cathedral to the church of São António.

Such was the scene of total destruction in the centre of the city which anyone on the castle walls would have seen below them. Only two or three thousand of the city's 20,000 houses had survived with no damage at all; 15,000 were completely destroyed or severely damaged. All the principal physical embodiments of authority in the city centre – royal, aristocratic, ecclesiastical and governmental – had disappeared. The entire infrastructure that had enabled people to eat, drink, buy clothes, be entertained, and worship was no more. Lisbon was a city whose very heart had been ripped out; and when, just before dawn on 8 November, it was rocked by the biggest aftershock since All Saints' Day the survivors in this *horroroso deserto* were reminded that their ordeal was far from over.

~ THIRTEEN ~

Laws and Disorder

ON 6 NOVEMBER THE *GAZETA DE LISBOA'S* 'coverage' of the earthquake comprised a single sentence. It read: 'The first day of this month
will forever be remembered because of the earthquakes and fires which
have ruined a great part of this city; but it is fortunate that the royal
coffers as well as those of many private citizens have been recovered
from the ruins.' Two things are surprising about this 'masterpiece of
understatement':[1] that there should be no mention of the health of the
King in a journal which was effectively a Court circular, and that the
Gazeta was produced at all that week.

Even if the *Gazeta* had published details about the government's
attempts to re-establish law and order in the city it is very unlikely that they
would have represented fact. All anecdotal evidence suggests that for
the first five days the situation in Lisbon was one of utter lawlessness
and hopelessness, the former exacerbated by escaped prisoners, deserters and looters and the latter by the actions of those priests more determined to goad the population into a religious frenzy than encourage
practical responses to the dire situation. But on 5 November Abraham
Castres was assured by the King that 'the best orders [had] been given
for preventing rapine and murder';[2] and one of the English merchants

wrote that by then soldiers summoned from Peniche, Elvas and Olivença had at last been posted in locations that were not still burning and the Evora dragoons were stopping anyone on the roads out of the city 'who seemed inclined to run away into the neighbouring countries, particularly labouring men and artificers'.[3] Lord Drumlanrig also confirmed, in a letter to his parents dated 8 November, that 'the Ministry have exerted themselves within this day or two, and have put in execution several regulations to collect provisions, and put a stop to the horrid scenes of villany that were perpetually committed while all was in confusion'.[4]

The humanitarian challenge confronting 'the Ministry' was even greater than the task of restoring order. Almost all stocks of timber and sailcloth, required for making shelters, had been consumed by the fire and those that remained were used up within the first few days. There was no firewood for cooking or for keeping the very old, the very young, the injured and the infirm warm at night. Nor were there any provisions in the huge encampments at Campo Grande to the north, in Cotovia to the north-west and elsewhere except those that people had managed to bring with them. Rumours soon circulated of instances of cannibalism in the city itself. As all the existing hospitals had been destroyed, field hospitals had to be established at the convent of São Bento and at the Jesuit *Misericórdia* attached to the church of São Roque, but there was little that could be done for the wounded other than offer comfort and absolution and wait for gangrene to bring a slow and agonizing end to their suffering.

A number of the more enterprising members of the Church and nobility distinguished themselves. To the fore were the Marquês de Alegrete, the *Monteiro-mor* or Huntsman of the Royal Household and Mayor of Lisbon; the Duque de Lafões, Dom Pedro de Bragança, the Chief Justice; his younger brother Dom João Carlos de Bragança; Monsenhor Sampaio of the Patriarchal church, who was said to have personally buried 240 of the dead, and was present when a fifteen-year-old girl was dug out of the ruins after eight days without food or water; the Palhavā Princes, the King's illegitimate brothers, who provided a refuge to more than a thousand people in the grounds of their palace; and, among less aristocratic citizens, the young lieutenant whom Mr Braddock had encountered guarding the Mint who stayed alone at his post for three days, beating back the flames whenever they encroached and thereby earning himself a promotion to captain for his bravery and devotion to duty. The hanging of looters, including four English sailors, at various prominent sites around the city was another measure which had an immediate effect, and by the end of the first week soldiers 'with swords drawn' were forcing 'the common people'[5] to assist in the mass burials of rotting corpses. Those found nearest the water were taken onto the river in boats, weighted and thrown overboard. Elsewhere pits were dug and the bodies were covered in lime 'to destroy the putrid exhalation'.[6]

Decrees gushed forth from the Court at an extraordinary rate, announcing measures to tackle hunger and stop the spread of disease; to prevent the population abandoning the city altogether; to tackle the looting, to summon troops and re-establish religious life in the few churches that still stood; to forbid priests from stirring up undue consternation among the population; to authorize the Royal Treasury to buy up all available bricks, tiles and other building materials; and to proclaim that plans for reconstruction were already being assessed. In all, more than a hundred such ordinances would be announced before the end of the year.

Many of the decrees are more evidence of the persistence of particular problems than of their solution. By the time attempts were made to try and stem the exodus of refugees into the provinces, for example, so many had already fled that some merchants estimated that only half the city's survivors remained within its environs; and it was only on the fifth day that the urgency of burying the dead was communicated to heads of convents – a clear sign that progress with burials was pitifully slow. Others brought swift results, especially those relating to the supply of provisions. By the second week butchers and bakers were at work in all of the encampments in and around the city, and a good harvest ensured plentiful supplies of corn from stores in the countryside outside the city. English corn merchants added to the stockpiles by offering all they had in store to the King, an offer which was 'very well taken'.[7] As far as the spread of disease was concerned, there was little that could be done other than disposing of the bodies as fast as possible; but at least the fire had had a positive effect in this respect by burning many corpses to a cinder.

By the end of the second week Edward Hay remarked in a letter to his brother Lord Dupplin, Commissioner of Trade, Lord of the Treasury and soon to be appointed joint-paymaster of the Forces, that 'the general consternation seems to be pretty well over' and said that he believed that 'if it please God we have no return of any great shock peoples minds will be daily more composed'. Hay's wife and baby Mary were doing well in the *quinta* at Marvila, and he told his brother that his wife was 'determined not to leave me, and I dare not persuade her to it. Poor dear woman'.[8] Castres also pronounced himself in 'tolerable health, and infinitely better than I could expect considering the anxiety and fatigue I have undergone'.[9]

Castres and Hay received further encouraging, if astonishing, news when they went to see the King after the massive aftershock on Sunday, 8 November. The purpose of their visit was to deliver the formal message of condolence from the English Factory to the Royal Family but while they were at the Palace they were told that the King was adamant that the city should be rebuilt exactly where it had stood. As most foreigners shared the opinion that 'one century [would] not put things to right', and that the future could only be one of 'total Bankruptcy and Stagnation'[10] for Portugal, such a scheme sounded like wishful thinking verging on the delusional. The fire alone had caused what would later be described as 'as savage a gutting of the heart of a city as [could] be found anywhere in the previous history of Europe',[11] destroying a considerably greater acreage than had been lost to London's Great Fire. Edward Hay could not envisage how such a project could possibly be realized, and Castres, though he had no doubt about 'M de Carvalho's facilitating the proper means towards it',[12] wondered what would finance a new city as there was 'hardly a merchant in a hundred of any nation that [had] saved anything', and the Portuguese themselves were so undone that they were thought to be unable to pay 'one single shilling'[13] of what they owed the English merchants.

However, both men admired the determination of the Court 'to encourage the merchants to make new settlements, and drive on the same trade here as usual'; and there was a chance that as long as the gold and diamond mines of Brazil continued to churn out their riches, *some* sort of trade might continue. Indeed if that were to happen, Hay thought that any English merchants brave enough to stay on in Lisbon might even 'do better than they ever did'. 'We must', he bravely declared, 'now look upon ourselves as an infant Factory.' That such a 'considerable branch of commerce'[14] as the Portugal trade might be lost altogether to Britain was a possibility too shocking to contemplate.

Although Abraham Castres was 'in tolerable health' he was still sick with worry about a plethora of concerns more immediate than the future rebuilding of the city. There was still no news from either Cádiz or Gibraltar to confirm that they had not been destroyed by the earthquake or tidal waves; and there was no sign of HMS *Bedford* or any other English man-o'-war with the supplies and craftsmen he so desperately needed for the refugee camp that had formerly been his home – and room below-decks to remove some of those clamouring to return to England. Carvalho's insistence on maintaining the ban on shipping leaving the Tagus was a further concern: although the Minister had assured him that as soon as another search of all vessels for plunder had been completed the embargo would be lifted it was, in the meantime, preventing news of the disaster from reaching the outside world by the speediest means. Furthermore, his cash resources were almost exhausted and by nature he could not, with the imminent onset of winter, adopt the approach later suggested by Benjamin Keene and send 'the horses of the Factory that are eating you up all together agrazing'.[15]

On Sunday, 16 November the Royal Family, all the nobility and clergy solemnly processed from Alcântara to the church and convent of Necessidades to beg for mercy and seek forgiveness of their sins. That very afternoon there was an aftershock that was felt as far away as Santiago da Compostella and La Coruña, and the Tagus rose so alarmingly that it was feared another tidal wave was about to race upriver. Two days after that there was an aftershock as great as the one of 8 November. Worse still, it began to pour with rain, making for execrable conditions in the open. 'No body yet ventures to lie in houses', wrote the physician Richard Wolfall, 'and though we are in general exposed to the open sky, for want of material to make tents, and tho' rain has fallen several nights past, yet I don't find but the most delicate tender people suffer difficulties as the most robust and healthy. Everything is yet with us in the greatest confusion imaginable: we have neither cloaths nor conveniences, nor money to send for them to other countries'.[16]

Two days later Captain Clies received permission for the *Expedition* to sail for England, taking with her Benjamin Farmer, sixteen other passengers, and the cash of those merchants who had nowhere secure to keep it or saw no future in the Lisbon trade. Lord Drumlanrig, who had spent ten days living on the packet, was not among those able to sail. Dr Scrafton and his friends still feared that if the journey didn't kill him the English winter certainly would, so he was installed in a 'very large cabin' on the merchant ship *St Ignatius*. He wrote to his parents assuring them that he was 'surehearted and well' and that it was 'warm and not crowded' on board. There was still no sign of a warship which might be able to take him 'towards Italy in the most safe and commodious manner imaginable'; but he courageously declared that if none appeared he was 'not at all apprehensive of the consequences of returning to England at this bad season'. Indeed his principal concern was for the friends he had made among the English merchants. 'I cannot express', he wrote, 'how much I have and do feel for the poor Colony of Merchants who are totally undone by this calamity and support themselves under their misfortunes astonishingly.'[7]

By the end of November the King decided that he was going to build a new palace of timber in the grounds at Belém. Suggestions that he might wish to move to Mafra were dismissed: according to the Queen he had no desire to live in a high-ceilinged large building ever again.

FOURTEEN

News Spreads

WHEN THE FIRST REPORTS OF WHAT HAD HAPPENED in Lisbon reached Madrid, Castres's despatch to Sir Benjamin Keene was not among them. This put Keene in a very concerned state and on 10 November he wrote to his old friend telling him that he knew their friend the Conde de Perelada was dead, saying:

> I console myself from this very silence that no harm is personally
> taken upon you, and that your house is situated in such a manner
> as not to be exposed to the flames which we hear are consuming
> the miserable remains of what survived the earthquake . . . I dread
> the account I may expect of the death and ruin of so many of our
> poor countrymen. Their Catholic Majesties have been affected with
> this news as souls like [theirs] should be affected in such terrible
> calamities.

In a brave attempt at sounding cheerful Keene added, 'I imagine you are collecting your flock who are burnt out of their houses, and planting them in tents in your *quinta'.* By 19 November Keene had at last received two letters from Castres, the one written on 4 November and another dated 11 November, and this time he replied 'What can I say to you? What is to be said in particular upon such a general calamity?'[2]

A courier who left the Spanish capital on 8 November arrived in Paris two weeks later in time for the news that 50,000 people had perished in the Lisbon earthquake to be inserted in that day's *Gazette de France*; and after that, as Goethe later wrote, 'the Demon of fear had never so speedily and powerfully diffused his terror over the earth'.[3] In two days word finally reached London – three weeks and three days after the disaster – and with the arrival of each new report confusion increased. In the *Whitehall Evening Post* of 25 November it was reported that a quake in which 60,000 had perished was believed to have struck Lisbon, but a postscript added that there were 'letters in town . . . much more favourable than heretofore related'.[4] Then the next edition of the paper claimed that 100,000 lives had been lost as 'the earth opened, and swallowed up great numbers of houses, and flames issuing at the same time, set on fire those that stood'. The most important, and shocking, details for the readership of the time were those relating to the high-born: the tragic death of the Conde de Perelada was mentioned – he and his whole family had been 'swallowed up' – and the King, it was said, had been 'obliged to run out in his shirt, and sat in it without any cloathing for three hours in his coach'.[5] The postscript to that day's edition contained even graver news from Amsterdam: although it was now believed that 'only' 50,000 had died it was said that the Royal Family had all been killed in the aftershock on 8 November.

The next edition carried news of a letter from the Papal Nuncio 'intimating that the survivors of the late calamity were fearful of being put to the sword by the neighbouring barbarians', by which it meant Barbary corsairs rather than Spaniards; and mention was made of 'necessities' being gathered together for the Portuguese 'which the British heart is (as usual) most ready to grant'.[6] Finally, on 2 December, it was reported that 'not above 10,000' had been lost in the 'calamity', but rather ominously it was also noted that there was no word of 'any ship sailing from

Lisbon to any place since the misfortune', and in the postscript fresh news from Amsterdam claimed that half the city had been destroyed and that 'upwards of 50,000 have perished'. Amid the welter of contradictory but all equally shocking reports the only solace that the *Whitehall Evening Post* could offer was that Sir Everard Fawkner, the head of the Post Office, was 'so deeply affected with the late calamity, and the importance of the Portugal trade to this nation, that he gives his constant attendance at the Post Office . . . to see that all orders received from the government, and from traders to Lisbon may be executed with the greatest exactness, and forwarded with the utmost expedition'.[7]

To confuse matters further, Sir Benjamin Keene's official despatch from Madrid had not arrived by the time the *Whitehall Evening Post* and other journals carried their first reports, and when he penned it on 10 November he had still heard no word from Castres. So although his information, printed in *The London Gazette* on 29 November, was expected to be the most authoritative and up-to-date, it was neither. But it was, even in the absence of any intelligence from Castres, accurate enough. Keene reported that 'the palace, churches and most of the stately buildings' in Lisbon were destroyed and that at the time the Spanish messenger had left, 'the flames [were] still destroying the remains of the city'. The port of Setúbal, he added, was 'entirely destroyed', although Porto, to the relief of everyone involved in the wine trade, had experienced 'very little damage'. The new dimension that Keene added was his testimony about the effects of the earthquake in Spain: the 'fine causeway of two leagues' from Cádiz to the Isle of Leon had been swept away, together with 'a great many people who were upon it', and all towns on that part of the Spanish coast had 'shared more or less in this calamity'.[8] With this news it became clear to Londoners that the 'Lisbon earthquake' had destroyed a lot more than Lisbon and its environs alone.

Edward Hay had predicted that when the news reached London it would 'raise a great consternation in the city',[9] and he was correct. There was pandemonium. It began to circulate at change-time on 25 November, and was reported as having 'struck such a general panic that the merchants withdrew immediately, the 'change [was] shut up, and no business [was] transacted'.[10] Not a single person attended that day's meeting of a club of Lisbon merchants at the Fountain Tavern in Bartholomew Lane, and rumours of colossal losses among individual merchants spread rapidly. On 29 November the bluestocking Mary Delany wrote to her sister that 'Mr [Joseph] Mellish's loss will be very considerable' and that his partner David de Purry, who was in London, had 'lost *friends, fortune, family, every connection in life!*'[11] She had also been told that John Gore (who was related to the Mellishes) and John Bristow, both heavily involved in the diamond trade, had lost £30,000 and £100,000 respectively, and that even Edward Hay's brother, the Bishop of St Asaph, had lost an investment of £7,000 which was 'part of his wife's fortune'.[12]

The coffee houses hummed. One minute it was said that every merchant of the English Factory had lost everything, the next that the losses were lower than previously thought. One story which did the rounds even claimed that all of Lisbon was under water. The details, as well as the generalities, were also earnestly discussed – the *Whitehall Evening Post* reported that some coffee house men were 'asking about the Spanish and French ministers, saying, that the son of the former was saved by the latter; others about the King's being saved in his shirt, and the Royal Family's living three days in a coach'[13] – and the financial implications of each titbit were weighed up. With each day's news the 'skeptics'* became fewer and fewer and by the end of the first week in December Horace Walpole was confident enough of the facts to tell his

* Samuel Johnson was said by Macaulay to be 'in the habit of sifting with extreme severity the evidence for all stories which were merely odd. But when they were not only odd but miraculous, his severity relaxed'. Thus he once declared 'half testingly, we suppose, that for six months he refused to credit the fact of the earthquake at Lisbon, and that he still believed the calamity to be greatly exaggerated'; and yet was prepared to go 'on a ghost-hunt to Cock Lane' and to be 'angry with John Wesley for not following up another scent of the same kind with proper spirit and perseverance'.[17]

friend Sir Horace Mann, the Consul in Naples, that 'the catastrophe is greater than ever happened in your neighbourhood.* Our share is very considerable, and by some reckoned at four millions.'[14]

Quite apart from the commercial damage that seemed likely to ensue, there was a genuine humanitarian concern. Mary Delany told her sister that 'the dismal fate of Lisbon [has] sunk my spirits to such a degree that for my part I have not been able to raise them since'; and every day seemed to bring 'some new unhappy discovery', leaving her 'so thoroughly touched' that she 'could hardly think of anything else'.[15] Londoners had a collective memory of the Great Fire less than a hundred years earlier. They also had a more recent collective memory of earthquakes. At about noon on 8 February 1750, and again a month later, the city had been shaken by quakes of sufficient violence to set the dogs howling and causing fish to jump half a yard clear of the Thames. The first one had not excited any great reaction, but the population found the second, which was more severe, impossible to ignore; and when a mad Guardsman with the *nom de plume* 'Military Prophet' started to trumpet his certainty that a third shock would occur a month after the second, London was gripped by a terrible panic.

In early April Horace Walpole witnessed 730 coaches leaving London in three days, 100,000 people were camping in the open in Hyde Park, and up to a third of the city's inhabitants were said to have fled to the country. According to the Methodist preacher Charles Wesley, London 'looked like a sacked city'.[16] When the third shock failed to materialize the populace returned rather ashamed. But the memory of the terror stayed fresh in the minds of Londoners, as did the prophecy of the eccentric William Whiston, Isaac Newton's successor as Lucasian Professor of Mathematics at Cambridge, that one of the ninety-nine events presaging the imminent end of the world would be a terrible

---

* Walpole's words were carefully chosen: recent excavations near Naples had unearthed the ruins of Herculaneum and Pompeii.

earthquake in which a tenth part of an eminent city would be destroyed killing 7,000 or more.

On 28 November Henry Fox, the new Secretary of State for the Southern Department and Leader of the House of Commons, delivered a message to the Speaker which was then read to both Houses of Parliament. It was a request from George II for permission 'to give such assistance to the distressed people of Portugal, as His Majesty shall think fit; and that such expenses as shall be incurred by His Majesty in relieving the misery to which they may be reduced by this deplorable calamity, shall be made good out of the next aids'.[18] The measure was unanimously approved with 'a universal shout of joy'[19] and the following day an extraordinary meeting took place under the direction of the Prime Minister, the Duke of Newcastle, at which the first emergency relief initiative of its kind and size in history was planned. Merrick Burrell, John Gore and John Bristow – three of the leading Lisbon merchants in London – were invited so that their opinions as to what the city would need most could be canvassed.

The provision of foodstuffs was the main item on the agenda: the viability of ensuring rapid shipment of 6,000 barrels of 'good beef' and 4,000 firkins of butter from Ireland was discussed, as well as large quantities of wheat, flour, biscuits and rice from England. It was known that a Newfoundland fishing fleet was bound for Iberian ports, so fish would be in plentiful supply, but tools – pickaxes, spades, crows and screws – were added to a list of essential items that might be required, as were 'shoes, if necessary'. Finally, it was agreed that the sum of £50,000 in specie should also be sent, making the total value of the assistance amount to £100,000; and Burrell, Bristow and Gore were authorized to begin procuring the supplies, to make the necessary shipping arrangements, and to ensure that everything, including the cash, was 'distributed for the use of the sufferers'.[20] Josiah Mellish's wife, and many others among the great and the good of London, then set to 'busily packing boxes with all sorts of wearing apparel and necessities for work, to send to the poor miserable Portuguese'.[21]

By the end of the month the news had reached almost every corner of Europe, generating the same degree of interest as in London. In France the *Mercure de France* would carry over a hundred articles about the earthquake in the coming year, the *Gazette de Cologne* and *Courrier d'Avignon* more than fifty each. In the United Provinces, the merchants of the Amsterdam exchange were as nervous as their English counterparts of the likely financial repercussions from the blow to Europe's supplier of gold. And in England, according to Horace Walpole, 'the earthquake, the opposition, and the war' remained the 'only topics'[22] ever discussed for weeks to come.

It was not until he reached Malta in the second week of December that Augustus Hervey heard 'the sad news of the fatal earthquake that happened at Lisbon, with many particulars of that misfortune, and that it had been felt in many places of Europe, and even across the ocean to Barbary'. His diary entry continued, 'these are frightful events, and ought to inspire reflections that should mend the lives of individuals in order not to deserve such chastisements from Providence'. At Cagliari, just before Christmas, he heard further details from the Viceroy which made him 'very uneasy' about the fate of João da Bemposta and all his other old friends.[23] As only a handful of members of the 'lesser' nobility had been killed he need not have worried about Dom João, but his mother had perished in Sant'Ana convent and many of the palaces in which Hervey had been entertained, including Dom João's in the Largo Paço da Rainha a little to the east of Castres's house and the Palácio de Bragança, were ruined or very badly damaged; and the same was true of his old haunts the convents of Chelas, Odivelas and Sant'Ana.

Just six days later North Americans also received word of the disaster when Capt Joseph Hibbert's brigantine *Hannah* arrived in Boston from Cádiz, and the first report appeared in *The Boston Gazette* on

22 December. It was greeted with astonishment not least because, at a little after four o'clock in the morning on 18 November, New England had itself been rocked by 'a most terrible shock of an earthquake'.[24] According to the account of Professor John Winthrop, the eminent Professor of Mathematics and Philosophy, who had lectured on earthquakes at Harvard eight days afterwards, it had been a 'perfectly calm and serene' night with an almost full moon when the quake began 'with a roaring noise in the north-west like thunder at a distance [which] grew fiercer as the earthquake drew nearer'. The first tremor resembled 'that of a long rolling, swelling sea', and lasted about a minute. Then, almost immediately afterwards, the next tremor came on 'with redoubled noise and violence'. Winthrop's bed was 'tossed from side to side' and his whole house was so 'prodigiously agitated' that 'the windows rattled, [and] the beams cracked, as if all would presently be shaken to pieces'. This second shock lasted four or five minutes before ceasing, with just one more 'little revival of the trembling'. An aftershock followed one and a quarter hours later.

The damage caused by the earthquake in North America was extensive and it was soon ascertained that the quake had been sensible along 800 miles of the coast and as far inland as 550 miles. In Boston, the public market-house was 'thrown down', a new distiller's cistern was 'burst to pieces by the agitation of the liquor in it', and in the harbour large numbers of fish floated to the surface. Stone fences throughout the affected area collapsed, and numerous reports were received of chasms spouting water and sand. Out in the Atlantic, seventy leagues east of Cape Ann, a ship's crew thought they had run aground, but on lowering the lead found they were in more than fifty fathoms of water. In the West Indies at two o'clock that afternoon the water withdrew from the harbour on St Maarten, 'leaving the vessels dry, and fish on the banks, where there used to be three or four fathom of water'. Having witnessed a similar occurrence just weeks earlier, many people fled inland before the water returned; and when it did so 'it arose six feet higher than usual, so as to overflow the low lands'.[25]

New England experienced further aftershocks on 22 November and 19 December, and by the end of the year there was huge interest in the Lisbon earthquake. Many New England ministers regarded the war that had begun the previous year as a Holy War to expel the Catholic interlopers from North America, and although Protestants had also been given warnings to repent of their sins in the form of Braddock's defeat and the quake, none of these were comparable to what had happened to Portugal's bastion of Catholicism. Before April 1756 New England printers had turned out three scientific tracts, the text of thirteen sermons and five poems, and they had reprinted four accounts of previous earthquakes. The first eye-witness account to be sold on the streets was a rather colourful, and in parts bigoted, one penned by Benjamin Farmer.

FIFTEEN

Aid and Anxiety

THOMAS CHASE HAD NOT HAD A CHANGE of clothing for almost a month when he was helped from the Hake *quinta* and put on board their ship *Tagus* on 29 November. The following day she sailed for home with twenty-four passengers, the first English vessel after the *Expedition* packet to have been allowed to leave. Before departing Chase had received some gratifying information. John Jorge was alive, and he had not deserted him in the Terreiro do Paço the day after the earthquake. When he had reached the other side of the river with his uncle and the lame old lady he had paid an English shoe-maker to go back and fetch Chase, but by the time the man returned to the square Chase had already set out for the Hakes. Chase knew that he had been exceptionally lucky to have crossed Jorge's path that day; many others had lain in the streets begging passers-by for help until they were eventually consumed by the fire. He was also fortunate to be leaving so soon and with such ease: when Edward Hay managed to hire a vessel to repatriate the first fifty of the poorest in the Irish community they spent twenty days on board waiting for the grant of a pass to leave the river, and finally had to disembark again.

As the *Tagus* left for home a very welcome sight was seen making its way up the river. Under the escort of Captain Rich Dorrill and HMS *Penzance* the English fishing fleet arrived from Newfoundland loaded with vast quantities of dry salted cod to bolster the stocks of provisions for the tens of thousands camped out in the fields; and Dorrill's crew were able to help Castres improve the shanty-town that had once been his beautiful garden. When Dorrill departed again on 12 December he escorted two vessels carrying the first Irish families to leave, and took Lord Drumlanrig with him. No British warship bound for the Mediterranean had appeared in the whole of November so, unable to wait any longer, Drumlanrig was forced to return home. His journey nearly ended in disaster before it had even begun. As *Penzance* departed she was not recognized as an English warship by the commanding officer of one of the forts even though she was flying the colours and, to Dorrill's disgust and dismay, was fired upon twice from the shore.

Three days after Dorrill's departure, and two days after the Patriarch ordered another penitential procession in the city, the next packet arrived having ploughed for nine days through 'severe and terrible storms'. This had brought on the most awful seasickness in John Dobson – but seemed to have 'strengthen'd rather than impair'd' the health of his sick companion, George Lucy. The desire of these two men to spend the winter in Lisbon seems extraordinary: they knew what had happened there before embarking and would have realized that finding food and shelter in a city ravaged by earth, water and fire was going to be difficult even for friends of the Goddard and Branfill families. Perhaps they simply sought 'adventure', in addition to a cure for Lucy's ailments. Whatever their motivation, a letter from Dobson to his uncle is the first eye-witness account of the impressions of someone arriving in Lisbon in the immediate aftermath of the earthquake:

> I would now say something [he began] of the city of Lisbon (which I have only seen at a distance) if words could paint the misery

which has oppress'd it: an earthquake of seven minutes began the
desolation on All Saints Day at 10 o'clock in the morning; a Moor
embraced this opportunity of glutting his national revenge and set
fire to a stable near the palace so between both almost everything
is destroy'd. The opera house (which was esteem'd the richest
building in Europe and cost the late King 300,000 sterling), the
custom house, the royal palace, and all the houses of the English
merchants are demolished: not above twenty English have
perished, tho' the whole Factory is in a manner ruin'd by the loss of
their effects to an immense value. The Portuguese ran with immediate haste to their churches, which fell first, and buried near
twenty thousand people in one confus'd heap of rubbish. Sir Harry
Frankland and his Lady were in a post chaise; the very moment
they got out of it, some stones from the houses killed the mules
and broke the chaise to pieces. A gallows is erected every five and
twenty yards to punish the villany of those wretches who take
advantage of this inexpressible distress. The King, Queen and
Royal Family are retired to the palace of Bellisle at some little
distance from Lisbon.

A postscript reads:

Since I wrote the above, I have heard that the Spanish Minister and
his family were swallow'd up alive in their coach. Goddard is
living: I hope to see him soon. Later accounts inform me that the
fire was spread by the wax of candles in the churches catching hold
of the paintings and tapestry; Report has increas'd the number of
the killed to fifty thousand. The sea ebb'd and flow'd three times in
less than an hour.'[1]

John Dobson was an erudite young historian, an author of verses and
ballads, and the winner of a £1,000 prize for his translation into Latin

verse of *Paradise Lost* while at Oxford. * He would also appear to have been Lisbon's first 'earthquake tourist'.

When Dobson and Lucy arrived, seven weeks after the earthquake, the plight of the populace had improved little. Although everyone now had shelter under tents or in wooden barracks – 9,000 of which were erected in the first six months – there was still a desperate shortage of clothing and blankets. It was 'the rigorous season of the year', and to add to the misery and fear there were almost daily 'tremulations'. Some had grown tired of the encampments on the outskirts and had chosen to return to the city and live among the ruins, despite the dangers posed by the after-shocks and by the continued 'great plundering and robbing' which Edward Hay reported. All this combined to 'disturb people's minds, and keep them in constant alarm'.[2]

The organization of trade remained problematic. An ordinance declaring that all provisions would be admitted free of duty and another confirming the establishment of a temporary customs house at Belém had been published early in November, and both measures were welcomed by all merchants. But thereafter chaos reigned. The Newfoundland fishing fleet was forbidden to leave the Tagus even though the cargoes of many of the vessels were intended for other Iberian ports which were equally in need; the fixing of retail prices discouraged merchants from ordering provisions from England and Ireland in case the wholesale price allowed them no margin; and a ban on erecting *barracas* at Belém precluded the building of warehouses or offices near the temporary customs house, which meant that all merchants remained 'dispersed about the country in a most inconvenient manner for the carrying on of their business'.[3] The circumstances were far from easy, and Benjamin Keene passed on to Castres the disturbing news that a prominent banker in Madrid was finding

---

* Dobson would later write *Chronological annals of the war; from its beginnings to the present time* (1763).

that 'all those [in Portugal] he is owing money to have lost little or nothing, but all those who are in debt are worse than ruined', and suspected that 'the truth is not being spoken in all circumstances'.[4] Most worrying of all for those English merchants who were trying to continue trading was the fact that there was no sign of the winter convoy from England that would bring huge cargoes of textiles and other goods for the Brazil fleets which, come the new year, would start to leave for the Atlantic crossing.

The process of assessing options for resurrecting the city continued apace. By mid-December Manuel da Maia, a portly, octogenarian military engineer who had overseen the construction of the magnificent aqueduct of Águas Livres (which had sustained no damage in the earthquake), presented to the Duque de Lafões and Carvalho his suggestions: to rebuild the city as it had been, to rebuild it with wider streets, to demolish the Baixa and rebuild it to a completely new design, or to abandon the city and rebuild a new one nearer Belém. Da Maia had assembled a team, including the Hungarian engineer Carlos Mardel (the architect of Carvalho's new palace at Oeiras) and Eugénio dos Santos (recently charged with establishing a new school of architecture and drawing, the Casa do Risco), who would work on producing different blueprints within these criteria and it was agreed that he should return in the spring with six plans.

On the morning of 21 December, further lives were lost when Lisbon was shaken by an aftershock greater than any since 1 November. But the contents of a despatch received that day by Castres were so important that he made straight for the 'Royal Tent' at Belém. Carvalho received him there and seemed 'extremely well pleased' as Castres read out the messages of condolence and support from George II and both Houses of Parliament and revealed that £100,000 worth of provisions and specie were being despatched to the city. Castres was asked to return the next day to convey the news to the Royal Family in person, and José was visibly moved as he delivered his response, declaring in front of the whole Court that, in the Envoy's words:

> . . . there was no need of the present melancholy occasion to
> convince him of the King of Great Britain His Good Brother and
> Faithful ally's sincere Friendship and Regard for Him and for His
> Family, having already had many proofs of my Royal Master's sen-
> timents and disposition towards him, and all that was his. That the
> concern His Majesty and the British nation had expressed for the
> distresses brought upon the people by the late calamity had made
> such an impression upon him as he should never forget, desiring
> me at the same time to renew to His Majesty the strongest assur-
> ances on his part of the friendship and esteem for his royal person,
> and of the continuance of his endeavours to preserve, by all
> possible means, the strict union and perfect understanding which
> had so long and so happily subsisted between the two crowns.

Castres added in his despatch to London that both the King and Queen expressed themselves with 'such a mixture of complacency and tenderness both in their looks and tone of voice, as plainly showed the emotion of their hearts', and that it was clear 'how sensibly they were touched with this most signal mark of His Majesty's attention to and compassion for the distresses of their subjects'. It was a satisfying end to the year for Castres, and he also took great comfort from a seasonal letter from Benjamin Keene in Madrid. 'I never find myself warm and comfortable', his old friend wrote, 'without thinking how you are deprived of these comforts; I never see superfluities upon my table or any other without thinking of your necessities, but I rejoice to see your firmness of mind, which is such as inspires itself into the timid.'[5]

As Castres left the royal tent a number of nobles and 'persons of all stations' approached him in the garden and expressed how thankful they were that the Envoy 'had not been charged with empty compliments';

and on 26 December, when he went to the Palace to convey festive greetings, Carvalho reiterated 'in the most solemn manner how much their most faithful majesties had been affected by his Majesty's most princely and affectionate behaviour towards them', and that he too was moved by the 'princely and extensive succours ordered to be sent hither with such expedition'. Similar scenes took place in London when George II had summoned the Portuguese Ambassador, Luís da Cunha, to tell him of the offer of assistance. According to Carvalho, the King's speech 'had drawn tears from [da Cunha's] eyes' and he had written to José declaring 'that it was beyond [his] power to give [his] sovereign a true and exact relation of the many affecting passages . . . which had touched them so'.[6]

Britain was not alone in offering assistance. Spain had at the outset pledged 'as much ready money every day as a messenger can carry' and promised that 'the *douanes* are open on the frontiers for all necessities to pass free without duties'.[7] Hamburg would send three large cargoes of timber, planks and other building materials as well as 100,000 *thalers*; and the United Provinces also undertook to despatch a large shipment of timber. José rather stubbornly declined any assistance at all from Spain in the beginning, even though his sister was Fernando VI's Queen and his Queen was Fernando's sister; later he accepted 150,000 dollars (£33,750) in specie, but refused any provisions on the somewhat dogmatic basis that to do so would infringe trade agreements between the two countries. Offers of help from France were politely declined, to the chagrin of the Comte de Baschi who soon afterwards ordered his Consul, Nicolas Grenier, not to attend any more of the regular consuls' meetings at Castres's house in view of the imminent outbreak of war.

The 'phony' war was intensifying by the day – there were 103 French prizes and 4,000 prisoners in Portsmouth alone by the end of December – but it was weeks of appalling weather and contrary winds, not the French fleet, that frustrated Britain's aid effort. Although the first ship from Ireland laden with beef and butter arrived in the second week of

January 1756, HMS *Hampton Court* nearly foundered soon after leaving
Spithead and she and the rest of the convoy were forced to turn back.
Five packet boat departures in a row were also cancelled, and for the
whole of January Lisbon was to all intents and purposes completely cut
off from England.

One ship that did reach the Tagus in the last week of 1755 had completed a passage from Boston in twenty-four days, and her crew brought
news of the New England quake. This was received with horror by those
not solely preoccupied with staying alive: the city had only just learnt of
another terrible earthquake in Morocco in the second half of November
which seemed to have occurred on exactly the same day. Reliable details
of this second visitation of God's wrath on Morocco were scarce. It was
said to have totally destroyed Meknes, leaving only eight survivors in
the Jewish quarter of the city, and there were reports of 'numberless'
deaths[8] elsewhere – far more than in the earthquake of 1 November.
This news was in turn transmitted back to New England, where it
appeared in the *Boston Weekly Newsletter* on 1 April 1756.

There were also further quakes in Europe: on the night of 26 December Liège, Maastricht, Nijmegen and Arnhem were all shaken; on
30 December it was the turn of the inhabitants of Glasgow and Greenock;
and on the afternoon of 9 December Switzerland experienced a
phenomenon which was, according to the account of Rodolf Valltravers
to the Royal Society, not only 'unusual' in his country but doubly fright-
ening after the news of Lisbon's misfortune had left the Swiss 'much
alarmed, and apprehensive of some other great misfortune'.[9] A remark
by Horace Walpole in a letter to George Montagu shows that people
were fully aware that the world seemed to be mired in a seismic crisis:
'there have been lately such earthquakes and waterquakes, and rocks
rent, and other strange phenomena', he wrote, 'that one would think
the world exceedingly out of repair'.[10] The anonymous author 'MP' agreed
with his 'friend in the country' that 'these last nine or ten years have

produced more earthquakes and other unusual phenomena in nature, than ever happened in the world in the same space of time since the general deluge'. Perhaps, he suggested ominously, the Lisbon earthquake was 'but the beginning of sorrows' and was 'preparatory to some great event, which seem'd near at hand'.[11]

As survivors like Benjamin Farmer and Thomas Chase began to arrive in England to tell their stories, the fear that worse may yet be to come was equalled by the worry of those who had still not heard whether their relatives had survived. The Duke of Queensbury had written a letter about his son to Benjamin Keene in Madrid which 'drew tears from [his] eyes' every time he thought about it. At least Keene was able to assure Queensbury that his son was on his way home on HMS *Penzance*, accompanied by a physician. He received many other 'melancholy letters'[12] which he was not able to answer with any words of comfort either because he had no information, or the truth was too terrible. The banker Benjamin Harboyne, for example, 'became a raving maniac'[13] during the quake and had to be shipped home in chains to live out his days under the watchful eyes of a keeper at his home in Yorkshire; and even in Drumlanrig's case a joyous reunion with his doting parents was short-lived. A combination of the hardships he endured in the aftermath of the earthquake and being forced to return to an English winter were more than his consumptive frame could bear. Ten months later he was dead, and a line unbroken for more than five hundred years came to an end.

By the time the first English refugees returned home religious shockwaves generated by the earthquake had spread throughout the northern hemisphere. In England the Reverend William Stukeley had asserted in a lecture to the Royal Society after the London tremors in 1750 that earthquakes were 'a plain and notorious proof of God's hand', and that 'of all the great and public calamities which affect us mortals, [they] claim the first title to the name of warnings and judgements'. This was religious and 'scientific' orthodoxy – God spoke through earthquakes – and the question thrust to the fore by the Lisbon quake was, what was His message? And to whom exactly was it addressed? The ensuing debate was not confined to some remote theological backwater. Britain may have been a more secular society than Portugal, but religion was still its bedrock and, as Tobias Smollett wrote in his *Complete History of England*, 'the public was overwhelmed with consternation by the tidings of [the] dreadful earthquake'.[14]

An inscription on the Monument, in the City of London, blamed 'the treachery and malice of the Popish Faction' for the Great Fire of 1666, and the most extreme reaction to Lisbon's fate suggested that it was no surprise God had targeted a city whose name was a byword for idolatry and superstition. *An Address To The Inhabitants Of Great-Britain; Occasioned By The Late Earthquake at Lisbon*, an anonymous tract sold in the pamphlet shops of the Royal Exchange, declared that it was 'no wonder Lisbon is fallen. God has justly made it like unto Sodom and Gomorrah.' It was a city ruled by the Inquisition, in which 'numbers of virgins have been sacrificed to the brutal lusts of the wretched monsters, the Inquisitors'.[15] In similar vein the Methodist leader George Whitefield characterized Lisbon's religion in his *Letter To The Remaining Disconsolate Inhabitants of Lisbon* as being that of 'Mahomedan Christians, nay worse! Far worse than any Mahomedans'; and he too blamed the Inquisition, with its 'tedious years of dark imprisonment, subterraneous tortures, [and] flagellations of these most unhappy wretches',[16] for what had happened.

Most of the sermons and pamphlets were not so quick to condemn Lisbon, and interpreted what had happened as an unequivocal warning to *everyone* to mend their ways and repent of sins before it was too late. As war with France drew closer there was a profound sense among the religious that a day of reckoning was approaching. There had been the Jacobite rebellion ten years earlier, then an epidemic of cattle disease, then the London earthquakes, then defeats at the hands of the French and Indians in North America – and these were signs, proclaimed 'Citizen', the author of *An old remedy new reviv'd; or, an infallible method to prevent this city from sharing in the calamities of Lisbon*, that 'Wrath is gone out against us, and the Hand of the Lord is now upon the Earth'. It was a mistake for anyone to think 'that God loved us more than them', he continued, 'or that they were greater sinners than ourselves'; and he warned that if people did not repent 'we shall all likewise perish'. 'Citizen' also directed a particular message at merchants, warning them that not to repent would mean that 'a stagnation in trade will ensue' or, worse still, that the Lisbon trade would 'be lost to another nation'.[17]

The Congregationalist preacher Samuel Hayward was another who pointed out that although 'this ruin hath not fallen on [Lisbon] undeservedly' the message was directed at Britain as well. Indeed visible manifestations of God's wrath had extended 'even to [Britain's] shores' in the form of the disturbances on inland waters and the tidal waves, and they conveyed 'an alarming notice of what God was doing in the Earth, and that thou also wert not beyond His reach'.[18] There had even been a tremor in Cumberland on 17 November, suggesting that God might be about 'to revisit this nation with a heavier hand'.[19] Hayward's words were principally directed, as were those of many others, at London and Londoners. Amidst 'the Age of Gin', London, with its luxury and irreligion, its love of pleasure and masquerade balls and plays, its 'houses of lewdness' and the ubiquity of 'the sin of Sodom',[20] was going to bring Judgement down on everyone's heads if people did not change immediately.

This sense of urgency, that Lisbon showed that time was running out, was a central theme in Whitefield's fellow Methodist John Wesley's *Serious Thoughts Occasioned by the Late Earthquake at Lisbon*. God, wrote Wesley, was 'now making an Inquisition for blood', and for anyone to claim that the earthquake was simply the result of 'natural causes' was wrong because it was simply 'untrue'. Nature was, after all, nothing less than 'the art of God', 'God's method of acting in the world', and the next natural sign was known to be imminent: Wesley reminded his readers that in 1757 or 1758 Halley's Comet would pass through the skies and that if people had failed by then to 'acknowledge the hand of the Almighty' God might well direct the Comet to 'set the earth on fire and burn it to a coal'.[21]

On 18 December the Church of England, with the approval of George II, announced that 6 February 1756 would be a public Fast Day on which the 'most dreadful and extensive earthquake' would be remembered and the 'manifold sins and wickedness' of the nation examined. In the meantime the disaster which the Rector of St Paul's, Deptford declared had no equal 'in sacred or prophane history, save only Noah's flood'[22] did have an immediate effect on how people conducted themselves. Amid fears of an imminent invasion of the south coast, Horace Walpole remarked to a friend that 'between the French and the earthquakes you have no notion how good we are grown; nobody makes a suit of clothes now but of sack turned up with ashes'.[23] A masquerade ball was cancelled after the Archbishop of Canterbury protested, and such events fell out of fashion; and the Vice-Chancellor of Cambridge University reported in January 1756 that among the undergraduates there was 'not the least irregularity . . . it is rather fashionable to be decent'.[24]

The religious impact was the same all across Europe. In Holland, where Lisbon's destruction was loaded with particular significance as seeming to mark the end for a once great trading power, ministers declared the quake to be both a punishment and a warning in sermons with titles like 'On the Terror of God's Coming'. In Switzerland, the earthquake of 9 December was followed by another in early January, causing even more people to listen to or read the sermons of Élie Bertrand and other leading pastors. In Cologne it was said that no other subject was discussed in January; and in New England sermons with titles proclaiming 'Earthquakes the works of God and tokens of his just displeasure', 'Divine Power and Anger displayed in Earthquakes', and 'The Expected Dissolution of all things, a motive to universal holiness' were delivered from every pulpit on their own Fast Day. As an indication of the immense interest, and fear, generated in England, Thomas Sherlock's *A Letter from the Lord Bishop of London, to the clergy and people of Westminster* had sold more than 100,000 copies in less than six months after London's earthquakes in 1750, and five years later the demand of the public and the penitent remained insatiable.

Back in Lisbon Kitty Witham, one of the English nuns at the Bridgettine convent, wrote in a letter home, 'only God knows how long we have to live for I believe this world will not last long'.[25]

~ SIXTEEN ~

The Toll

THE EXACT NUMBER OF PEOPLE WHO WERE KILLED by the earth-quake, tidal waves and fire will never be known. In the immediate aftermath some traumatized eye-witnesses overestimated the fatali-ties; others deliberately exaggerated in order to make written accounts they intended for publication more dramatic; and some proposed figures which were so huge as to rob them of any semblance of cred-ibility. Although the initial reports that reached the capitals of Europe suggested that 100,000 people had perished, by mid-December this figure was known to be far too high. But the range of estimates pre-sented by the reliable eye-witness reports was wide. The Genoese Consul, the Papal Nuncio and Miguel Pedegache (a Swiss-Portuguese correspondent of the *Journal Etranger* who was a close friend of Carvalho) reckoned one tenth of the city's population had perished, or 20,000–25,000 souls. A well-informed article in the December edition of *New Universal Magazine* recorded that 'by the accounts of some passengers arrived from the Tagus it appears that nine thousand corpses, picked up in the streets of Lisbon, have been buried; and it is computed that above three times that number still lay under the rubbish'.[1] Edward Hay thought it unlikely that the figure was less than

40,000. Thomas Chase's impression, after listening to all the reports brought into the Hake's *quinta* during November, believed the death toll might have been as high as 50,000. The only anomalous estimate among foreign dignitaries was that of the Comte de Baschi, who reported 12,000 deaths to a French government keen not to see undue sympathy extended on the eve of war to a country it regarded as a colony of England.

When Carvalho wrote to all European governments on 18 November his estimate of 6,000–8,000 deaths was much lower than those of foreigners in the city. But practical considerations were foremost in his mind: his main concern was damage limitation. If Portugal's trading partners were allowed to believe that Lisbon really was 'no more', then a resumption of trade and the process of reconstruction would become impossible. Furthermore, Portugal was known to be under-populated and lived with a constant threat of annexation by its larger Iberian neighbour. Benjamin Keene, for one, recognized what Carvalho intended and wrote in a letter to Castres that he could 'perceive a desire in your Court to hide part of its misfortunes'.[2]

As for other official or semi-official Portuguese estimates, none appeared in writing for two years. There were a number of explanations for this delay. Portuguese pride was severely dented by what had occurred – the words *humilhado*[3] and *desgraça*[4] appear in many of the Portuguese accounts – and there was an understandable reluctance to relive the disaster. Indeed, when Joachim Moreira de Mendonça of the Royal Archives received official clearance in 1758 to publish his *História Universal dos Terremotos*, arguably the most reliable and informative of the contemporary Portuguese accounts, his estimate of 10,000 deaths on 1 November and a further 5,000 in the month as a whole was only marginally higher for the quake day itself than that given by Carvalho to foreign governments in the immediate aftermath. Lower estimates would have been ridiculed, but Carvalho regarded anything higher as being inadmissible on the grounds of endangering Portuguese national interests.*

Even if Carvalho had wanted to present a death toll that was reasonably accurate, as opposed to politically expedient, he could not have done so. There was no census of the city's population, and even the demographic information provided by those parishes whose records had survived the fire was of dubious value.[5] Many people had succeeded in fleeing to the provinces and to Spain, in spite of Carvalho's measures to prevent them or recall them; and Lisbon had many tens of thousands of residents who did not appear on any civic or ecclesiastical record – slaves, Gallegos, *ciganos* and street orphans, to name just four categories. There was also no record of the many visitors to the capital that All Saints' Day, and so great was the chaos throughout the country that their deaths may not even have been registered by their home parishes: people disappeared all the time into the city, as was true of any European capital. The only way to have recorded all fatalities with something approaching accuracy would have been for those burying or disposing of bodies each to have kept a tally. But there is no evidence that this was done: no records at all have survived which even mention the existence of the mass grave recently unearthed under the Convento de Jesus which is estimated to hold parts of more than 3,000 individuals, and cannot have been the only such grave. Even had a rough count been carried out as bodies were interred, there could be no counting those swept away by the tidal waves or incinerated in the fire.

Children were another group, like slaves and itinerant labourers, who suffered far more than could ever be evident from parish records for

---

* Among 'unofficial' Portuguese estimates to appear in print at the time were the following: José de Oliveira Trovão e Sousa, *Carta em que hum amigo dá noticia a outro do lamentavel sucesso de Lisboa* – 70,000; 'D.J.F.M em A', *Theatro Lamentavel, Scena Funesta: Relaçam Verdadeira Do Terremoto* – one third of the city's inhabitants; Anon., *Destruição de Lisboa, e Famosa desgraça, que padeceo no dia primeiro de Novembro de 1755* – one in eight; Miguel Tibério Pedegache, *Nova, e fiel relação do terremoto* – one in ten; Padre Fr. António do Sacramento, *Exhortação Consolatoria* – 18,000; Fr Manuel Portal, *História da ruina da cidade de Lisboa* – 12,000–15,000.

the simple reason that unless they were undergoing instruction they were not registered. Given that children accounted for an even greater proportion of the population than was the case in the cities of northern Europe, and that they were least able to flee and most likely to become separated from their parents during flight, the number who died must have been very considerable indeed. Furthermore, Lisbon's rate of child mortality in a normal year cannot have been any better than London's, where a third of all deaths were children under the age of two and forty per cent were children under the age of five; and this implies that the survival rate of children in the aftermath, living in the open on a meagre diet of whatever could be scrounged, must have been very poor.

One section of society that may well also have sought to play down its casualties quite deliberately was the ecclesiastical establishment. No source counts more than a few hundred deaths among *religiosos,* but given that at least one in ten people on the streets of Lisbon were clerics or friars or nuns of some description, and that the great majority of them would have been in church on All Saints' Day, such a low death toll is simply implausible. Taking one parish alone, that of Santa Catarina, the most popular profession at the time of the quake was that of *padre,* or priest: there were 223 listed in the parish records, as opposed to 174 shopkeepers and 117 sailors. The reason why religious communities understated their losses is simple: admitting to a high death toll was not compatible with the message that the Church wanted to impart to the people, namely that it was their appalling sinfulness that had brought the wrath of God upon the city.

As far as the English and Irish communities are concerned, Castres and Hay found it impossible to make a reliable head-count even among a population numbering no more than 2,000. A list of seventy-seven dead was drawn up by the end of the year, but of British subjects known to them as many as sixty remained unaccounted for among those 'so obscure as not to be known to any but the Irish friars'. As for deaths among the 'extremely numerous'[6] English and Irish 'lower sort', there was no way – as was true of Gallegos, street children, *ciganos* and slaves – of telling how many had died.

A year after the quake Francisco Xavier, the self-styled Chevalier de Oliveira, a Portuguese convert to Protestantism living in exile in London, wrote in his *Pathetic Discourse on the present Calamities of Portugal* 'it was calculated, but only by guess, that about 30,000 perished'.[7] That appears to have been the generally accepted death toll in England at the time. A century later Charles Dickens wrote that the quake had 'swallowed at one gulp forty thousand people';[8] and Murray's *Handbook For Travellers In Portugal*, noting that 'the number of victims has been estimated as high as 80,000 and as low as 10,000', concluded that 'the truth lies probably half way between the two'.[9] In the early twentieth century Francisco Luiz Pereira de Sousa, in his meticulous study of the earthquake, estimated a death toll of 15,000–20,000, to which subsequent fatalities among the 40,000–50,000 injured have to be added. All in all it seems likely that 30,000–40,000 people were killed in Lisbon, and a further 10,000 in the rest of Portugal, Morocco, and Spain. In a single month the population of Lisbon had been reduced by a number at least one and a half times greater than that of those who died in London, a city four times larger, in the whole of 1755; indeed, the death toll was considerably higher than that wrought on London in the peak month of the Great Plague. It was nothing short of a demographic catastrophe.

SEVENTEEN

Rain, Ruination and Revolution

THE NEW YEAR WAS USHERED IN by substantial tremors on 1 and 2 January, but Carvalho continued to push ahead with the formulation of plans for Lisbon's reconstruction. A detailed survey was ordered of all the ruined areas of the city, construction of buildings outside the city walls was forbidden, and then all building activity was forbidden pending the announcement of Manuel da Maia's suggestions for the design of the new Baixa.

Although Dom Pedro de Bragança, Duque de Lafões and head of the Royal Judiciary, was closely involved with this process, the man who had orchestrated all the emergency measures implemented since the earthquake, and who had emerged as the country's unrivalled helmsman, was Carvalho. The disaster had presented him with the opportunity he had long awaited, and the extent to which the King now relied on his common sense and practicality is demonstrated by the tale that, when asked by a distraught José what he should do in the immediate aftermath of the quake, Carvalho had replied simply, 'Bury the dead, and take care of the living'. The heroic myth that would later cloak Carvalho's conduct in the wake of the disaster was destined, with his considerable assistance, permanently to eradicate most traces of what really happened (and the heroism of others). Even within his own lifetime it was said that for two whole days and nights after 1 November Carvalho ate nothing except a single 'basin of broth, which his wife carried unto him herself'; that for several days his carriage was 'his cabinet, his bed, his only abode' while he laboured ceaselessly at drafting and executing dozens and dozens of decrees and emergency regulations on behalf of the King; and that it was 'by his courage, his perseverance, and his firmness, he prevented the people from abandoning a city'.[1] The impression of one man stepping forward and succeeding in bringing the situation entirely under control at the flick of his pen may be an exaggerated one, but there was no doubt that Carvalho was a man of uncommon intelligence, dedication and determination whose actions may well have saved the Portuguese nation.

In January Carvalho took a cue from the Spanish Court, which had sent out a questionnaire in November to every parish in the land and ordered the circulation of a similar one in Portugal. The thirteen questions asked each parish for details about the time at which the earthquake had struck; the direction from which it seemed to come; the number of deaths and buildings ruined; the effects on all bodies of water, fountains and wells; the damage caused by fire; whether the sea rose or fell immediately before the tidal wave, and by how much; whether fissures occurred; what measures were taken by civil, military and ecclesiastical authorities in the immediate aftermath; aftershocks and previous earthquakes; demographic information; and whether there were food shortages. The results of this comprehensive survey would later be described as 'the birth certificate of modern seismology';[2] of more immediate and widespread importance, it marked the beginning of a new era of government in a country whose authorities traditionally had so little interest in, or grasp of, or so great a fear of, the nation's demographic profile that even forty years later, long after Carvalho's death, 'official' estimates of the nation's population ranged from two million to 3.7 million.* The answers to the

* These estimates were issued by the Royal Academy of Sciences in 1789.

questionnaires may have been of limited use in determining an accurate final death toll, but their mere existence established that Carvalho meant not only to make the power of the centre felt in every corner of the country, but also to introduce method and modernity to government.

Torrential rains fell in the spring, making for miserable living conditions in the wooden encampments surrounding the city and causing the collapse of many ruins and the appearance, according to the Papal Nuncio, of many more bodies. Captain Thomas Brodrick's HMS *Hampton Court*, the warship charged with carrying the specie and escorting the convoy laden with much-needed supplies from England, was finally able to make landfall at Lisbon on 19 February, and five days earlier five more Irish ships had arrived with great quantities of beef and butter. The *Hampton Court* was, like the departing *Penzance* in December, fired upon by the fort at Belém, forcing Brodrick to anchor in deep water. After all the difficulties of assembling and transporting the provisions he did not appreciate this welcome but, more importantly, he wanted no delays in unloading the cargoes. Unfortunately Carvalho had worked himself sick since the earthquake, and Brodrick noted in his log on 24 February that 'the ill state of the Portuguese Secretary of State has prevented any orders being given for the delivery of the money or provisions which I brought with me . . . neither has anything been done with the provisions &c which came by the merchant ships'. Whether Carvalho really was ill, or simply delaying issuing instructions until the King returned from a hunting trip to Salvaterra, is a moot point.

When the King did return in early March, authorization to unload the beef, bread, butter, oatmeal, flour and grotts was immediately received; and when the specie left *Hampton Court* in thirteen chests on 8 March the delivery of Britain's aid was largely completed. Only two Irish ships were still to come, and they arrived in April. Brodrick was keen to be away again: he noted in his log on 16 March there had been quakes 'almost every day since we have been here',[3] and two days later Lisbon was struck by the biggest aftershock yet. One of Lord Tyrawley's illegitimate sons, who was serving on board *Hampton Court*, painted a ghostly picture of the city by night. 'The howling of dogs', he wrote, 'the stench of dead bodies, together with the gloom which now diffused itself around, from the moon's being sometimes obscured, gave me some idea of that general crash, when sun and moon shall be no more; and filled my mind with meditations, that only such a scene could inspire.'[4]

The Comte de Baschi, the French Ambassador, claimed that the delay in unloading the provisions meant that they were all spoiled and had to be thrown in the Tagus. This was not true, but his point about the unreliable workings of the port was a valid one. The needs of Lisbon's huge refugee camps were not being well-served by the port authorities. The forty English fishing vessels from Newfoundland, which had arrived in Lisbon on 29 November, were still being detained at the end of January, unable to obtain *franquias* to leave with their cargoes for other Iberian ports until Castres raised the matter with Carvalho himself. Several of the fleet were then suddenly cleared to leave, but the rest had to wait many more weeks before they could follow. Even a valid *franquia* did not guarantee departure. Once a ship had been searched for plundered or contraband goods it had to cross the Bar on the same day – but tides, winds and the short winter days often rendered this impossible, and skippers were then obliged to return to Belém and take their place in the queue for *franquias* all over again.

Another unpopular regulation was the imposition of a new four per cent duty on all imports except comestibles. This measure was described by Carvalho as a *'don gratuit'* – a contribution by the whole merchant community towards the costs of building a new customs house, exchange and warehouses. But the English merchants regarded it as an ill-timed body blow and began to campaign vociferously for their exemption from the tax, arguing that it breached existing trade treaties between England and Portugal. In December Lord Tyrawley had been asked by the English

government to give his advice, as an old Lisbon hand, on the future of the
Portugal trade and this was exactly the sort of hot-headed behaviour that
he had warned against two years earlier. In his view a faction of English
merchants had in recent years put their whole community 'in perpetual hot water' and cost their country 'the esteem of the Portuguese'.[5]
Edward Hay agreed, and at a meeting of the English Factory he told the
merchants that it would be very unwise for them to be seen behaving
churlishly about the *don gratuit*, especially as Brazil was contributing
generously to the fund. The merchants backed down. It was just as well:
when the English and Irish provisions were at last safe onshore, the
Portuguese Court insisted that 'out of gratitude as much as decency' to
Britain the poorest English and Irish victims of the disaster should be
the first to be helped. This was a generous and magnanimous gesture,
and the English Factory accepted one thirtieth of the comestibles and
£2,000 of specie for distribution to the most needy.

The commercial life of the city remained severely disrupted by more
weighty handicaps than onerous regulations and bureaucratic ineffi-
ciency. In a detailed despatch outlining the challenges facing all merchants Edward Hay confirmed that the cargoes of sugar, hides and
tobacco that had arrived with the Brazil fleets the previous autumn had
mostly been lost in the fire at the Customs House; and that all goods in
the King's warehouses were also lost, as were almost all the goods in
merchants' private warehouses and those in the city's shops. The stocks
of silk from a new government-run factory in Rato, north of the Bairro
Alto, had all been destroyed when the fire swept through a store in the
Largo do Pelourinho. There was also the question of debts to consider. It
was the shopkeepers and merchant tailors whom Hay thought least able
to pay as they typically had no capital and ran their businesses on credit
from foreign suppliers. As for the debts owed by the Portuguese Brazil
merchants, he hoped that they could not be greater than the annual
value of English exports through Lisbon to Brazil. As most of the English

merchants involved in the Brazil trade were 'substantial people', he also hoped that they would be able to recover these losses.

Hay concluded that despite the 'very great loss our trade has sustained I am far from thinking it total'. It was his job as Consul to be as optimistic as the facts allowed about the prospects, and among the positives he mentioned the fact that no ships had been lost in the Tagus, that the Mint had survived intact, that 'several people' had saved their cash chests, and that it was no bad thing that there was so little English cargo for onward shipment to Brazil that year because it would allow de-stocking to occur and thereby 'put trade upon a better footing [for] another year'. Addressing the question of whether some form of relief should be offered to the stricken merchants by the home government, Hay found himself 'at a loss to judge in what manner this can be afforded them'. He saw no equitable way of distributing any 'pecuniary gift from Parliament', and thought that any such gift 'might not have the effect intended by it',[6] the more so as the position of most merchants was complicated by their acting both as principals trading on their own accounts and as agents for others. Who, then, would be compensated first – the merchant for his losses or the client for his?

The full extent of the losses of the English merchants was beginning to be revealed. There were known to be 'some houses'[7] of English merchants who had lost £50,000–£80,000 in goods and debts. George Wansey, a Wiltshire woollens merchant, recorded in his diary, 'how greatly does this stroke of God's providence affect our family and much embarrass me in my affairs'. Not only did he have goods and outstanding debts in Lisbon worth £1,000 but he was also owed money by his brother William, Warden of the Society of Merchant Venturers, and William had been 'ruined by this affair',[8] declaring debts of £23,000 that he could only honour at a rate of 14s:£1. An injunction from Henry Fox, the Secretary of State for the Southern Department, was desperately sought by two London merchants to prevent Daniel Hoissard from selling the £4,500 of textiles they were shipping to him in Lisbon because they had heard that he was bankrupt. For gun-maker James Farmer, Benjamin's brother, who was already in financial trouble in the summer of 1755, the earthquake proved the final straw and he too had to seek an accommodation with his creditors.

As the domino effect of the disaster spread far and wide it was often the smallest traders, those unable to ask for support and patience from their creditors, who suffered worst of all. As sad as any case was that of Captain Thomas Bean of the *Bean Blossome* who was owed £32 by the great house of Bristow & Ward for 'Demoredge at Madiera' which he was unable to extract from them, and he judged that there was 'Sunck of my last Vige in all at Lisbon 100 [pounds]'. The *Bean Blossome*'s owner had also 'not saved one penny worth of his Efects in Lisbon, and he is Computed abought £300 Sufferer there and at [Faro] abought ye Same Sum, having three where houses of Luse wheat intierly Down and great part of that lost in ye Rubbedge and his household furniture smashed all to peaces'.[9] No matter how hopeful Edward Hay tried to be, the losses incurred by everyone from substantial merchant to humblest ship's captain who leased his vessel threatened to bring about a very serious collapse of 'that most advantageous branch of commerce' – the Portugal trade – with equally serious ramifications for the English textile industry and the lucrative importation of Brazilian gold.

A century after the earthquake its financial cost was quantified in *The Stranger's Guide In Lisbon* at precisely £536,360,000. The implausibility of this figure is best demonstrated by an examination of the categories of loss making up the total. Diamonds belonging to the Crown were valued at £2 million, diamonds and precious stones belonging to others at £4 million, the damage to the Paço da Ribeira, the Patriarchal church, the customs houses and the new Opera at £10 million. None of these figures appear unrealistic; but the estimate of £480 million attributed to the losses of 'furniture, stores and other goods' rather undermines the credibility of the whole, the more so as it is a sum equivalent to six times Britain's worryingly high national debt in 1755. It may be that the figure was a misprint. A more likely explanation is that the author of *The Stranger's Guide* omitted to translate the figure for 'furniture, stores, and other goods' from *cruzados* into sterling; and this oversight went largely unchallenged. Even in the twentieth century respected academics continued to cite a figure of £536 million without demur.[10]

Few contemporaries were as exact about the extent of the damage as the author of *The Stranger's Guide*. One French eye-witness put a value of just twenty million *livres*, or less than £1 million, on the houses, churches, monasteries, convents and major public buildings, a figure which was perhaps a reflection of his opinion of their architectural merit; but he also cited a figure sixty times as large as this for 'value of furniture'[11] – possibly the origin of the anomaly in *The Stranger's Guide*. One recent study has computed the damage to Portuguese property at 64,000–72,000 *contos* (about £18 million–£20 million),[12] and another at 100,000–150,000 *contos* (£27.8 million –£41.7 million).[13] Both would seem to confirm that the estimate of 86,000 *contos* (£24 million) provided by the astute and sensible Edward Hay to the British government, and a figure of 'twenty millions sterling'[14] cited in a well-informed letter in the December 1755 issue of *New Universal Magazine*, were of the correct order of magnitude (and three times London's losses in the Great Fire, or twenty times the value of the cargoes of that autumn's Brazil fleets). The losses of the English merchants, the hardest hit of all the foreign merchant communities, have been variously estimated at £6 million–£10 million, an amount equivalent to six to ten times England's total exports to Portugal in 1755. This was a potentially ruinous loss to bear, as were the costs of the damage in Spain, which have been estimated at 70 million *reales* (one fifth of total state expenditure for the year).[15] But as Benjamin Keene told Castres, such figures were 'quasht to nothing by what happened [to Portugal]'.[16]

Portugal did not produce any form of public finance figures, and Carvalho remained tight-lipped. His silence may unintentionally have been the most accurate representation of the situation: in one sense the losses were simply incalculable. The cost of reconstructing some buildings, like the magnificent Opera House and the Cais da Pedra, could be accurately assessed because they were new. But what realistic value could possibly have been assigned to the Paço da Ribeira, the product of two centuries of extension and modification? And while the belief of the British merchants that the Mint contained £2 million on 1 November would have been verifiable because it and its records survived the triple disaster, there are no records for the contents of the Casa da Índia (thought to have contained more than £1 million of diamonds) or the Customs House (known to have held 12,000 crates of sugar), or for any of the hundreds and hundreds of warehouses and stores which were destroyed. What value could be put on the vast collections of manuscripts, the libraries, the 4,000 early-seventeenth-century items in João IV's musical library, and the city's precious relics? Or the Casa Dourada, the gilded room, and the eighty-six panels of Flemish tapestry at the palace of Dom Fernando de Mascarenhas, the Marquês de Fronteira, in the parish of Chagas? Or the 200 paintings by European masters, the exquisite tapestries telling the story of Troy, and the vast library of the Marquês de Louriçal? Or the collection of Dutch and Flemish masters in the palace of the Conde de Coculim by the Praça da Ribeira? Furthermore the loss of productivity in the workforce, the extent of the interruption of cross-border trade, and the long-term damage to the kingdom of the Algarves (which still looked as devastated in the early twentieth century as it did the day after the quake and tidal wave) were all consequences whose value could only be guessed at.

Despite the ruination of so many merchants Edward Hay persisted in his belief that the situation *was* recoverable. Fleets for Pernambuco, Bahia and Rio departed between January and April 1756, and in early

May a Portuguese man-o'-war arrived from Rio with two million *cruzados* on board. So there had been no interruption in the outward Brazil trade even if British merchants were not able to send as much cargo as they usually did; and as far as the inward trade was concerned the Brazilian goose was still laying its golden eggs. As the months passed most British merchants were also able, with the support of their creditors and financiers in England, to resume business by agreeing to make staged payments of their debts or redrawing partnerships in the hope that future trade would repay all historic losses. Jackson, Branfill & Goddard, for example, were able to reschedule a debt of £12,500 to Benjamin Branfill's uncle, City merchant William Braund, which he later wrote down by half and then made payable in instalments over the next eight years. Furthermore, demand was stronger than ever: there was a desperate shortage of clothing in Lisbon from which woollens merchants like Jackson, Branfill & Goddard were able to benefit, and great quantities of foodstuffs, building materials and English artisans were urgently required.

A steady stream of snippets of good news also helped to bolster confidence and morale. In May, the *Gazeta de Lisboa* suddenly reported that most diamonds that had been stored in the Paço da Ribeira had been recovered as well as 1,500 *arrobas* of melted gold plate worth over £2.5 million. Such things convinced merchants like Edward Burn, Lawrence Fowkes, Joseph May, Gerard Devismes, David de Purry, the Hakes and Goddards and many others whose names appear on English Factory documents from 1756 that it was worth staying in Lisbon. Even poor Benjamin Farmer returned to pursue his claim for reparations for his schooner for a good many more years without success, although there is no trace of Thomas Chase ever doing so. The worst fears about how Portuguese customers and debtors might behave also proved unfounded. Textile merchant Edward French, for example, was very moved by the great 'friendship and respect from the natives of this country since the late misfortune'.[17] Some of his Portuguese customers had even offered to lend him money and to bring forward their orders; and the Judge Conservator, who oversaw and regulated English trading affairs, promised the merchants that all creditors who could pay would be made to honour their debts. By May Edward Hay was so encouraged on so many fronts that he breezily reported to his superiors that 'in general our affairs are upon no bad footing in this country. We have the *pas* of all other nations in point of trade'.[18]

Within weeks of Hay's optimistic pronouncement José announced that Carvalho would take the place of the deceased Pedro da Mota as the Minister of Home Affairs; and that Carvalho's former office, that of Foreign Affairs and War, would be taken by Luís da Cunha, the Portuguese Ambassador in London. By the end of the summer the pro-French Diogo de Mendonça Corte-Real, the third Secretary of State, had been arrested and exiled to Cape Verde on Carvalho's orders for his part in a plot by a group of nobles, including the Duque de Aveiro and the Duque de Lafões, to unseat the autocratic busybody in their midst. Although Carvalho had been recognized both internally and externally as *de facto* Prime Minister for some time, these events were significant in that they confirmed that a creeping, silent revolution at Court – a coup – had been triggered by the earthquake. 'Common report' by now had it that the King was only interested in his hunting, music and mistresses and that 'Mr C', as Carvalho was often referred to among English merchants, now ruled 'with unbounded sway'.[19]

Almost as if the Lisbon earthquake had shaken up European alliances to such an extent that all that was awaited was the report of the starting gun, war was finally declared between England and France in May. After French troops seized Menorca and a fleet led by Admiral John Byng, with Augustus Hervey's ship in the line, failed to relieve the British garrison, Byng was infamously court-martialled and executed for his failure to 'do his utmost'. As the conflict gathered momentum, turning into the first truly global war, Carvalho had to consider Portugal's position even more carefully. With an army and navy barely worth the name the country was self-evidently a tempting target for Spain. But relations between the two countries were amicable at the outset – Fernando VI had dismissed his pro-French Prime Minister, the Marqués de la Ensenada, in 1754 and had offered to mediate between England and France earlier in 1756 – and both governments reassured each other that they had no intention of being drawn into the fray.

Unfortunately neither Spain nor Portugal was the real master of her neutrality. As Benjamin Keene well knew, the Bourbon Pact was only dormant, not dead, and if Spain were pushed or pulled into war by France then Portugal would immediately feel threatened and would enlist help from England. In 1753 France had even tried a more direct approach with Portugal by sending the agent, adventurer and man of letters Ange Goudar to try and persuade the independent-minded Carvalho that it was time for Portugal to forge her own political and economic destiny, free from the yoke of England, and that an alliance with France could mean an end to the fear of annexation by Spain for good. Carvalho had not taken the bait and, as a result, when Goudar published his *Relation historique du tremblement de terre survenu à Lisbonne le premier Novembre 1755* in The Hague in 1756 it contained a 'political discourse' which suggested that the earthquake should be welcomed by Portugal as a wake-up call.

Goudar declared that during his mission to Lisbon he had found nothing but 'political ineptitude', 'a monarchy that had run out of steam, weakened by revolutions, disturbed by hidden sects and impoverished by its own wealth'; and a 'people repressed by superstition, a nation whose customs bore a striking resemblance to those of Barbarians, and a state governed by Asian half-breeds whose only Europeanness was in the form of a puppet monarchy'. As if this was not a bad enough state of affairs, he continued, England had brought its ancient ally to its knees by ensuring Portugal remained industrially backward so that she could siphon off Brazilian gold. 'The mines of Brazil can be said to belong entirely to England', Goudar asserted, 'and Portugal is merely an administrator of its own wealth.'[20]

If Goudar was hoping that this diatribe might lead to a new Franco-Portuguese dialogue, or might goad Carvalho into the French camp, he was very much mistaken. Even if there were a few enlightened souls who saw elements of truth in what he wrote, his rhetoric was so offensive to Portuguese *brio nacional* that none would admit as much, least of all Carvalho. The Portuguese Minister's reaction was condign, and seemed to confirm an intention, expressed in an aside to Castres made when Britain had announced a treaty with Prussia earlier in the year, that 'as a good Portuguese he would always show himself as a hearty Englishman'.[21] Goudar's book was immediately banned and an edict from the Inquisition, which the Frenchman had heavily criticized, condemned it as a tissue of lies, insults and falsehoods. The Comte de Baschi's departure followed soon afterwards: he too had done little to advance France's cause with what Castres described as his 'turbulent temper', 'perpetual disputes about trifles', and his 'free and unguarded reflexions upon the customs and manners of the country'[22] and its Royal Family. Carvalho was notoriously inscrutable but for the time being it appeared to Castres that there would be no change to Portugal's diplomatic status quo; whether he would use the state of emergency after the earthquake as an opportunity again to attack the use and abuse by some English merchants of their trading privileges, and their increasing incursion into markets that were traditionally the preserve of Portuguese merchants, remained to be seen.

When Caleb Whitefoord, a young wine merchant from Edinburgh, arrived in Lisbon in August 1756 he wrote to his partner, Thomas Brown, 'I am now landed, I wish I could say on *terra firma*'. Aftershocks were still being felt regularly in the city, * keeping the populace in a state of 'continual terror' especially in the days before each full moon. Five hundred were recorded in the first year after the earthquake, and this meant that even if Carvalho had had the materials, money and manpower to begin the repair and reconstruction of the city it would have been impossible to do so. 'Twill be a great many years', Whitefoord opined in his letter, 'before the place can recover the late disaster', as even the few houses which still stood had the appearance of 'a lame beggar, propped upon crutches'. There was evidence of some clearing-up going on in the main streets of the Baixa, but Whitefoord thought he detected a distinct, perhaps understandable, nervousness about the way any such work was carried out. It was as if the ruins were declaring '*noli me tangere*', making people 'very cautious how they handle them'.

As Whitefoord wandered about the city he happened across the ruins of the great convent and church of the Trinidade in the Bairro Alto and found his nose 'saluted with a very offensive smell'. Nine months had elapsed since the earthquake, and his grisly experience made him wonder 'what would be the consequences if all [the] bodies were to be uncovered'. He also came to the conclusion that the houses still standing in the city were 'not sufficient to accommodate one fifth of the inhabitants'. A few days later, after seeing more of the city, his conclusion was even bleaker: 'I can venture to assure you', he wrote in another letter, 'in spite of what has been published to the contrary, that there are not three houses left in all the city of Lisbon, and that even in the suburbs where there [are] a few standing . . . they are so rent and shattered as not to be inhabitable.' The only people to be seen in the streets were 'the lower sort', of whom at least a third were Africans, living in ruins and 'quite eat up with vermin'. Even the English merchants were still reduced to living thirty to a home built for a family of seven or eight in the undam-

* 'Will your Earth never be quiet?' Benjamin Keene asked Castres in a letter of 21 July 1756 (see Lodge, (ed.), *The Private Correspondence of Sir Benjamin Keene, KB*, p. 486).

aged extremities of the city, in conditions which were more 'like a hospital' than a private residence. All their business was done on the hoof, in the open, or at 'a dirty little coffee-house at Beleir', as Whitefoord described the long-suffering Mr Morley's public house.

Despite its shattered state Lisbon still exercised a certain allure on anyone seeing it for the first time. The epidemic that everyone had thought bound to break out in the summer never materialized, the sky was 'always serene', and after the extreme heat of the day Whitefoord found the evenings 'delightful'. Among the *alfacinhas* some aspects of life continued unhindered: he observed, a little tastelessly, that 'there have been as many marriages within these few days as would cause an earthquake'; and even the ruins were attractive in a grim sort of way, although he did not think that they '[afforded] such fine views as Palmyra and other cities which have shared the same fate'. But Whitefoord's conclusion was emphatic. 'Never', he wrote, 'was seen or I believe ever heard of so universal a ruin'.[23]

On 8 November 8 1756 sixteen ships arrived from Rio with a cargo of 3,000 chests of sugar, 46,000 hides in hair, one and a half million *cruzados* in gold for the King and eight million *cruzados* in gold and silver for merchants. England's exports to Lisbon rose from £1.1 million in 1755 to £1.5 million in 1756. Castres was presented with a portrait of himself by merchants grateful for everything he had done for them in the aftermath of the quake; and Edward Hay's confidence that the 'considerable branch of commerce' would not disappear seemed to have been justified. As Manuel da Maia's team of designers created six potential blueprints for a new city there was, in spite of the scepticism of Whitefoord and everyone else who saw the ruins, a chance that in time the great city of Lisbon might be rebuilt after all.

~ EIGHTEEN ~

Fasting and Philosophy

ON THE PUBLIC FAST DAY IN FEBRUARY 1756 the 12,000 parish churches in Britain were packed to the rafters, and John Wesley remarked that such a glorious day had not been known since the Restoration. The texts of sermons with titles like *National wickedness the cause of national misery, A speedy repentance the most effectual means to avert God's judgements* and *An alarm to a careless world* were rushed into print soon afterwards, some of them many times over; and congregations everywhere became familiar with the special Fast Day prayer which beseeched the Almighty 'to awaken our consciences yet farther, that we may see and duly consider thy hand, which, in the most astonishing manner, hath been lifted up so near us'.

There were constant reminders of the event universally acknowledged as 'the most severe judgment of God's wrath that was ever inflicted on sinners'.[1] The seven years after Lisbon's disaster would prove to be not only years of universal war but also of an unprecedented 'seismic crisis' in Europe. France experienced more than forty earthquakes in 1756 alone. In Germany eighty-eight tremors were recorded between November 1755 and March 1757; and in Brig, in Switzerland, 135 tremors were felt between December 1755 and February

1756. Such widespread disturbances made it difficult for any preacher to continue to claim that Lisbon had been destroyed because it was 'a most remarkably wicked place, being a mart and seat of trade to all nations [which has] imported their vices along with their other commodities'.[2] Most leading churchmen preferred, like the Canon of Lichfield, to declare that 'the late dreadful earthquake' was 'no proof of God's particular wrath against the Portuguese';[3] and, like the Canon of St Paul's, to call for 'a truly Christian spirit' in considering 'the calamities of a people, connected to us by all the ties of alliance, friendship, and mutual interest'.[4]

One religious response that was even less welcome in Lisbon than that of reactionary European Protestants was that of the Chevalier de Oliveira, the former Portuguese diplomat now living in London. In his *Pathetic Discourse*, published in London and Holland in 1756, the Chevalier placed the blame for the earthquake squarely on the shoulders of Portugal's idiosyncratic brand of Catholicism and the Inquisition. 'By the force of absurd devotions, terrible sacrifices, and vain prayers, unworthy to be heard' the Portuguese were, he alleged, 'plunged in the most shameful superstition, and the most gross idolatry' and had 'mutilated, mangled, and disfigured the Law of God'.[5] However much he may privately have agreed with some of his opinions, Carvalho did not take kindly to open criticism from a fellow Portuguese: it amounted to treason and would not be forgotten.

At home Carvalho's largely successful attempts to muzzle the clergy and emphazise that the earthquake had been a natural, rather than providential, catastrophe received a more serious setback in October 1756 with the publication of a tract by the influential Italian-born Jesuit Gabriel Malagrida entitled *Juízo da verdadeira causa do terramoto* – 'Judgement on the true cause of the earthquake'. Malagrida had consistently preached against the 'heresy' of natural explanations for the disaster, declaring that 'not even the Devil could invent a false idea so liable to lead us to irreparable ruin'. For him, it was the sins of *alfacinhas* alone that had brought such a terrible destruction upon them. It was their love of comedies and all theatre, the immodest dancing in the streets, the love of playing cards, their licentiousness – these were the destroyers of the city; and he proposed that the only course of action open to such sinners was to pray, and process, and beg forgiveness. Carvalho, on the other hand, in his relentless determination to re-establish normal daily life and begin rebuilding the city, wanted the population to be active and hard-working, not indulging in ceaseless, unproductive self-recrimination.

The appearance of Malagrida's tract at a time when Jesuits were putting up armed resistance to Carvalho's reforms and seizure of their territories in Brazil, and as the first anniversary of the quake loomed, sealed his fate. On 29 October the Secretary of State countered the prophesies of many clerics that Lisbon was about to be struck by a disaster as terrible as that of the previous year by publishing an order forbidding anyone from leaving the city and placing troops all around it. Then, when no great quake came to finish off the remaining inhabitants of the city, he had Malagrida banished to Setúbal and excluded all Jesuits from the Court in which they had been so powerful during João's final years. The next phase of the revolution caused by the earthquake had begun.

The effect of the shockwaves from Lisbon on European thought was every bit as great as its impact on religious life: 1 November 1755 would come to be regarded as 'one of the birthdays of the modern age'.[6] For many years before the earthquake Europe was dominated by the philosophy of 'optimism', the term used to encapsulate the ideas contained in Gottfried Leibniz's 1710 treatise *Theodicy* and subsequently expounded by Alexander Pope's verse *Essay on Man*.

Theodicy was an attempt to reconcile belief in an omnipotent God with human suffering, to affirm God's essential goodness and justice in spite of the existence of evil, by asserting that man inhabited 'the best of all possible worlds' (in the words of Leibniz) and that 'whatever is, is right' (in the words of Pope). This proposition could be interpreted in different ways. It could simply be taken to mean that things could not be different, that they were what they were; or it could be seen as an affirmation that everything that happened in the world was for the best, even to the extent that 'all partial evil' was part of 'a universal good'[7]. This philosophy, essentially one of passive acceptance of a world governed by divine Providence that was unquestionably benign, was strongly underpinned by Christian doctrines of submission and resignation; and so persuasive had it proved that it appealed across even the most rigid political and religious lines of demarcation. Catholicism or Protestantism, absolutism or parliamentarianism, noble or peasant – no creed or station precluded adherence to optimism. It was, quite simply, 'a notion that had the western world in its grip'.[8]

For a growing number of sceptics the seemingly paradoxical notion that a perfect God had wilfully created evil and suffering had started to become untenable by 1755; and for the most famous and influential among them the earthquake was the straw that broke the camel's back. François-Marie Arouet, better known as Voltaire, had little quarrel with the notion that things were what they were and could not be any different because it was a truism, no more than a statement of the obvious. What he found untenable was the idea that everything, including evil of the magnitude of what had been seen in Lisbon, was 'for the best'; and within days of hearing the first reports of the disaster on 24 November 1755, Voltaire wrote from his home near Geneva to his friend Élie Bertrand in Berne posing the question: 'Would Pope have dared to say whatever is, is best if he himself had been in Lisbon?' That same day, in a letter to Jean-Robert Tronchin, a banker in Lyons, he pursued this further:

. . . this is indeed a cruel sort of physics. People will really find it difficult to divine how the laws of motion bring about such frightful disasters in 'the best of all possible worlds'. A hundred thousand ants, our neighbours, suddenly crushed on our ant-hill and half of them probably perishing in inexpressible anguish amidst the debris from which they cannot be extricated . . . What a sad game of chance the game of human life is! What will the preachers say, especially if the palace of the Inquisition remains standing? I flatter myself at least that the reverend Fathers, the Inquisitors, will have been crushed like all the others. That ought to teach men not to persecute men, for while some holy scoundrels burn a few fanatics the earth swallows up the lot of them whole.[9]

In another letter written on 30 November Voltaire called the disaster 'a terrible argument against optimism',[10] and he set to work on what would become the most famous, and influential, intellectual response to what had occurred – his 180-line *Poème sur le désastre de Lisbonne*.

The subtitle of the poem, *Éxamen de cet axiome: 'Tout est bien'*, named Voltaire's target, and in the preface he set out his stall. 'If the question of physical evil has ever deserved the attention of man', he began, 'it is when those melancholy events occur which put us in mind of the feebleness of our nature – such as plagues, which have carried off a quarter of the inhabitants of the known world; or the earthquake which swallowed up four hundred thousand people in China in 1699, or those in Lima and Callao, or, most recently, those in Portugal and the kingdom of Fez'; and such catastrophes, he continued, made 'the maxim "whatever is, is right" . . . seem a little peculiar to those who have witnessed such calamities'.

At the outset Voltaire seemingly made it clear that he was not calling into question the existence of divine Providence; his concern was 'that all is not ordered in such a manner as to promote our present happiness'.

Nor, he also stated, was he attacking Alexander Pope, whom he had always admired. It was the fatalism, the passivity implicit in the tenet 'all is well' which he lambasted as 'simply an insult to the suffering in our life';[11] and he challenged the acceptance of the notion that 'whatever is, is right' as being antithetical. If God was both benign and all-powerful, how could this deity let such things happen? Was it not monstrously cruel to maintain, as he suggested optimists might, that the quake could be financially advantageous for the survivors, that reconstruction would create a boom, even that animals would benefit by being able to feast on corpses? To claim as much was, in Voltaire's opinion, 'as cruel as the earthquake was fatal'.[12] And why, he asked, even if the earthquake was intended as some sort of punishment, were so many little children killed? And why was Lisbon chosen – was it *really* more sinful than London or Paris?

The initial draft of Voltaire's *Poème* was completed by 4 December and the first copies appeared anonymously in Paris in January 1756. The questions it raised were deeply shocking, subversive, and even blasphemous. What Voltaire was asking for was 'a god who speaks to the human race', not the god of optimism, which was nothing but a 'cruel philosophy under a consoling name';[13] and he was bent on forcing nothing less than a reconsideration of the nature, and place in the world, of evil. The extent to which similar questions entered the minds of Mr Braddock in the weeks after he watched the church of São Paulo collapse on its parishioners and the tidal wave roll in from the Tagus, or Lawrence Fowkes at the moment when it was realized that Mrs Morrogh and her child were dead, or Benjamin Branfill when dear old Mrs Hussey expired, would never be known; and the faith of *alfacinhas* in the immediate aftermath was even more 'blind', submissive and accepting than ever. But for educated people throughout Europe, shocked and desperately frightened by the reports of what had happened in Lisbon, Voltaire's devastating attack on optimism could not be ignored.

Voltaire offered few crumbs of comfort to those whose world view he was setting out to destroy, and he had no ready explanation for the coexistence of God and evil in the world. Even after he had changed the end of the poem in response to the advice of friends that the original version, 'Man must suffer/ Submit, adore and die', was so bleak that it would undermine the impact of everything else he was trying to say, the conclusion was hardly encouraging. The word 'hope' – 'man's sole bliss below' [14] – appeared in the new version but without any great conviction. 'The goodness of Providence' was 'the only sanctuary' that Voltaire could suggest, a sanctuary 'in which man can take shelter during this general eclipse of his reason, and amidst the calamities to which his weak and frail nature is exposed'. [15] But offering words of comfort was not his objective. Voltaire wanted to introduce doubt, to disturb, to *destroy*, so that something new would replace facile optimism.

Voltaire's attack on optimism soon prompted a forceful counter from another influential contemporary, Jean-Jacques Rousseau. In a letter written to Voltaire in August 1756 Rousseau rejected Voltaire's black depiction of man's existence, and expressed disappointment that the great *philosophe* had not found it within himself to display greater humanity in his argument. 'You reproach Alexander Pope and Leibnitz', he wrote, 'for belittling our misfortunes by affirming that all is well, but you so burden the list of our miseries that you further disparage our condition. Instead of the consolations that I expected, you only vex me . . . [Your poem] makes my affliction worse, prompts me to grumble, and leading me beyond a shattered hope, reduces me to despair.' Just for good measure, the impoverished and rather bitter Rousseau added that Voltaire's arguments were 'the product of an unnatural and unhealthy life of a pampered and privileged intellectual'.

Rousseau's 'eternal and beneficent Being' had created a universe with 'the minimum evil' and 'the maximum good', and he had 'done no better for mankind because [He] can do no better'. For Rousseau the 'source of moral evil' was in man, not in God, and one novel argument that he deployed in his defence of a benign Providence concerned the role of man in disasters like that of Lisbon. 'Most of our physical ills', he wrote, 'are still our own work.' In Lisbon it was man, not nature, who had built 'twenty thousand houses of six to seven stories', Rousseau pointed out; and if the populace had been more spread out and housed in lower buildings 'the damage would have been much less and perhaps of no account'.[16] Furthermore, how many casualties were due to man's deliberate, considered decisions – to return to a house for money, or to grab clothes, or to save papers?

Earthquakes were not rare events, and they were slowly becoming less mysterious. It was therefore not the immensity of the Lisbon quake that would make the tragedy that had befallen the city resonate through the ages. This, in the opinion of Theodore Besterman on the 200th anniversary of the quake, was 'only of relatively modest importance' in the long run. It was the 'moral repercussions', the impact on Western thought, which 'surpassed by far those of a physical and even human nature'. In Voltaire's deft hands the Lisbon earthquake became the vehicle for an assault on optimism and the orthodox view of divine Providence which would change the way people thought for ever; and in turn it arguably became the last disaster in which God held centre stage. In the meantime Voltaire's initial response to the younger upstart Rousseau comprised just two dismissive sentences, concluding 'you will pardon me for leaving there all these philosophical discussions which are only amusements'.[17] For a full, blistering response, Rousseau would have to wait another two years.

Oh wretched man, earth-fated to be cursed;
Abyss of plagues, and miseries the worst!
Horrors on horrors, griefs on griefs must show,
That man's the victim of unceasing woe,
And lamentations which inspire my strain,
Prove that philosophy is false and vain.
Approach in crowds, and meditate a while
Yon shattered walls, and view each ruined pile,
Women and children heaped up mountain high,
Limbs crushed which under ponderous marble lie;
Wretches unnumbered in the pangs of death,
Who mangled, torn, and panting for their breath,
Buried beneath their sinking roofs expire,
 And end their wretched lives in torments dire.
Say, when you hear their piteous, half-formed cries,
Or from their ashes see the smoke arise,
Say, will you then eternal laws maintain,
Which God to cruelties like these constrain?
Whilst you these facts replete with horror view,
Will you maintain death to their crimes was due?
And can you then impute a sinful deed
To babes who on their mothers' bosoms bleed?
Was then more vice in fallen Lisbon found,
Than Paris, where voluptuous joys abound?
Was less debauchery to London known,
Where opulence luxurious holds her throne?
Earth Lisbon swallows; the light sons of France
Protract the feast, or lead the sprightly dance.[18]

Voltaire, *Poem on the Lisbon Disaster*

(lines 1–23)

PART THREE

AFTERMATH

'In view of our contemporary experience with such disasters, it does not surprise the writer at all that what may have been one of the greatest of all quakes . . . has left no special tradition in its wake'

Bahngrell W. Brown, 'The Quake That Shook Christendom – Lisbon 1755',
The Southern Quarterly, Vol. VII (July 1969) No.4, p. 425

NINETEEN

Executions

I have now pretty nearly finished my voyage from Falmouth to
Lisbon; and as I have almost overcome all sea sickness, will give
you the paper now due. On Sunday last, the day after Christmas
Day, about three o'clock in the afternoon I embarked for Lisbon.
I thought, indeed, I should have been left behind; for I had hardly
finished dinner, when word was brought that the ship had weighed
anchor and was under sail.

By making, however, the boatman row stoutly, we got up with our
packet before she was out of the harbour. Indeed, as it happened,
there was no danger of our being left behind, for the Captain of the
ship was still on board, and she could not go out to sea till he was set
on shore. To explain this seeming paradox you must know, that the
Captains of these packets have sometimes the indolent desire of
remaining by a comfortable fire-side, while their vessels, under the
command of masters, buffet the relentless waves. Their interest
likewise in this respect, if I am not misinformed, coincides with
their inclinations, as they find it, I believe, to better account to act at
home as merchants than abroad as sailors. Our sails being at length
unfurled, we glided out of Falmouth harbour, with two vessels in our
company . . .[1]

In (the unrelated) Christopher Hervey's account of his 'Grand Tour', which began in Lisbon on the last day of 1758, there is no mention of Henry Fielding's *Journal Of A Voyage To Lisbon*, published three years earlier. But there are great similarities between the styles and initial observations of the great novelist and the young tourist. Hervey was more fortunate in that his passage only lasted seven days; and four years after Fielding's death the interest of travellers was principally in Lisbon's ruins and the possibility of acquiring earthquake souvenirs – melted coins, china bowls and the like. 'It is generally allowed', wrote another visitor of the time, 'that, from a very indifferent city, Lisbon is become one of the most extraordinary ruins in the world'.² For the intrepid traveller the capital of Portugal was, in other words, the new Pompeii or Herculaneum.

At Belém, Hervey was less interested in the Jerónimos monastery which had caught Fielding's eye than a structure 'something like a prodigious long stable building'. This was the wooden barrack on a rise in which the Royal Family still lived four years after the earthquake; and although the Tagus, 'the *golden* Tagus', struck him as 'one of the most delightful sights ever beheld', when he climbed into a *chaise* onshore it was a different sort of 'nastiness' that transfixed him to that which Fielding had criticized. 'Heaps of ruins lay on all sides', he wrote, 'or where a few houses remained, they were so propped up with large pieces of timber, that they rather added to the horror of the scene.' This was profoundly moving, and Hervey's letter continued, 'melancholy reflections occupied me, and I considered that under my feet might lie hundreds of carcases, some of which, by the houses falling hollow upon them, were destroyed by the slow-consuming hand of famine, as the fire subsequent to the earthquake might not reach these now subterraneous regions'.

As Hervey's *chaise* conducted him eastwards towards his host's home in Santa Apollónia the book-keeper who had collected him from the packet pointed out one of the streets running north from the riverside and told him that it had once been 'the most populous street in Lisbon'. Now it was little more than 'a mass of broken walls, with open windows, through two or three rows of which you discovered still farther ruins: a harbour for thieves, owls and goats; in short, the seat of desolation!'. *Some* progress had been made in clearing the city. Most of the ruined streets had had a passage driven through 'the confused materials of the overthrown buildings'. But the Baixa was still uninhabitable, as the vast number of 'temporary houses'[3] built between the Terreiro do Paço and Santa Apollónia – and far beyond – attested; indeed, it appeared that nothing of the new city had 'been put in execution'. Hervey was told that a shortage of funds had precluded any further progress, and that the special duty Carvalho had placed on imports and exports was 'by no means sufficient to answer such expenses'.[4]

It wasn't that progress had slowed as much as not yet begun. In May 1758 the legal conditions for the reconstruction of the private quarters of the Baixa had been published and landowners were given five years in which to rebuild or have their land confiscated. Loans would be provided to those landowners who could not afford the costs. Furthermore the new Baixa was to be built to exact specifications which aimed to replace the ramshackle medieval quarter with the most modern city centre in Europe. The basic design which Manuel da Maia and his team had produced was rectilinear. Five broad main streets would run all the way north from the Terreiro do Paço to the Rossio; a further three would start one third of the way up, also ending at the Rossio; and this grid would be intersected at right-angles by seven cross-streets. Most of the des- ignated names of the streets running north – such as Rua Áurea (Gold Street), Rua dos Sapateiros (Shoe-makers' Street), Rua dos Correeiros (Saddlers' Street), Rua da Prata (Silver Street), Rua dos Douradores (Gilders' Street), Rua Fanqueiros (Cloth-makers' Street) – were delib- erately functional, proclaiming to residents and visitors alike that Lisbon now had a *commercial* centre worthy of its centuries-old reputation as a trading entrepôt. By the same token, the new square on the riverside was to be called the Praça do Comércio (or as Carvalho, mindful of his royal patronage, was always careful to refer to it, the *Real* Praça do Comércio). To show that the religious life was not being wholly superseded by the secular, the cross-streets which passed through the destroyed parishes bore the names of those parishes – Rua São Julião, Rua de Conceição, Rua de São Nicolau and Rua de Santa Justa. Similarly, the easternmost street running north to south through Thomas Chase's former *bairro* was designated as the new Rua da Madalena.

All buildings in the new Baixa were to be built four storeys high with an attic, and were intended for both residential and commercial use. Each had to contain a timber framework called a *gaiola*, or 'birdcage', so that the damage wrought by any future earthquakes might be limited by height and elasticity, and they were to be painted ochre. Fires would be contained by the broader, straight streets and firebreak walls between each building. To ensure adequate building materials were available a decree of 1757 had encouraged 'the multiplication of factories of lime, bricks, wood and stone', and as many components as possible were to be mass-produced or prefabricated and stockpiled in the Praça do Comércio, around which the principal public buildings would be constructed. The whole area comprised almost sixty acres and in its uniform, stark, utilitarian design clearly reflected the background of the military engineers involved in its creation. For a nation that was usually depicted as a laggard in everything from the arts to sciences to commerce to religion, the plan was astoundingly bold and innovative. If completed, Lisbon would become the first city in the world designed to be as earthquake-proof as technology would allow, and would thereby be making the most defiant response imaginable to the disaster that had befallen it. But the question on every visitor's lips was – would it, could it, ever be completed?

The talk all over the city when Christopher Hervey arrived concerned not the rebuilding, or commerce, or some new law promulgated by Carvalho. He first caught wind of it from those on board the *Hanover* as the two packets passed each other crossing the Bar. The affairs of the kingdom were said to be in a 'critical situation' and, with the usual exception of the Falmouth packets and English men-o'-war, an embargo had been placed on all shipping for the most shocking reason. Some members of the most illustrious families in the kingdom, whose names, he was told, were 'known in the triumphant days of Portugal', had been 'taken up and thrown into prison'.[5] There they had been accused of attempting to assassinate the King. On the night of 3 September 1758 José had been on his way back to the royal barrack at Belém at about eleven o'clock, accompanied by a valet but no guards, when his coach had been ambushed by three armed men. The coachman was shot and a blunderbuss 'full of sluggs'[6] was discharged into the back of the carriage. The King and his valet were both wounded but had the presence of mind to dive onto the floor of the carriage, thereby avoiding a further volley of shots, and the coachman managed to take them all straight to the royal surgeon's house nearby.

The episode remains so completely shrouded in mystery that there is scant proof even for this approximate version of events.[7] After the death in 1757 of poor Abraham Castres, who had increasingly suffered from a terrible 'asthmatick disorder' and hideously swollen legs since the earthquake, Edward Hay had been promoted to Envoy Extraordinary in Lisbon (and Sir Harry Frankland to Consul), so it fell to Hay to try and recount the events to the British government. In his despatch of 13 September 1758 he wrote that the King had been on his way 'to visit a mistress' attended by his 'favourite servant', Pedro Teixeira, and that they would normally have been in two carriages, the King in the first and Teixeira in the second, when they came across three mounted men wearing masks. The ambushers let the first carriage pass – the one that would normally have carried the King – and fired at the second. Hay therefore concluded that 'this blow is thought to have been designed against the man, not against the master'. The King was believed to be wounded in the right arm 'but not dangerously', and Teixeira was 'much hurt'.[8]

As was true of London, there was a long tradition of violent hooliganism among the noble classes of Lisbon: in his youth Carvalho had himself led one of the gangs which routinely attacked people, taverns, brothels or private homes for 'sport'. Assassinations, often prompted by sexual liaisons, were equally commonplace, and Teixeira certainly had enemies as he was thought to have 'grown insolent from the king's patronage'.[9] Some said that he had personally insulted Dom José Mascarenhas, Duque de Aveiro, one of the foremost (and least popular) *fidalgos* (nobles) in the land. Others said that the King was the target, that the Duque de Aveiro had never forgiven him for exiling his uncle, a favourite of João V, at the beginning of his reign; or that the Duke had had ambitions to marry José's daughter, the princess of Brazil, before she was married to her uncle instead; or that he sought revenge for the King's refusal to allow a cross-marriage that would have cemented a powerful alliance of his family with that of the Duque de Cadaval. Another possible explanation was that an attack on a confidant of the King – Teixeira – was intended as a warning to another – Carvalho – that the nobility had had enough of the reforming zeal of the latter; two years earlier the Duque de Aveiro had been implicated in the plot to oust Carvalho that had led to the exile of Secretary of State Diogo de Mendonça Corte-Real.

For three months after the attack nothing happened except an announcement that the King had been injured in a fall and the Queen, Mariana Vitória, would stand as regent until his condition improved. It was as if, in the words of one English merchant, 'the government seemed to give itself no concern at all to come to the bottom of this affair';[10] and neither the Duque de Aveiro nor any other noble fled the country as might have been expected after a bungled assassination attempt. Perhaps, some would later suggest, the conspiracy was so widespread and so watertight that no one felt the need to flee; others pointed out that the innocent have no reason to flee. Then, in mid-December, four days after the publication of a decree offering a reward for any information about an attempt on the King's life, troops surrounded the houses of all members of the Távora family; that of the Duque de Aveiro and his son, the Conde de Atouguia, head of the Palace Guard; and two men suspected of setting the ambush. The ladies were all taken straight to convents while the men were subjected to weeks of torture at the hands of the Inquisition.

One 12 January 1759, six nobles and five commoners were sentenced to execution and the following morning ten figures were led from jails around the city to the square in front of the royal palace at Belém. Despite the cold a vast crowd had assembled by 8.30 a.m. – some said the whole city, others 70,000 – to witness the most sensational event since the earthquake. A large scaffold, standing twice as high as a man, had been erected by the waterside with eight wheels and a number of poles on it. In one corner there was an effigy of José Policarpio, who was still at liberty, and in another sat António Alvarez Ferreira. Both were retainers of the Duque de Aveiro, and both were said to have been the would-be assassins. The first noble to be led to the scaffold was the Marquesa de Távora, matriarch of the eponymous family, who had been incarcerated since her arrest at the Grilas convent. Nearly sixty years old, she had been a great beauty in her time and was still a striking figure. Led by two Jesuit priests, she mounted the scaffold. Prayers were said and then she was seated on a stool and with a single blow of what foreigners took to be a 'very large knife' she was beheaded. Her body was placed in a corner and covered with black silk.

The next to be led forward was the Marquesa's youngest child, twenty-two-year-old José Maria de Távora. He looked so young and innocent that many in the crowd thought he could not be more than sixteen, and it was hard to imagine him being involved in any skulduggery. His mother's execution had been, in deference to her gender and standing, relatively dignified. José was bound to a St Andrew's cross and had a cord placed round his neck which was twisted until the life was strangled out of him. His upper and lower arms, his thighs and his shins were then smashed with an iron bar and his body was thrown on a wheel. After José Maria it was the turn of Luís Bernardo de Távora, José Maria's elder brother and the cuckolded husband of one of the king's mistresses; the Conde de Atouguia, the husband of Maria Bernarda de Távora; the Marquês de Alorna; Bras José Romeiro, who served in Luís de Távora's militia; and another servant of the Duque de Aveiro.

Then came the Marquês de Távora himself, the former Governor of Portuguese India who had returned in 1754 and was a General in the King's Horse. He was paraded bareheaded to increase his ignominy and after mounting the scaffold he walked round all the wheels, lifting the sail-cloths to inspect the bodies. When he came to that of his youngest child, José Maria, he knelt down and wept. His own execution followed: the Marquês was fastened to a cross and after his right arm and right leg had both been broken top and bottom, to the accompaniment of screams 'horrible beyond expression', he was given the *coup de grâce* with a blow to the chest. No such mercy was shown to the Duque de Aveiro, Master of the Royal Household, who remained alive, 'his shrieks terrible indeed', as all his limbs were broken.

The last victim, António Alvarez Ferreira, was the 'conspirator' for whom the climax of this grisly piece of theatre was reserved. He was seated on a high step and chained to a pole as the bodies of all the others were uncovered for him to see while brushwood and resin was spread over the scaffold. It was then set alight and Ferreira was burnt alive, 'shrieking amidst the flames for five minutes'. When the whole scaffold had been razed to the ground the ashes were swept into the Tagus, and that same day the Duque de Aveiro's palace was demolished and the ground salted.

Benjamin Farmer, who had returned to Lisbon to pursue his claim for compensation for the seizure of his schooner in the Cape Verde islands and was still there hoping for redress, did not witness the execution. But on his way back from a walk in the hills he came across a vast crowd returning to the city from Belém. 'Their pace was slow', he wrote, 'their eyes fixed on the ground. There was a perfect silence. Except some sighs and the pattering of their feet nothing was heard. Their countenances without exception were filled with the deepest melancholy but no rage.' Farmer was 'wonderfully affected' by the sight and recalled that he had 'once before felt the effect of such communication of feeling. For at the time of the great earthquake, when the new quay was swallowed up and the sea threatened the lower part of the city, a multitude like this fled to the hills.'[11]

Christopher Hervey, whose understanding of the enormity of what had occurred was not as great as that of someone as *au fait* as Benjamin Farmer, remarked after the executions 'how mysterious everything is here – but such is the government of Portugal'. He was told that 'still more . . . are to die; but who or when God knows'. All of the executed nobles were closely related by blood or marriage ties. But that counted for nought in the face of Carvalho's ambition to be rid of anyone who was not his ally or might be powerful enough to see him removed from Court; and Hervey's information was correct. Many other nobles were rounded up and imprisoned for life or exiled at the same time as the 'conspirators' to add to those, like the illustrious Duque de Lafões and his brother, who had already decided it was safer to leave Carvalho's Portugal. Even the Palhavã Princes, José's illegitimate half-brothers, were banished to their estates. Hervey was thankful to say that as 'the lightning blazes around me . . . its bolts reach not my humble situation',[12] and all foreigners reacted by turning a blind eye. Indeed Carvalho handled – or perhaps even created

– the 'Távora Affair' so dexterously that the only reaction shown abroad was disgust with the 'traitors' and satisfaction that they had met the same fate as sundry Jacobite rebels in England in 1746, and Robert-François Damiens for his attempt to kill Louis XV in Paris in 1757. For this Carvalho was himself ennobled by José and styled the Conde de Oeiras. In truth, as Benjamin Farmer noted at the time, he was more than a Count: Carvalho was 'master of the king' and the King now 'had no one he could rely on beside Carvalho'.[13]

After nine years of shrewd and patient manoeuvring 'King Sebastian', as the new Conde de Oeiras was increasingly referred to on the street and behind his back at Court, was now so powerful that he was able to do as he pleased. The salutary effect of the executions reduced the rest of the nobility, in Benjamin Farmer's words, to 'a condition very little above menial servants'. Carvalho's brother Paulo was made Inquisitor-General, and the 200 year-old Inquisition was gradually transformed into a 'political engine';[14] another brother, Francisco Xavier de Mendonça, returned from Brazil to become Secretary of State for Marine Affairs and take charge of all colonial administration; Lisbon's first police force was created under the direction of an intendant answerable to Carvalho; and the establishment of the Colégio Real dos Nobres, for the education of nobles, and the Aula do Comércio, a business school, were intended to produce a generation of entrepreneurs and educated nobles.

Most important of all, in Carvalho's eyes, was the opportunity the conspiracy gave him to deliver the decisive blow in his struggle with the Jesuits, whose temporal power in Brazil had finally been suppressed in 1758 after a five-year battle on the margins of the empire. Gabriel Malagrida, who had been such a thorn in Carvalho's side in the aftermath of the earthquake, was also the Marquêsa de Távora's confessor; and this provided the pretext for his arrest, as well as that of many other leading Jesuits, on charges of complicity. On the first anniversary of the attempt on José's life, a date chosen very deliberately, a royal decree announced that the Jesuit order was considered to be in a state of rebellion against the Crown. All Jesuit property in the Portuguese empire was confiscated and the entire order expelled from Portuguese territory. When Pope Clement XIII expressed approbation of Carvalho's purge the Papal Nuncio in Lisbon, Filippo Acciaiuoli, was promptly expelled.

News of the expulsion of the Jesuits created a far greater sensation in Europe than the execution of the nobles, the more so after Malagrida was subjected to an *auto-da-fé* in September 1761, then garrotted and burnt at the stake alongside an effigy of the Chevalier de Oliveira who, from the safety of London, had been so critical of Portugal after the earthquake. The irony that the victim of Portugal's last 'religious' execution was a Jesuit priest was not lost on Catholics or Protestants alike, and Carvalho did not let his vendetta rest with the death of Malagrida. As if intent on replacing the Jews with Jesuits in the national psyche as an outlet for suspicion and hatred, he relentlessly campaigned against the Society of Jesus throughout Europe. In France the Society was abolished in 1764, and four years later Spain, Naples and Sicily followed suit. In 1773 it was suppressed by the Pope. Portugal had seemingly become a leader of, rather than a laggard to, its peer group of nations with Carvalho's fierce vendetta – to what positive effect, other than reinforcing the absolutism of the Crown still further, remained uncertain. Meanwhile the ramifications were summed up by a correspondent to Edward Cave's *Gentleman's Magazine* after the executions who wrote that it had become 'evident to the world that within these ten years past, a total alteration of measures hath taken place in the political system of Portugal' and that the country was now 'in the steel grip of a destroying angel, scattering vengeance through the land'.[15]

TWENTY

The End of Optimism,
the Birth of a Science

THE STIR CAUSED BY AN ATTEMPT ON a sovereign's life was as
nothing compared to the impact of the *opus* that Voltaire produced at
the same time. *Candide, ou l'Optimisme* was first published secretly, and
anonymously. But by the spring the identity of its author was known,
and before the end of the year the novella was earnestly, or with amusement, or with horror, being discussed throughout Europe.

If the tragedy of the Lisbon earthquake had provided the catalyst for
Voltaire's initial assault on the philosophy of optimism with his *Poème*,
much had happened in the intervening years to confirm his abhor-
rence for the resignation with which mankind suffered. The execution
of Admiral Byng, about which he famously wrote 'it is considered useful
now and again to shoot an admiral *"pour encourager les autres"*',[1] and
other horrors of the Seven Years' War were events that had increased
Voltaire's rage with 'the mania for insisting that all is well when all is by
no means well'.[2] Now the executions in Lisbon fortuitously provided
him with the most apposite backdrop he could have wished for, one
which could only have been better if there had been a widespread

realization of the extent to which the charges were primarily a Machiavellian fabrication of Carvalho.

Candide was the most scornful, scathing, devastating reply to the fatalism expressed in Rousseau's letter of August 1756 and by all other optimists; and its story soon became familiar to educated readers right across Europe. The naïve young protagonist Candide embarks on an odyssey (or Grand Tour) with the optimist Dr Pangloss as his guide (or Leibnizian bear-leader). Progress from country to country is at a breathtaking pace, the tempo giving added emphasis to the plethora of misfortunes and untold suffering that they encounter. Earthquakes, rape, dismemberment, slavery, shipwrecks, exploitation, disease, persecution, ignorance, selfishness, disenchantment, despair – these are the markers along the way; but the irrepressibly cheerful Candide never loses faith in Pangloss's absurd assurances that no matter what happens, 'all is for the best in the best of all possible worlds'. In two of Voltaire's most darkly witty passages a slave in South America with no right hand or left leg – the first lost in an accident, the second cut off for trying to escape – is made to utter the appalling line, 'it is the price we pay for the sugar you eat in Europe';[3] and Pangloss asserts that syphilis, with which he is afflicted, is a good thing because if it had not come to Europe from South America then Europe would not have chocolate.

It is in the fifth chapter that Candide and Pangloss arrive in Lisbon, where the first thing that happens is that their companion Jacques the Anabaptist saves a sailor from being thrown overboard but is then pitched into the water himself and drowns. Candide is prevented from trying to rescue him by Pangloss, who tells him that 'Lisbon harbour was built expressly so that the Anabaptist should one day drown in it'. To anyone who had witnessed the tidal waves rolling up the Tagus on 1 November 1755, it is hard to imagine any more shocking statement; but it would have been hooted at by sceptics of the philosophy of optimism, and worse is to come. After Candide and Pangloss land in Lisbon they are immediately caught up in the earthquake: 'they feel the earth tremble beneath them; a boiling sea rises in the port and shatters the vessels lying at anchor. Great sheets of flame and ash cover the streets and public squares; houses collapse, roofs topple on to foundations, and foundations are levelled in turn; thirty thousand inhabitants without regard to age and sex are crushed beneath the ruins.' This description would have been familiar to every reader. But, once again, the next sentence – true though it undoubtedly was to real life – is breathtaking in its cynicism: a sailor says, 'with an oath and a whistle . . . there'll be things for the taking here'.

Candide is injured 'by some falling masonry', but Pangloss is too busy with philosophical musings to answer his request for oil and wine; only after his young charge has fainted does he bring him a little water. Meanwhile the sailor has responded to Candide's cry that 'the end of the world is here' by 'braving death in his search for silver', finding some, getting drunk and 'after sleeping it off, [he] purchases the favours of the first willing girl he finds in the ruins of the fallen houses, in amidst the dead and the dying'. When Pangloss remonstrates with him, the sailor retorts 'you've picked the wrong man, with your drivel about universal reason'.[4] Pangloss, undeterred, reassures people when the quake is over with the words 'this is all for the best . . . for if there is a volcano beneath Lisbon, then it cannot be anywhere else; for it is impossible for things to be elsewhere than where they are. For all is well.'[5] Before they move on to equally bleak pastures, the Inquisition arrests Candide and Pangloss; and the authorities decide that 'the most effective means of averting further destruction' is to hold an *auto-da-fé*, as 'the spectacle of a few individuals being ceremonially roasted over a slow fire was the infallible secret recipe for preventing the earth from quaking'. A Biscayan and two Portuguese who 'were seen throwing away the bacon garnish while eating a chicken' are burnt, Candide is flogged, Pangloss is hanged and 'that same day the earth quaked once more with a terrifying din'. Candide asks himself, 'if this is the best of all possible worlds, what must the others be like?'.[6]

Voltaire's famous ending to *Candide* – his assertion that, having rejected Pangloss's philosophy, 'we must cultivate our garden', is only marginally less enigmatic than that of the *Poème*. Whatever it is taken to mean – extolling the merits of a practical (as opposed to philosophical) approach to life, or of retreating from life to one's own backyard, or of cultivating one's own alternative to optimism, or of tackling despair through one's own best efforts – it does mean *something* to every reader. It was therefore more than simply a nihilistic demolition of optimism, even if Voltaire wished the reader to choose his own meaning rather than have one prescribed, and he stated that his purpose in writing *Candide* was 'to bring amusement to a small number of men of wit'. This was somewhat disingenuous: Voltaire knew that it would scandalize, that it would be banned as blasphemous and treasonous by some religious and secular authorities, and that many of his fellow intellectuals would regard it as insufferably denigrating. He also knew that it would be widely read. But he cannot have guessed that at least seventeen editions would be required in 1759 as a staggering 30,000 copies were sold across Europe to a reading public which delighted in its 'amusement'. The combination of the Lisbon earthquake and Voltaire's acerbic pen in time consigned Leibnizian optimism to oblivion: as Theodore Besterman wrote on the 200th anniversary of the earthquake, 'the *Poème* opened the assault on optimism, *Candide* finished it off for good'.[7] A watershed in Western thought had been marked, and the beginning of a new 'modern' era.

Candide was not the only great *oeuvre* of its type to appear in 1759. By an extraordinary coincidence, Samuel Johnson produced *Rasselas* the same year.[8] It was written in a week to pay for his mother's medical bills and funeral, and is also an odyssey – the story of an Abyssinian prince who, like Candide, leaves his home in the 'happy valley of Amhara' to 'see the miseries of the world, since the sight of them is necessary to happiness'. In Imlac, Rasselas, like Candide, has a supposedly wise companion; and Rasselas arrives at a similar conclusion to Candide at the end of his travels. Unlike Candide, who ends in a different place to that from which he started out, Rasselas returns home. He has learnt that things elsewhere are no better than in Abyssinia, that the secret of happiness is not to 'endeavour to modify the motions of the elements, or fix the destiny of kingdoms', and that it cannot be attained by going on any sort of journey. It is found within, by '[considering] what beings like us may perform; each labouring for his own happiness, by promoting within his own circle, however narrow, the happiness of others'.

Leibnizian optimism was Johnson's target as well as Voltaire's, but the extreme cynicism and ridicule deployed by Voltaire is absent from *Rasselas*, and by addressing 'the human condition' rather than seeking to destroy a doctrine, Johnson's 'little story book', as he called it, was arguably more gentle, accessible, loveable and, in many ways, substantial. *Rasselas* is more lightly crafted, less obvious, than *Candide* but it may well stand alongside the great Dictionary he had published in the earthquake year as Johnson's finest work. And for some *Rasselas* would be 'brandy to Voltaire's thin beer'.[9]

The scientific aftershock of the Lisbon earthquake was not as quick to force change as the philosophical aftershock, but it was no less significant for that. Scientists, or natural philosophers, of the time did not question the theological explanation that earthquakes were the speech of God, but this did not preclude investigation into their secondary, natural causes. No inherent contradiction was seen between the notion of God's intervention and modern, Newtonian ideas about the universe: it was fact that God had spoken and the role of science was simply to ascertain the exact means by which his speech had been articulated by nature. Explanations were many and varied, commonly featuring the interaction of a concoction of Aristotelian and 'modern' wisdom that included subterranean winds, underground fires, the expansion of vapours, electricity and explosions. A number of features of earthquakes were more or less correctly identified by the mid-eighteenth century – for example that a hollow, thundering noise typically preceded one, that they could cause lakes and rivers to disappear, and that there was usually a considerable elapse of time before very big earthquakes struck the same place again – but many other, more far-fetched ideas would persist either in popular belief or 'scientific' theory for a long time to come. Some natural philosophers held that quakes were always preceded by fireballs, meteors or strong winds; others, that they always occurred in calm weather. Some sought to establish a causal link between earthquakes and famines or outbreaks of disease; others, that quakes only hit large conurbations, typically ones situated by the sea or rivers.

In the wake of the London tremors in 1750, which generated huge interest in the history and causes of earthquakes, the Reverend William Stukeley proposed in *The Philosophy of Earthquakes, Natural and Religious* that it had to be electricity from the atmosphere that provided 'the snap, and the shock' which triggered them as it was the most powerful of all natural forces – although the means by which 'the atmosphere and earth are put into that electric and vibratory state which prepares them to give or receive the snap' was, he admitted, no more definable than 'the cause of magnetism, or of gravitation, or how muscular motion is performed, or a thousand other secrets of nature'.[10] As lightning and earthquakes were generally thought to have the same cause, Stukeley's theory appeared to be supported within the next two years by Benjamin Franklin's famous kite experiment, demonstrating that lightning was an electrical rather than a chemical phenomenon. But others persisted in their view that earthquakes must be caused by a chemical reaction.

The importance of Lisbon to this ongoing debate was as a catalyst. No earthquake in history had generated such interest and, as a result, such a substantial body of significant and relevant observations. It is not known to what use the answers to the questionnaires sent out to Portuguese and Spanish parishes were put: they were certainly not published or circulated. But the publication in 1755 by the Royal Society of a substantial body of eye-witness testimony relating to the quake and the tidal waves was a ground-breaking event in the history of seismology. The accounts gathered by the Society's Fellows came from all over Britain, giving valuable information about the seiches visible on inland waters and the tidal waves which hit the coast later in the day; and they were augmented by observations in Switzerland, Madeira, Porto, Lisbon itself, and even as far afield as Barbados. In 1756 the Reverend Zachary Grey, vicar of the parish of St Giles and St Peter in Cambridge, updated his important catalogue, *A Chronological and Historical Account of the most remarkable earthquakes to the year 1750*; and in Königsberg Immanuel Kant produced three essays dismissing the idea that earthquakes were caused by the gravitational pull of heavenly bodies and arguing that it was the action of water on sulphurous and ferrous deposits in subterranean caverns which triggered them, and that they then spread through passages which ran parallel to mountain ranges and river systems. Kant also correctly asserted that the origin of the Lisbon earthquake must have been under the sea, and that it was the disturbance of the ocean floor which had created the tidal wave.

Two years later the publication of *The History and Philosophy of Earthquakes, from the Remotest to the Present Times* by 'A Member of the Royal Academy of Berlin' – the astronomer John Bevis – gathered together ten papers about the causes of earthquakes by 'the best writers on the subject' and included the body of work presented by the Royal Society in Volume 49 of its *Philosophical Transactions*; and that same year Voltaire's friend, the Swiss pastor and naturalist Élie Bertrand, produced his *Mémoires Historiques et Physiques sur les Tremblements de Terre*, a catalogue of Swiss earthquakes. In Portugal Joachim Moreira de Mendonça published his *História Universal dos Terremotos* in 1758, which included a dissertation on the causes of earthquakes; and works printed in Germany and Spain contributed to the unprecedented outpouring of work on the subject.

The work of two individuals would come to be remembered as particularly significant. The first was John Winthrop, Professor of Mathematics and Natural Philosophy at Harvard, who had observed how far objects were thrown during the New England earthquake; and in a letter to the Royal Society written in 1758[11] he not only suggested – as had Pliny – that the movement of the ground had been 'undulatory', like the waves of the sea, but also omitted any reference to the 'primary' cause and concentrated solely on the secondary, natural causes. This was a change of emphasis from a lecture he had delivered immediately after the New England earthquake and may have reflected the different audience he was seeking to address. In concluding in that lecture that some good must have been intended by God, he had given what has been called 'as optimistic a view of a natural catastrophe as [had] been committed to print since the drowning of Pharaoh's army';[12] but by bringing science to the fore in his letter his presentation was novel.

This 'scientific' approach was also demonstrated by the Reverend John Michell, a thirty-six-year-old Fellow of Queen's College, Cambridge, who was recognized chiefly as an astronomer in his own lifetime (and was rather unkindly described by the antiquary William Cole as being 'a little short man, of a black complexion and fat'). During the spring of 1760 Michell presented a series of papers to the Royal Society. He introduced them by explaining that it was his intention to use the facts gathered in the wake of the Lisbon earthquake to prove, rather than merely theorize, that 'earthquakes owe their origin to some sudden explosion in the internal parts of the earth'; to explain 'the more particular effects' caused by such explosions; and to establish 'the connexion of them with the phaenomena' itself. It was a bold move to discard, as far as was possible, Aristotle, Seneca and Pliny in favour of up-to-date observations; but by doing so Michell went even further than Winthrop by developing a new theory altogether.

Michell adhered to the idea that large quantities of water, being suddenly deposited on 'subterraneous fires', released 'vapour whose quantity and elastic force' was capable of 'shaking the earth'. But it was his explanation of how this 'elastic force' operated that was novel:

> Suppose a large cloth, or carpet, (spread upon a floor) to be raised
> at one edge, and then suddenly brought down again to the floor,
> the air under it, being by this means propelled, will pass along, till
> it escapes at the opposite side, raising the cloth in a wave all the
> way as it goes. In like manner, a large quantity of vapour may be
> conceived to raise the earth in a wave, as it passes along between
> the strata, which it may easily separate in an horizontal direction,
> there being, as I have said before, little or no cohesion between one
> stratum and another[13]

This was not only the origin of modern wave theory, but also the closest that anyone had yet come to understanding the role of 'faulting'. From his considerable knowledge of geology Michell knew that the strata of the earth were 'frequently much bent, being raised in some places, and depressed in others', and posited that if 'the difference in the strata . . . should be very considerable, it may have a great effect in producing some of the singularities of particular earthquakes'.[14] Furthermore, Michell used the available information regarding the times at which the quake was felt in different locations, the direction of its approach, and the elapse of time between the earthquake and the tidal wave to calculate, not entirely erroneously, that the earthquake's epicentre was beneath the Atlantic between Lisbon and Porto at a depth of between one and three miles. Had Michell not adhered to the traditional notion that an earthquake was caused by an explosion and accepted that faulting alone could cause his seismic waves, he would have pre-empted the theory of geological faulting by 130 years. As it was his *Conjectures* ensured his election to the Royal Society, and in the twentieth century they would earn him recognition as the 'Father of Seismology' and Lisbon the distinction of being the first earthquake 'to be investigated on modern scientific lines'.[15]

~ TWENTY-ONE ~

Slow Progress, Slump and
a Reign of Terror

AS SEBASTIÃO JOSÉ DE CARVALHO E MELO, Conde de Oeiras, pushed on with his drive to modernize Portugal progress on the rebuilding of Lisbon remained slow. Despite England's great military successes in 1759 – the so-called 'year of victories' – the war rumbled on, requiring travellers from England who wanted to visit Italy either to try and seek a passage all the way by ship or to sail to Lisbon and then proceed overland through Spain. Even the packets were not entirely safe: the *Prince Frederick* was taken by the French with a cargo of £80,000 'in the hole', an amount nearly as large as that donated by England to Portugal in the immediate aftermath of the quake. One who would not be deterred was the Piedmontese man of letters Giuseppe Baretti, a close friend of Henry Fielding, Samuel Johnson and David Garrick, who knew the streets of London better than those of his home city of Turin. Baretti had just received great acclaim for his *Dictionary of the English and Italian Languages*, with its dedication by Johnson, and had taken the job as 'bear-leader' to Edward Southwell, the future Lord Clifford, as a means of securing a free journey home in August 1760.

Baretti was a very astute, and acute, observer – despite suffering from extreme short-sightedness – and was also very well-travelled. Like so many who had gone before him he was awe-struck by the view of Lisbon from the Tagus. 'Nothing can equal it that ever I saw', he gushed in a letter to his brothers, before adding the partisan rejoinder, 'except Genoa with its suburbs'. But when he had seen the damage wrought by the earthquake Baretti found himself almost unable to find words to describe 'such a scene of horrible desolation'. He thought that the devastated area was twice as big as Turin and saw nothing therein except 'vast heaps of rubbish, out of which arise in numberless places the miserable remains of shatter'd walls and broken pillars'. His account continued:

> My whole frame was shaking as I ascended this and that heap of rubbish. Who knows, thought I, but I stand now directly over some mangled body that was suddenly buried under this heap! Some worthy man! Some beautiful woman! Some helpless infant! A whole family perhaps! Then I came in sight of a ruined church. Consider its walls giving way! The roof and cupola sinking at once, and crushing hundreds of thousands of all ages, of all ranks, of all conditions! This was a convent; this was a nunnery; this was a college; this a hospital! Reflect on whole communities lost in an instant! The dreadful idea comes round and round with irresistible intrusion.

Given the scene before him Baretti was surprised that everyone he spoke to was so adamant that the city would be rebuilt 'quite regular, quite fine, finer than ever it was' – as if national pride depended on it. Indeed the notion seemed so at odds with the evidence of his eyes that he doubted the common sense, and even the sanity, of those who spoke in such terms.

> How is the rubbish of 15,000 houses to be removed', he asked, 'along with that of some hundred of large churches, two royal palaces, and many convents, nunneries, hospitals and other public edifices? If half the people that have escaped the earthquake, were to

be employed in nothing else but in the removal of that immense rubbish, it is not very clear that they would be able to remove it in ten years. Then where are the materials for rebuilding sixteen thousand houses and some hundreds of other edifices? The making of millions and millions of bricks . . . is not the work of a day. Where is the wood for kilns? Thousands of brickmakers, the lime? The iron?

As he wandered about the ruins Baretti could tell that a start had now been made, but it seemed to him a very odd one. Rather than begin with something of the greatest practical use, such as housing or warehouses, the first building nearing completion was the vast new naval Arsenal. When he questioned anyone about the logic of proceeding in this way they seemed to 'have another way of thinking', leaving him to ponder whether 'as soon as that wonderful Arsenal is completed they set about to rebuild their Inquisition, their cathedral, or some stupendous convent'. From his window in Kelly's inn in Buenos Ayres he could see what *he* thought needed dealing with first – the plight of the thousands dwelling in the 'clusters of wooden huts and cottages' on the outskirts of the city.

Giuseppe Baretti did not confine his remarks to the physical state of the capital. He enjoyed meeting Eugene Nicholas, the Irish organ-builder at Mafra who stood just four feet tall; he marvelled at the enterprise of the pickpockets at a bullfight who spread panic and confusion with a cry of '*terramoto!*'; and he was very moved by the stories of the survivors he met, especially an old lady still living in the cellar out of which she had been dug nine days after the quake to discover that the other twelve members of her family had perished. But the prevalence, as he saw it, of lawlessness, the very large number of Africans, superstition, and other features of society prompted him to remark that the country was 'rather too much in the neighbourhood of Africa'; and he was not impressed by the inhabitants' apparent propensity to live 'without thinking much of tomorrow'. 'The Portuguese', he added, 'do not look as if they were

disturbed by desire of change or fear of want', raising questions about the
dynamism of society, the country's ability to progress. It seemed to him
extraordinary that so many shops were owned by foreigners – even
tailors and shoe shops; that there were a multitude of *French* barbers
and hairdressers; and that most shoes were imported. 'One is apt to
suspect', he concluded, 'that the industry of this nation is not so great.'[1]

That same year twenty-three-year-old Thomas Pitt, the nephew of the
man largely orchestrating England's war strategy, William Pitt the Elder,
recorded impressions that were equally derogatory about the Portuguese
and sceptical about the prospects of ever seeing the city rebuilt. After
being presented at Court in the royal *barraca* at Belém on his first day
young Thomas decided there and then that 'the ladies of the court made
a most ridiculous figure', comparable to 'the wicked fairies in a French
romance'; that the men were hopelessly ignorant, having never travelled
anywhere; and that superstition, laziness, pride and a thirst for revenge
were defining characteristics of the Portuguese nation. 'Debauchey [*sic*]
of every sort is said to flourish in this climate', he remarked, before concluding that 'upon the whole, I am afraid the proverb is not so much
mistaken, which strips a Spaniard of his good qualities to make a
Portuguese'. Although he too found much to admire during his stay,
and especially enjoyed his enterprising visit to the great monasteries at
Alcobaça and Batalha a hundred miles north of Lisbon, he was convinced
that 'the prospect of this great city rising from its ruins is at a great distance'; and that, even if finished, it was likely to suffer from the 'want of
taste' which he thought characterized 'all the buildings that still remain'.
As for the Arsenal, he agreed with Baretti: 'it has', he wrote, 'cost a great
deal of money to lodge [ropes], anchors etc which they have not'.[2]

Thomas Pitt's diary was not intended for publication, but had it been
printed Carvalho would have considered him not only impolite, after
the Minister had done so much to help him during his stay, but also
dangerous enough to warrant a serious protest to Pitt's uncle. When

Giuseppe Baretti tried to have his letters published Carvalho lodged a complaint with the Austrian Governor of Lombardy and then, when he tried to publish in Venice, he found he was prohibited there too. Only after he had deleted any criticism of Portugal did the *Lettere familiari ai suoi tre fratelli* reach the printer's press. * It was probably not Baretti's observations that at the bullfight he had never seen 'so many fat men in one place', or that Portuguese cart wheels seemed to be 'made of two boards nailed together, and clumsily cut in a circular form' which caused most offence. But in suggesting that Carvalho's 'exaltation', the expulsion of the Papal Nuncio and the Jesuits, and the 'Távora Affair' were all subjects 'worth enquiry, especially as care has been taken to throw a veil over them, which will obstruct future historians',[3] he overstepped the mark. A manic determination to censor anything and everything that denigrated Portugal and himself had overtaken Carvalho, and his reach was impressive: there was no corner of Europe to which he would not pursue transgressors.

On board the same ship that brought Thomas Pitt to Lisbon was Edward Hay's elder brother, the Earl of Kinnoull, who had been sent on a very delicate mission. When the French fleet based at Toulon had left port the previous year to take part in a planned invasion of England, it had been engaged by Admiral Boscawen off Lagos, on Portugal's Algarve coast. The French flagships, *L'Océan* and *Redoutable* were driven onshore and two other ships captured before the fleet turned tail and sought refuge at Cádiz. Kinnoull's problem, and England's, was that the engagement took place in Portuguese waters and Boscawen had landed on 'neutral' Portuguese soil without permission in order to torch the two French ships. José and Carvalho accepted Kinnoull's apology graciously, but when a dialogue about the trade situation between the two nations was opened Carvalho became rather less amenable.

---

* When Baretti's unexpurgated text was finally published in England in 1770 with the title *Journey From London To Genoa*, Samuel Johnson described it as 'one of the best travel books ever written'.

For five years Carvalho had pursued an economic programme which amounted to an attempt to regain control of all facets of Portuguese trade and strengthen indigenous participation. The creation of the Companhia de Grão-Pará e Maranhão in Brazil had been the start, followed by the establishment of the new Board of Commerce, the Junta do Comércio, and the creation of another Brazilian monopoly, the Companhia de Pernambuco e Paraíba. At home the Brazilian companies had their equivalent in the new Companhia Geral das Vinhas do Alto Douro, through which Carvalho sought to concentrate control of the wine-growing regions around Porto, and the wine retail trade, in the hands of large local growers and merchants.

This highly controversial initiative was ostensibly motivated by a desire to control quality and pricing. But English merchants found themselves squeezed out of the Brazil trade by the new company, and lost their ability to regulate prices or sell Douro wines in Portugal. Many Portuguese also suffered from the new monopoly, especially the tavernkeepers. The most disaffected among the latter group responded by instigating the *Revolta dos Borrachos* – the so-called 'Revolt of the Drunks' – during which they burnt down the offices of the new company. Carvalho's response was swift and brutal: hundreds of the rioters were arrested and thrown in jail and seventeen or eighteen of them were executed. An attempt to stimulate manufacturing, most notably by resurrecting a national silk industry, and a ban on certain luxury imports were two other initiatives taken by Carvalho in his quest to reduce Portugal's dependence on imported goods – and thereby cut the trade deficit and the export of gold this forced upon the country.

Many English merchants had done very well in the years since the earthquake, as Edward Hay had hoped they would. Their trade was buoyed by demand from Brazil, and by the war, and English exports to Portugal in the years 1756 and 1757 had been as high as ever – exceeding £1.5 million in each year – while Portuguese exports to England failed to improve. But then English exports started to contract, and the merchants blamed the earthquake and, first and foremost, Carvalho's initiatives. Disputes put before Hay and his successor as Consul, Sir Harry Frankland, multiplied and became increasingly acrimonious, and Kinnoull found himself plunged into an atmosphere of extreme rancour. Carvalho's response to each issue raised by Kinnoull was that he had no intention of breaking any treaty agreements, but that the Portuguese interests were paramount. He also reminded Kinnoull, with the faintest hint of menace, that Portugal was England's only source of the gold which supported her ballooning wartime national debt.

The weather in Lisbon had been unseasonably warm for a number of days when, at about noon on 31 March 1761, the city was hit for the third time in the century by a quake measuring greater than seven on the Richter Scale. It lasted more than three minutes, possibly as much as five, and in the process brought down many of the ruins of 1755. An eye-witness on an English boat in the harbour watched 'the ruins of the last earthquake falling heap upon heap'. Even the new houses that had been built in the Rua Augusta were 'shattered in such a manner' that they had to be pulled down. Once again prisoners escaped from the jails, soldiers were placed around the city to stop a general flight, and the whole populace was gripped by 'terrible apprehensions';[4] and once again the quake was strong enough to be felt throughout Portugal, destroying what little had been left unscathed in 1755 in the port of Setúbal and causing a great deal more damage to Porto than six years earlier. On the *Expedition*, which had left Lisbon two days earlier, Captain Woodward noticed that 'the sea swelled to a great degree, with a rumbling noise' off the Rock of Lisbon, and the packet was 'tossed about, as if in a storm'; even HMS *Gosport*, which was also off the Rock at the time, 'felt two violent shocks of an earthquake and one of the vessels in its convoy was shaken so badly that the crew threw out their longboat and prepared to abandon ship'.[5]

The quake was strong enough to be sensible in Madrid, Bayonne and

Bordeaux, in Amsterdam, and even as far afield as Cork, in southern Ireland, and Madeira; and once again seiches were visible on Loch Ness. An hour afterwards a tidal wave of eight feet left a number of ships high and dry in the Tagus; later in the day waves also reached the Cornish coast (five measuring over six feet hit Penzance in the space of an hour), the southern Irish coast and, eight hours after the quake, Barbados. One English visitor in Lisbon wrote, 'as the rebuilding of the city went on so very slow before this shock I suppose now an entire stop will be [made] to it for some time'.[6] Churchmen were rather more cautious in their response than they had been six years earlier, but this did not prevent the whole population from wondering what this latest visitation from God might portend.

One year later the global conflict that Voltaire had described as 'the most hellish war that ever was fought'[7] finally came to Portugal and put all Carvalho's plans in jeopardy. In 1761 peace negotiations between England and France ended when France and the new King of Spain, Carlos III, resurrected the Bourbon Family Compact. The neutrality which Benjamin Keene had worked so tirelessly to encourage that it hastened his demise in 1757 from a 'convulsion fit', and which Augustus Hervey's brother George, Keene's successor as Ambassador in Madrid, strove to maintain, was no more. Despite the lamentable state of the Portuguese army, Carvalho called Spain's bluff and refused to bow to Franco-Spanish demands to abandon the alliance with England. Lord Tyrawley was sent to Lisbon to arrange for the country's defence; and in April 1762 Portugal was invaded through the province of Trás-os-Montes. But the Bourbon hope that Portugal might prove to be England's 'Achilles heel' proved wishful thinking. By the end of the year the campaign was a stalemate, and elsewhere England had captured the Spanish possessions of Havana, Manila and the Philippines. The Treaty of Paris, which saw England make substantial territorial gains and emerge as the leading power in Europe while also ending France's colonial ambitions in America, brought to a conclusion a war which had cost over a million lives.

Portuguese territory that had been occupied by troops of both sides was ravaged, but by the time hostilities ended there was a far bigger concern. The main factor behind the fall in English exports was not Carvalho's economic programme but a decline in the production of Brazilian gold and an end to the sugar boom. This cause of so many of their woes went largely unnoticed by the English merchants, who simply saw lower orders for goods from their customers, even when exports had fallen to a level half that of the late 1750s. The Portuguese empire was experiencing a very severe slump, and this meant that just as Carvalho wished to push ahead with the rebuilding of Lisbon in earnest, he was finding that his principal source of funding, the Brazilian 'goose', was broody. In the 1760s gold, for decades the mainstay of royal income, accounted for no more than one sixth of it. Furthermore, England had emerged even more powerful from the war and Carvalho's hopes of reducing Portugal's dependence on her ally were replaced by an increasingly acute mistrust. To demonstrate that he was still set on making Portugal as strong and independent as possible within the alliance, and thereby retain his room for manoeuvre, Carvalho announced a major overhaul of the army.

When twenty-nine-year-old Henry Hobart, son of the Earl of Buckinghamshire, arrived in Lisbon in 1767 he was impressed to find that the city appeared to be 'rebuilding very fast', and thought that 'in a few years [it] will be finished'. The public buildings of the Praça do Comércio, 'viz the Marine Arsenal, the Change, the Custom House, the Courts of Justice etc' were all functioning, 'a very large triumphal arch' was being built at the entrance to Rua Augusta, and north of the Rossio a new Passeio Público – a Public Promenade – had been laid out. The grid of streets in the Baixa, with its houses all 'uniform and built of stone . . . covered in white stucco', would, Hobart thought, 'make a very handsome appearance' when finished. But progress was not being made quite as fast as it seemed. Due to the lack of funds only fifty-nine houses had been completed in the Baixa, of which thirty-one were in Rua Augusta, an increase of just twenty-seven in five years; and on the outskirts of the city the 'temporary' townships in parishes like Santa Isabel, to the north-east, had become permanent. As for the city centre, it remained unlit, 'very nasty, and seldom cleaned'. Indeed Hobart was 'certain Edinburgh cannot stink more', although he was told that Carvalho's new police imposed 'severe penalties' against anyone caught throwing their sewage out of the window.

Hobart's mother and wife were both Bristows, a family long promi-nent in the Lisbon trade, and his observations on the changes wrought by Carvalho were revealing. He wrote that 'the whole kingdom is under the government of Carvalho, who knows every individual thing that passes in the country'. The church was 'diminishing in power every day', the Inquisition was – as a religious authority – 'not so troublesome a tribunal as some years ago', and superstition was 'not near so pre-dominant as formerly'. Furthermore there was now 'no danger of being robbed', murder was 'hardly . . . ever heard of', and ladies were 'allowed to appear more in publick'. As for Carvalho's reform of the army, the soldiers were said to be 'well paid and clothed' for the first time in several decades and to 'make a military appearance'. These struck Hobart as positive developments, even if Carvalho's economic measures were criticized by his friends among the English merchants for being 'a very great detriment to our trade'. But there was, as Baretti had suspected and Hobart now knew, an increasingly heavy price for all the changes. Carvalho was 'much dreaded' and kept 'the nobility &c &c in great sub-jection'. Anyone removed to the prison at Junqueira was 'seldom heard of ever again' and it was said that 'the best thing the family can do upon the occasion is not to make any enquiries'.[8] A dozen years after the earth-quake Portugal was in the grip of a reign of terror.

~ TWENTY-TWO ~

The End of Pombal

SEBASTIÃO JOSÉ DE CARVALHO E MELO was created Marquês de Pombal in 1769, and thereafter would always be referred to by friend or foe as 'Pombal'. His zeal for reforming education, commerce and Portuguese society in general, and his determination to see the country 'modernized', showed no signs of diminishing at the start of the new decade. At the same time Anglo-Portuguese commercial relations continued to worsen due to the deepening recession.

Shortly before Sir Harry Frankland died in 1768 a pamphlet entitled *Occasional Thoughts on the Portuguese Trade and the Inexpediency of Supporting the House of Braganza on the throne of Portugal* proved embarrassing for the Consul, and attested to the low ebb to which trade had sunk. The author suggested that Spain would be a far better long-term ally for Britain than 'the sinking crown of Portugal' and expressed disgust at the 'extraordinary aid we must ever and anon send to Portugal'. Worse still, Portugal was not only a 'needy dependant' but 'was always asking, and never can give us any assistance in our wars'. *

As for Portuguese gold, the author reckoned that the riches of Brazil would flow back to Britain regardless of any unwritten agreement between

* *Occasional Thoughts* pp. 4–9 *passim*.

the two nations for the simple reason that the Royal Navy, as ruler of the seas, would of necessity remain Portugal's bullion carrier of choice. English bottoms still accounted for more than half of the shipping to anchor in the Tagus, but it was half of a much-reduced whole. Brazilian exports had slumped by nearly fifty per cent during the 1760s; ship movements in and out of the Tagus were a third lower than at the time of the earthquake. In a desperate attempt to tackle the trade deficit through import substitution, Pombal ordered an expansion of domestic manufacturing which saw more than seventy new businesses set up by the Junta do Comércio in the 1770s – an initiative which English merchants regarded as a deliberate attempt to undermine their trade.

On the King's birthday in 1775, despite these problems, an eighty-four-ton bronze statue of José on horseback was unveiled in the centre of the Praça do Comércio. The celebrations lasted three days, with fireworks, processions and 'every device for pleasure that imagination could conceive'.[1] It was as if the reconstruction of Lisbon were finally complete. But, as was true of much that Pombal instigated, the task was far from finished. One English visitor at the time, who had no commercial axe to grind, thought that the city was by and large in 'the same ruinous state [as] the day after the earthquake' and it reminded him of a 'similar situation [he] had seen in the city of Dresden, caused by war and fire'.[2]

Two years later the King, who had lived in a wooden barrack ever since the quake, was dead and at the coronation of José's daughter as Maria I the self-styled 'Duc du Châtelet' also remarked that 'frightful traces' of the earthquake which had 'so excited the most celebrated philosophers'[3] were still everywhere to be seen. Rua Augusta, the main street running from the Praça do Comércio to the Rossio, was substantially complete, although its triumphal arch would not be finished for another hundred years; about half of the Baixa was built, its streets considered by the Duke to be 'broad and handsome, [with] pavements, like those of London, for foot passengers';[4] a great deal of private construction had reinvigorated damaged areas outside the Baixa; and the foundations had been laid for three new markets at the Ribeira Velha, the Ribeira Nova and the Praça da Figueira. If the remarks of visitors were a little harsh, it was certainly the case that Lisbon was still 'work-in-progress', and that the publication of Miguel Mauricio Ramacho's epic poem *Lisboa Reedificada* three years after José's death was premature.

The death of his ultimate protector left Pombal fighting for his life. The prisons in which the enemies of the Crown, or rather *his* enemies, languished were opened by Maria to reveal some unfortunates who had been incarcerated since the 'Távora Affair' nearly twenty years earlier. Pombal was banished to his country estates by the Queen, who was so incensed by many of his actions that she also ordered him not to come within twenty miles of her. If she approached his home, he would have to move. The Duc du Châtelet noticed that on coronation day, 'amidst the general joy occasioned by the fall of Pombal, an air of sadness universally prevailed'.[5] It was an undignified end for a man who had brought so much indignity to others, and it became more so when Pombal was subjected to three months of interrogation at the end of 1779 – the same year that Augustus Hervey, Earl of Bristol, died of 'gout of the stomach' and Edward Hay died while Governor of Barbados – after vehement denunciations of his conduct poured in from all corners of the kingdom. By now he was eighty years old, but he put up a spirited defence of everything he had ever done, claiming with a disingenuous degree of truth that all his actions had been approved by José.

In 1781 Maria put a stop to what she regarded as the unseemly process of accusation and counter-accusation and refused to accede to the demands of those who wished to see Pombal executed. He died the following year, by which time the bronze medallion bearing his image that had been placed on the statue of José in the Praça do Comércio had long since been removed. So acute was the shortage of funds that all work on rebuilding the city came to a halt, with two notable exceptions.

Construction of a magnificent basilica at Estrela – a new Mafra – was begun with the money that Pombal had set aside to build a bridge across the Tagus; and before long Maria also started to turn José's wooden 'palace' at Ajuda into something altogether more monumental. It was as if João had returned from the grave to rule again.

When Thomas Pelham, the son of the Earl of Chichester, visited Lisbon two years before Pombal's fall he described him as 'a remarkable well-bred man' and 'a most agreeable companion'.[6] This complimentary opinion was shared by the majority of foreigners who met the man who was Portugal's *de facto* ruler for two decades. But Pombal's actions and methods had made many enemies and ensured that his legacy would always remain controversial. At the end of João's reign Portugal had been, in the words of one English visitor, 'so much reduced as to have fallen into a worse state than infancy';[7] and it was this condition that Pombal had set out to tackle with a programme of reforms which sought to achieve the seemingly impossible.

The extent to which he realized his goals varied. There were certainly improvements to the education system; the stigma attached to trade by the higher strata of Portuguese society was much diminished and a broader middle class emerged; and the worst excesses of the Church and Inquisition were curbed. But in many respects it was as if the cards were simply shuffled. The Jesuits became a scapegoat to replace the Jews, and their dominance in education passed to the Oratorians; one third of the nobility were replaced by appointees loyal to Pombal; and the monopoly companies did not transform Portuguese commerce, they merely handed the spoils to different people many of whom, like Gerard Devisme and David de Purry, were foreigners and not Portuguese nationals.

Many other reforms existed only on paper. The reorganization of the army only took place after invasion during the Seven Years' War, and was largely cosmetic; and Pombal was slow, and ultimately unsuccessful, in building up Portuguese domestic manufacturing (although his efforts in this and other projects were hampered by the economic slump which accompanied much of his 'reign', and from which Portugal did not recover until the final decades of the century, when Brazil became prosperous again on the back of a booming cotton industry and sugar exports). At the time the Duc du Châtelet remarked that 'twenty years longer would scarcely have been sufficient for him to accomplish what he had only time to plan. The diseases were inveterate; a long course of medicine could alone have effected their cure';[8] on the other hand, it has been suggested more recently that 'if he had employed constant prodding instead of the mailed fist, perhaps the transition from the old to the new would have been more effective and less painful for all concerned'.[9]

Mixed though the legacy was, there is one achievement that cannot be disputed: Pombal played a leading role in rescuing Lisbon as a trading metropolis at a time when it could have atrophied, and in so doing he may have saved the Portuguese nation by ensuring that England saw the alliance as worth preserving. The rebuilding process may not have occurred at the pace which Pombal sought to project, and it may not have been carried out as he would have wished in every respect, not least due to the perpetual shortage of funds. But by his death the construction of the new city had developed sufficient momentum to ensure that it would eventually be as *nearly* completed and as *nearly* to plan as any other urban project of such magnitude. For that the Baixa would rightly become known as 'Pombaline' Lisbon, and 'the first modern city of the west'.[10]

In 1789 the young Irishman, and bricklayer turned eminent architect, James Murphy arrived in Portugal after completing his work on various additions to the House of Commons. His prime purpose was to fulfil a commission to draw the church and monastery at Batalha; but when he passed through Lisbon he brought a trained eye to bear on the state of the capital city three decades after the rebuilding had begun. Murphy's was an unusually impartial perspective, in that he actively sought to counter the prejudices and preconceptions displayed by most eighteenth-century travellers irrespective of their nationality or destination. 'We are apt to see defects in our own neighbours', he wrote in his account of his travels, 'whilst we are blind to our own. Like the Lamina witches, who, according to the facetious Rabelais, in foreign places had the penetration of a lynx, but at home they took out their eyes and laid them up in wooden slippers.'[11]

The Lisbon Murphy found was still 'the constant resort of merchants and travellers from every part of the globe'; the view from the river was still one of a 'magnificence of wealth and grandeur', even if this impression 'greatly diminished upon a closer inspection';[12] and the effects of the earthquake, five years before Murphy's birth, were still very visible 'in many parts of the city'. As he wandered the streets he encountered many an inhabitant who was keen to relate 'the dreadful scene which attended that melancholy disaster'. November 1 1755 was, he noted, 'the epoch whence [the people] date all modern events', and he found that everyone appeared to be easily startled by sudden loud noises like the passing of a carriage or the retort of a cannon. But they also recognized that the destruction of 'the ancient contracted lanes and unhealthy habitations' of the old city was evidence that even 'the severest visitations of Divine Providence are attended with manifold blessings'.[13] Under Pombal's direction they, like Londoners after the Great Fire, had seemingly 'turned the temporary evil into a permanent good'.[14]

Murphy the architect found much to admire in the 'capacious, regular and well-paved' new streets of the Baixa with their 'convenient pathways for foot-passengers, as in the streets of London' and the 'lofty, uniform and strong houses'. The new homes of the nobles and merchants that he visited he found to be 'furnished in a magnificent manner' with artefacts from India and China; but despite their considerable number he felt that there was a 'democratic' air to the city, by which he meant egalitarian. With no Royal Palace in the centre there was no 'court-end', and the fact that one of the new main thoroughfares was allocated to mere 'copper-smiths and tin men' appealed to him as much as the ordered layout of the Praça de Comércio, or 'Black Horse Square' as it was known to the British. The statue of José at its centre he complimented as 'a very noble production';[15] and the sight of the 'New Church', the Basílica da Estrela being built by Maria which he considered 'the most magnificent edifice raised in Lisbon since the earthquake', and which had cost more than half a million pounds – prompted him to ask 'where shall we meet with such excellent stone-cutters as in Portugal?'.[16] Such laudatory remarks earned Murphy the enduring gratitude of the Portuguese. Even in the twentieth century he was fondly remembered as 'one of the few foreign travellers who didn't automatically speak ill about our country'.[17]

He thanked Providence that the earthquake had spared the 'beautiful structure' of the Jerónimos monastery, and he saw great merit in Pombal's design for the Passeio Público, the public promenade running northeast from the Rossio. Perhaps most telling of all was that, in Murphy's opinion at least, Lisbon had at last thrown off its reputation for being filthier than any other leading city in Europe. It was still in need of 'common sewers, pipe-water and *chambres des aisances*'; but the situation was so far improved that it was 'no longer the subject of animadversion for strangers'. As for the great aqueduct which had withstood the earthquake so impressively, Murphy praised it as being 'justly considered one of the most magnificent monuments in Europe; and in point of magnitude . . . not inferior, perhaps, to any aqueduct the ancients have left us'.[18]

Murphy the traveller was as fascinated by all he saw on the streets, by the little ceremonies of life, as any who had gone before him. Outside the warehouse of a Hamburg merchant at the Ribeira Velha he mistook huge cheeses for cannonballs, remarking that 'each was about the size of a thirty-two pounder and very nearly as hard'.[19] He marvelled at the sight of ladies 'casting love-signals in their silent language of the fingers' while sitting in the Moorish fashion, cross-legged on cushions, on their balconies; at the gaudy apparel and golden trinkets and bracelets of the fish-wives, the boots and black conical hats of the fruit-sellers; at the appearance of people in their Sunday best – even a barber wore a sword, cockade, and not just one but two watches on chains. To visit anyone in boots, he was told, 'was an unpardonable offence unless [wearing] spurs at the same time'.[20] Gallegos were everywhere to be seen, ferrying the whole city's water about in wooden barrels (one of which they had to take to their lodgings every evening to use in the event of fire); but, to Murphy's disappointment, it was once again unusual to see ladies, blessed with eyes 'black and expressive' and teeth 'extremely white and regular',[21] on the street in Maria's reign.

Everyone Murphy talked to as they played cards or rolled dice in the streets seemed convinced that Portugal was 'the blessed Elysium, and that Lisbon [was] the greatest city in the world',[22] a demonstration of national, or metropolitan, pride which he found as touching as the fact that most among the 'lower classes' seemed to be 'religious, honest and sober, affectionate to their parents and respectful to their superiors'.[23] But he was not completely taken in by this Elysian allusion. Lisbon beggars were formidable in number and conduct: they demanded rather than requested contributions, and gathered at night in threatening hordes outside the houses of the most wealthy. The peasantry seemed to Murphy to be more degraded and oppressed than in any other nation of his experience; travel among the middle classes was so rare that they seemed completely cut off from 'modern notions and customs' and content with 'the tranquillity of established opinions'; the *fidalgos* he dismissed as being little more than 'a band of petty tyrants';[24] and he was unimpressed by 'the humble state of the arts'.[25]

Above all, and for all its great charms, Murphy was disappointed that 'the advancement of the country [was] by no means proportionate to its vast resources'.[26] It was as if the country was exhausted by all its early endeavours, in the fifteenth and sixteenth centuries, and was now taking a rest. This he considered understandable, and only time would 'determine whether they will ever more re-establish the once respectable name of Lusitanians.'[27] The Baixa quarters between Rua Áurea and Rua dos Sapateiros were being worked on at the time of Murphy's visit, and the Rua da Prata had been completed. But there remained much to do: nothing north of the new church of São Nicolau in the Rua dos Douradores had been finished, the construction of Rua dos Correeiros had barely started, and even the Rossio and Praça do Comércio remained work-in-progress.

TWENTY-THREE

Memories and Memorials

IN 1842, ALMOST A CENTURY AFTER THE destruction of Lisbon, a terrible fire razed a third of Hamburg, and a London periodical declared that 'the only events in modern history which afford a fitting comparison to the recent conflagration [are] the Great Fire of London, the Burning of Moscow [and] the Earthquake at Lisbon'.[1] Six years later, as revolutions engulfed Sicily, France, the German states, the Habsburg empire and Brazil, Lisbon's disaster was commemorated in spectacular fashion. The Colosseum in Regent's Park, which had hosted more than a million visitors in the previous dozen years, had just undergone an expensive refurbishment and reopened with two new attractions which a correspondent of the *Illustrated London News* proclaimed worthy of 'particular attention'. The first was a panorama on a one-acre canvas of Paris by moonlight, as seen from a balloon above the Tuileries; the other was the 'Cyclorama of Lisbon', designed by Mr William Bradwell and executed by Messrs Danson & Son.

Visitors entered the theatre through the Albany Street entrance and went upstairs to the 'Refreshment Cottage', or 'Rustic Armoury'; and beyond that was the exhibition of 'moveable paintings'. The *Illustrated*

London News's account described the opening scenes of the toast of Victorian showbusiness as follows:

> We are presented with the beautiful, varied, and sublime scenery of the Tagus, the movement of which produces a peculiar feeling in the spectator. The theatre in which he sits seems like a vessel floating down the stream, and passing one object after another – the mountainous shore – the ships and vessels, the merchantmen and the *xebec* – the nunnery, the fort, the mansion, the palace, the various convents, the Consulate House, and, at length, the City, with its palatial, ecclesiastical, public and private buildings – all doomed to sudden destruction. The last scene presents the Grand Square of Lisbon with its gorgeous palaces and magnificent ranges of streets, massive arches and noble flights of steps, vases, and other colossal decorations, with the beautiful statue and fountain of Apollo.

The narrative sequence of the pictures, each of them 'on a vast scale of magnificence', was accompanied by music blasted out by a Bevington's Apollonicon – a 'grand machine organ' with sixteen pedals and 2,407 pipes – and included excerpts from Beethoven's *Pastoral Symphony*, Mozart's *Don Giovanni*, Auber's *Masaniello*, Rossini's 'Preghiera' from *Mosè in Egitto*, Mendelssohn's 'Wedding March', a Brazilian melody, a Portuguese dance, and Haydn's *Il Terremoto*. As the earthquake struck, the audience was suddenly assailed by a great 'subterranean roar' then plunged into pitch darkness accompanied by an 'appalling crash'. When light returned, a picture of 'the horror and the desolation'[2] was revealed. One spectator remarked that the performance showed 'with terrible minuteness the terrible scenes which marked the earthquake';[3] another that 'the manner in which the earth heaved and was rent, the buildings toppled over, and the sea rose, was most cleverly contrived, and had a most terrifying effect'.[4] The *Illustrated London News*'s correspondent continued breathlessly:

We next see the ships tossing upon the waves, fated to the destruction with which the lowering sky only too visibly threatens them.
All is terror and despair. But this passes, and the site of the city
returns, now covered with ruins where so lately we contemplated
the glories of architectural genius – all, by the visitation of an
inscrutable Providence, involved in one common wreck, with
more than thirty thousand of its dwellers.

It was generally agreed by those recovering afterwards in the
'Refreshment Cottage' that 'a more magnificent series of pictorial wonders
cannot be imagined', that 'the execution of this splendid task [did] the
highest possible credit'[5] to Messrs Bradwell and Danson. 'Never', wrote
one who saw it, 'was better value in fright given for money.'[6] The show
played on into the 1850s, even maintaining its popularity in the face of
fierce competition from the destruction of Pompeii show in the Great
Exhibition of 1851.

The great popularity of the Cyclorama at a time when 'catastrophism'
was all the rage in England ensured that a huge number of people were
taught, or reminded, of the location of 'the most fearful catastrophe that
history records'.[7] Just as Udal ap Rhys had lamented the lack of information about Portugal in his *Account of the Most Remarkable Places and
Curiosities in Spain and Portugal* a century earlier, the compiler of John
Murray's *Hints to Travellers in Portugal* described the country as 'a land
unknown to the great number of travellers who annually quit England'.[8]
Murray's *Handbook For Travellers In Portugal* considered it a shame that
'the history of Portugal is so little studied in England'[9] (while dating the
earthquake to 14 August 1755).

But knowledge of Portugal outside the wine trade, the commercial
community and the ranks of the armed forces had improved a little –
even if some of it remained misleading or inaccurate. George Whitefield's
A brief account of some Lent and other extraordinary processions and

ecclesiastical entertainments seen last year at Lisbon, first published in the spring of the earthquake year, was now in its umpteenth edition, with a 'Narrative of the Earthquake that totally destroyed the above City' appended and 'Mr Whitefield's remarks thereon'. The Lisbon Polka and Lisbon waltzes enjoyed a certain popularity in England; there was a modest demand for Portuguese melodies such as those collected by a Dr Browning in a volume entitled *The Lusitanian Garland*; Wilhelm's Oertel's novel *Earthquake of Lisbon* was published; and, to the great relief of travellers, a new *Pocket Dictionary of the Portuguese and English Languages* was even produced by António Vieira. Anglo-Portuguese trade and England's involvement in Portuguese industry was a hotly debated topic – an English contractor was in the process of building the new railway from Lisbon to Santarém – as was England's hand in Portugal's political affairs. A Saxe-Coburg-Gotha cousin of Albert and Victoria, Ferdinand, was King Consort to Maria II until her death in 1853, and it was only with the assistance of the Royal Navy and Spanish troops that a civil war started by radical 'Septembrists' – for whom there was considerable popular support in England – was ended in 1847.

The first half of the nineteenth century had not been kind to Portugal. There were further earthquakes in 1796 and 1801; Maria I had been declared insane; the Portuguese Court had been forced to flee to Brazil, escorted there by the Royal Navy when Napoleonic troops invaded for the first of three times; the English were *de facto* rulers of the country in their absence; and when the Court returned from Brazil there was civil war and Brazil declared its independence. All this left Portugal bankrupt, ravaged, and deeply divided. But one thing had not changed. The approach to Lisbon was still magnificent and, according to Murray's *Handbook*, 'for beauty of situation, disputes the second place among European cities with Naples, acknowledging Constantinople alone as its superior'.[10] Charles Dickens described how ships wishing to enter the Tagus found themselves surrounded by 'fleets of dragon-fly boats', and were hailed from what he called 'that little filigree matchpot of a tower' at Belém for an inspection by the quarantine boat. Swallows skimmed the surface of the water and there always seemed to be a 'tropical glow all over the city'.[11]

The massive monastery and church of Jerónimos had, after the abolition of the monasteries in 1833, been turned into a school for orphans, but it was no less striking an edifice for that; and beyond it the suburbs remained, by common consent, 'extremely beautiful'.[12] The reputation of the great aqueduct for being 'one of the noblest productions of modern architecture in all Europe'[13] endured. The handsome palace of Necessidades was the home of choice for Maria II until her death, in 1853, although above and behind it was the much larger palace of Ajuda, used only for grand galas, receptions and state occasions. Started in the 1790s on the site of the wooden barrack that José had chosen to live in until the end of his life, Ajuda was, even in its half-completed state, considered to be an extraordinary edifice in an extraordinary setting. William Thackeray, stopping in the city for a day on his way to the Mediterranean, mused that 'it must have been an awful site from this hill to have looked at the city spread before it, and seen it reeling and swaying in the time of the earthquake', and he was so bowled over by the scale of the palace that he thought 'no king of Portugal ought ever to be rich enough to complete [it]'. If ever completed, Thackeray added, it 'might outvie the Tower of Babel';[14] but it would never be the seat of an absolutist royal. Power was now once again shared with the Cortes, or parliament, which sat in the former convent of São Bento where thousands of the wounded had been gathered to await a slow death in the aftermath of the quake.

After landing at the Cais do Sodré or the Praça do Comércio, the same vitality was also evident. Red-sashed boatmen touted for business; swarthy, barefoot Gallegos – of whom there were still 20,000 or more in the city – were everywhere, crying 'Água! Água!' in 'deep, sonorous voices' or proffering their services to new arrivals; prisoners in chains, condemned to transportation to one of the remote reaches of the empire, clanked past on their way to the Limoeiro; and mules laden with oranges, lemons, figs and flowers plodded by on their way to market. Processions of priests – but not monks – were still a common sight, as were ladies in veils attended by Africans, beggars, and soldiers sitting about smoking cigars. There were posters advertising bull-fights, and Brazilian parrots in cages hanging from balconies. On street corners one might see stockingless boys 'roasting some kind of animal unheard of in the annals of gastronomy'. There were even greater surprises than this. Cows were milked right outside palaces; peculiar wagons and dirt-carts with bells trundled by, their wheels 'never greased until they threatened to catch fire'; and there were more people mounted on mules – and more feral cats and mangy dogs – 'than in almost any city of the world'.[15]

Set back from, and above, the Cais do Sodré in the Rua do Alecrim stood one of the the city's impressive new palaces. Built by the Barão de Quintella on the site of those of the Conde de Vimioso and Marquês de Valença destroyed in November 1755, it was here that Marshal Junot had made his home after the French invasion in 1807. Nearby stood the old Bragança palace, whose priceless royal treasures Augustus Hervey had been shown before they were all lost in the fire which followed the earthquake. Now a small part of it was the rose-coloured Bragança *Hotel*, Lisbon's finest, where for 7/6d one could secure a room for the night with a view over the Tagus. Around the Cais do Sodré, or the Remolares as it used to be known, there were still 'sailors of all nations and complexions, from the jet-black African to the white-hued Dane'. The majority were English or Irish and, as Dickens related, they made their presence known by talking 'very loud to make the English easier to the "d—— furriners", who could understand if they would'. As they had done for centuries, they were still prone, if caught ashore after curfew, to 'disarm the sentinels in the Praça do Comércio, drive off the relief guard, and force a way to their boat, pushing off with three cheers, their faces beaming with a sense of having properly and creditably done what England expects every man to do'. The street life of the city, all 'stir and bustle', was in many respects still that of 'the old Lisbon of Vasco da Gama, Cabral, the discoverer of Brazil, Dom Sebastian, and Albuquerque',[16] of Augustus Hervey, Lord Tyrawley and Thomas Chase. It was this, and its location, which continued to strike visitors as being 'of no ordinary interest'.[17]

It was a considerable achievement for Lisbon – in the course of a century which had begun with near-total chaos and destruction and proceeded in a more or less constant state of turmoil – to have been rebuilt to this extent. The two most important central locations were now finally finished. In 1845 the magnificent new National Theatre had opened on the former site of the Inquisition, bordering the northern side of what had been the Rossio and was now the Praça Dom Pedro IV, with its distinctive wavy bands of black and white paving stones. The south-eastern section of the old Rossio was another new square, the Praça da Figueira or 'Covent Garden of Lisbon', where market-stalls for fish, flesh, fowl and fruit were set up every day. North-west of the former was the new Passeio Público, with its trees and gardens, the promenade that Pombal had begun but not seen completed in his own lifetime.[18] At the other end of the Baixa the Praça do Comércio was an impressive, if austere, tribute to the man. On the east side, set around a small square planted with trees, and containing benches 'for the accommodation of idlers', stood the Customs House, India House, Exchange and Tribunal of Commerce which the author of *The Stranger's Guide* praised for arguably being 'not surpassed by any other edifice of the kind in the world'. A small brass cannon in the square fired a salute at nine, twelve and three o'clock every day, triggered by a mechanism that responded to the position of the sun. On the north side of the Praça were the offices of the Ministry of Justice, the Supreme Court, the Municipal Chamber and the Junta do Credito; and on the west side, where the Royal Palace had stood, the Ministries of Foreign Affairs, Finance, War, Maritime Affairs and the Treasury.

Further west, where the Patriarchal church and Opera had stood, was the new Largo do Pelourinho with its pillory in the centre, the colossal naval Arsenal with its room containing a full-sized model ship completely rigged and the docks on the south side; while on the east side stood the Bank of Lisbon and in the north-west corner the omnibus company offices. Beyond this, in the area in which Mr Braddock had spent 1 November 1755, lay the rebuilt church of the Irish Dominicans at Corpo Santo, the new quays at the Cais do Sodré, a fish market said to be stocked with a 'greater abundance and variety of fish'[19] than anywhere in the world, and the rebuilt church of São Paulo. The new city was said to be daily enlarging itself as a programme of *Regeneração* was put in train.

There were still remarks that were less than complimentary. One traveller was taken aback by the number of women sporting 'mustachios calculated to inspire in our military gallants no tenderer passion than that of envy' and he thought those parts of the city which had not been rebuilt were 'absolutely repulsive, being no better than a labyrinth of narrow, crooked, filthy streets, a chaos of habitations gloomy and dismal to the eye'. There was even some criticism that Pombal's 'grand designs' had been compromised by the 'total inadequateness of the means to do them justice', that, as was said of London after the Great Fire, 'the opportunity was lost of erecting one of the most beautiful cities in the world';[20] and Murray's *Handbook* warned that the visitor had to be 'prepared for the worst accommodation, the worst food, and the greatest fatigue, and he must not expect much that can interest in the way of architecture, ecclesiology, or the fine arts'.[21] But many similar allegations, unbeknownst to most Portuguese who took them personally, were aired by visitors to any foreign city. Lisbon received more plaudits than most, and even those who agreed with the criticisms would not have disputed that the view from the spot where Richard Goddard had watched the city collapse and burn in 1755 was 'a picture indescribably grand' and, for some, one that was 'unrivalled'.[22]

There were still ruins here and there in the city (and all along the Algarve). To the east of the castle, the church of Santa Engrácia in the Campo Santa Clara still lacked its dome and would not be completed for another century – by which time the phrase *obras de Santa Engrácia* had become synonymous with projects destined never to be completed. Most conspicuous of all was the sight of the ruins of the Carmo's great arches, overlooking the Baixa.

This great convent and church complex remained, in the words of an English visitor, 'in the picturesque state in which the wreck and the wreckers had left it'. One 'abortive attempt' had been made to restore it but all that had been achieved was the moving of some of the rubble from the interior onto the street, therby creating a new street level well above that of the church. The Guarda Municipal occupied the cloisters, and a chemist had erected a wooden hut as his laboratory in the church (next to some stabling for mules). Such ruins provided a constant reminder of that terrible day in 1755 and imbued the city with 'an air of desolation' which the same visitor described as '[appealing]' strongly to the feelings'. He could never pass any of them unmoved'.[23]

This visitor was not alone. Dickens also noticed that, despite all the apparent colour and exuberance on display in Lisbon, and despite the ebullient street life, 'the common people' seldom laughed; and Thackeray detected an atmosphere of 'human minds [heaving] a sigh for the glories of by-gone days'.[24] Since the 1820s there had also been a new sound on the streets after dark, particularly in the twisting lanes of Alfama and Mouraria: the sound of *fado* being sung. Its exact origins were fiercely debated; what it sought to express was not. *Fado* was the sorrowful vocalization of *saudade* – a feeling of longing, of nostalgia, of melancholy, of missing friends and family in far-flung lands – which had become the defining sentiment of this great city.

A century after the quake Lisbon resembled, to one traveller, 'an elderly matron who has seated herself in a garden of roses, where she meditates on her gay youth-time, when all the world contended for her smiles; perhaps, too, gives a thought to her children, who, far away from her, have established homes for themselves beyond the ocean, leaving the parent lonely and deserted'.[25]

'THAT NIGHT, LOOKING FROM THE BRAGANÇA WINDOW at the weltering bay which seemed turned to silver, over which highway I could see away to Belem, the guarded mouth of the Tagus, I beheld the tranquil terraced roofs below, quiet in the moonlight; for the wilful Mohammedan moon was in her crescent, and I could almost imagine myself in the old Moorish city. As I looked, I fell into a reverie in my chair in the Bragança balcony. Napier's *Peninsular War* dropping from my hand, I imagine myself, that November morning, on that safe roof-top watching that tranquil city. Suddenly, the houses all around me began to roll and tremble like a stormy sea. Through an eclipse dimness I saw the buildings round my feet and far away on every side, gape and split; the floors fell with the shake of cannons. The groans and cries of a great battle were round me. I could hear the sea dashing on the quays, and rising to swallow what the earthquake had left. Through the air, dark with falling walls and beams, amid showers of stones red with the billows of fire from sudden conflagrations, I saw the cloudy streets strewn with the dead and dying; screaming crowds, running thickly, hither and thither, like sheep when the doors of the red slaughter-house are closed.'

Charles Dickens, Household Words, 25 December 1858, p. 89

Notes

INTRODUCTION
Earthquake? What Earthquake?

1 Murray, p. 5

2 Reid, p. 80

3 'RDO', 'Recent Earthquakes' in *Geographical Journal*, Vol.27, No.6 (June 1906), p. 616

4 Boxer, 'Some Contemporary Reactions To The Lisbon Earthquake of 1755', p. 5

5 Baptista et al, p. 144

6 Chester, p. 363

7 Zebrowski, Ernest Jnr, *Perils of a Restless Planet* (CUP, 1999), p. 1

8 Gould, p. 402

9 Boxer, op. cit., p. 5

10 Téllez Alarcia, Diego, 'Spanish Interpretations of the Lisbon Earthquake, 1755-62', in Braun and Radner, p. 52

11 The title of Dynes, Russell, 'The Lisbon Earthquake of 1755: the first modern disaster', in Braun and Radner, pp. 34–49

12 Neimann, Susan, *Evil In Modern Thought: An Alternative History of Philosophy* (Princeton University Press, 2002), p. 1

13 Davison, *Great Earthquakes*, p. 3

14 See, for example, Wiesner-Hanks, Merry E., *Early Modern Europe, 1450–1789* (CUP, 2006); Marshall, P.J. (ed.), *The Eighteenth Century* (OUP, 1998); Outram, Dorinda, *The Enlightenment* (CUP, 2005); Claydon, Tony, *Europe and the Making of England, 1660–1760* (CUP, 2007); Schaich, Michael (ed.), *Monarchy and Religion: The Transformation of Royal Culture in Eighteenth Century Europe* (German Historical Institute (OUP, 2007); Lees, Andrew and Hollen Lees, Lynn, *Cities and the Making of Modern Europe, 1750–1914* (CUP, 2007). The author's remark is in no way intended as a judgement on the merits of these works.

15 Gattrell, Vic, *City of Laughter* (Atlantic Books, 2006), p. 204: 'After the shock delivered in 1751 by the divine judgement on Lisbon, when that city was demolished by earthquake . . .'.

16 Pessoa, Fernando *O Que O Turista Deve Ver* ('What The Tourist Should See'). In similar vein, the introduction to the papers of a symposium on the Lisbon earthquake held at the 2005 annual meeting of the Academia Europaea has the earthquake occurring on a Sunday rather than a Saturday (see *European Review*, Vol.14, No.2 (May 2006), p. 167); and G.W. Housner in his article 'Historical View Of Earthquake Engineering' in Lee, William H.K. et al. (eds), *International Handbook of Earthquake and Engineering Seismology* (Academic Press, 2002) refers on p. 15 to the 'famous 1775 Lisbon earthquake' (Livros Horizonte, Lisbon, 1997), p. 10

ONE
Quem nunca viu Lisboa não viu coisa boa:
He who has not seen Lisbon has seen nothing

1 Hervey, Letter 4, 6 January 1758

2 Murphy, *Travels in Portugal in the years 1789 and 1790*, p. 213

3 Young, p. 23

4 Montagu, John (Earl of Sandwich), *A Voyage performed by the late Earl of Sandwich round the Mediterranean in the years 1738 and 1739* (London, 1799), p. 520

5 'Scots Gentleman', pp. 560–63

6 Anon., *Explication de l'estampe de Lisbonne*, p. 25

7 Black, 'Portugal in 1730 by the Reverend John Swinton', p. 72 (and with thanks to the Warden and Fellows of Wadham College, Oxford)

8 'MP', p. 1

9 Anon., *Description de la ville de Lisbonne*, p. 6

10 Baretti, Letter XVI, 29 August 1760

11 'Scots Gentleman', pp. 560–63

12 Rhys, p. 237

13 Boxer, *The Portuguese Seaborne Empire*, p. 189

14 MS/Pitt (i)

15 APDG, p. 189

16 APDG, p. 190

17 Rhys, p. 219

18 Black, op. cit., p. 78

19 Sequeira, 'A Cidade de D. João V', p. 59

20 'Scots Gentleman', pp. 560–63

21 MS/Pitt (i)

22 Cheke, p. 13

23 'Scots Gentleman', pp. 550–63

24 APDG, p. 43

25 Black, 'Lisbon in 1730: The Account of a British Traveller', p. 11

TWO At the Court of King John

1 TNA/SP/89/37: Tyrawley to Duke of Newcastle, 22 September 1730

2 Merveilleux, p. 41

3 TNA/SP/89/48: Castres to Holdernesse, 3 July 1751

4 Courtils, p. 154

5 Villiers, p. 70

6 The title of Chapter 8 in Delaforce, Angela, *Art and Patronage in Eighteenth Century Portugal* (CUP, 2002): The Court of Dom José and the New Lisbon: Grandeur and Vanity

7 Murphy, *Travels in Portugal in the years 1789 and 1790*, p. 177

8 TNA/SP/89/37: Tyrawley to Duke of Newcastle, 12 November 1730

9 TNA/SP/89/48: Castres to Holdernesse, 3 July 1751

10 'Costigan', p. 384

11 Boxer, 'Lord Tyrawley in Lisbon: An Anglo-Irish Protestant at the Portuguese Court 1728–41', p. 794

12 Whitefield, *A Brief Account of some Lent and other extraordinary processions . . . seen last year at Lisbon*, Letters 1 and 2, March 1754

13 Ibid., Letters 1 and 2, March 1754

14 Cormatin, p. 85 and p. 87

15 Villiers (thesis), p. 155

16 Mercator

17 Dumouriez, *État présent du royaume de Portugal*, p. 21

18 Cormatin, p. 248

19 Pombal letter to Cardeal da Mota, 19 February 1742, quoted in Rodrigues, Lúcia Lima and Craig, Russell, 'English Mercantilist Influences on the Foundation of the Portuguese School of Commerce in 1759', *Atlantic Economic Journal*, Vol. 32, No. 4, (December 2004), p. 336

20 Birmingham, David, 'A World on the Move: The Portuguese in Africa, Asia and America 1415–1808', Book Reviews, *History Today*, Vol. 43 (June 1993), p. 59

21: TNA/SP/89/48: Castres to Holdernesse, 3 July 1751

THREE *Terra Incognita*

1 The Diary of Samuel Pepys, 17 October 1661

2 Markham, C.R., *Journal of the Royal Geographical Society*, Vol. 38 (1868), p. 1

3 Hanson, p. 3

4 Farmer, p. 3

5 Black, 'Portugal in 1730 by the Reverend John Swinton', p. 74

6 Dumouriez, *An Account of Portugal As It Appeared in 1766 to Dumouriez, since a celebrated general in the French army*, pp. 174–5

7 Courtils, p. 155

8 Black, op. cit., p. 80

9 Erskine, p. 76

10 Ibid., pp. 75–7

11 TNA/SP/89/37: Tyrawley to Duke of Newcastle, 11 February 1730

12 Boxer, 'Lord Tyrawley in Lisbon: An Anglo-Irish Protestant at the Portuguese Court 1728–41', pp. 791–8 passim

13 Walpole, Horace, *Memoirs of . . . George II*, (London, 1845), Vol. III, p. 14

14 TNA/SP/89/40: Tyrawley to Duke of Newcastle, 7 January 1741

15 Lewis, W.S. et al (eds), *Horace Walpole's Correspondence with Sir Horace Mann* (OUP, 1967), Walpole to Mann, 1 July 1762

16 Ibid., Walpole to Mann, 15 November 1742;

'singularly licentious, even for the courts of Portugal and Russia' was a footnote in Le Marchant's 1742 edition of Walpole's *Memoirs of . . . George II*, Vol. I, p. 144 n.

17 TNA/SP/89/37: Tyrawley to Duke of Newcastle, 11 May 1733

18 Erskine, p. 121

19 Hanway, Jonas, *Travels of Jonas Hanway, Esq* (Philadelphia, 1797)

20 Review of Smith, John, 'Memoirs of the Marquis of Pombal', in *Monthly Review* (May 1844), p. 6

21 Lodge (ed.), *The Private Correspondence of Sir Benjamin Keene*, p. 72, letter from Keene to Castres, October 1745

22 Lewis et al, op. cit., Walpole to Mann, 4 December 1755, pp. 121–7 *passim*

23 Erskine, pp. 121–7 *passim*

24 Ibid., p. 143 and p. 150

25 *London Gazette*, 2–5 November 1754, quoting a report in the *Gazeta de Lisboa* dated 24 September 1754

26 Erskine, p. 175

27 Leake, p. v

28 Fielding, pp. 16–19 *passim*

29 Ibid., p. 23

30 Ibid., p. 29

31 Ibid., pp. 103–7 *passim*

32 Ibid., p. 9

33 See Battestin and Probyn, Letters 75–77, pp. 109–19 *passim*

34 Fielding, p. 24

FOUR The Gathering Storm

1 TNA/SP/89/50: Hay to Sir Thomas Robinson, 2 April 1755

2 Lodge (ed.), *The Private Correspondence of Sir Benjamine Keene*, p. 402, letter from Keene to Castres, 11 April 1755

3 Erskine, p. 179

4 TNA/SP/89/48: Castres to Amyand, 29 January 1753

5 TNA/SP/89/50: Castres to Sir Thomas Robinson, 12 August 1755

6 Lodge, op.cit., p. 407, letter from Keene to Castres, 22 May 1755

7 TNA/SP/89/48: Castres to Holdernesse, 16 June 1755

8 Ibid., Castres to Holdernesse, 16 June 1755

9 Courtils, p. 124

10 Ibid., pp. 146–61 *passim*

11 Erskine, p. 179

12 Lodge, op. cit., p. 416, letter from Keene to Castres, 7 July 1755

13 TNA/SP/89/48: Castres to Holdernesse, 16 September 1755

14 Erskine, p. 183

15 TNA/SP/89/48: Castres to Holdernesse, 16 September 1755

16 *London Gazette*, 2–6 September 1755, quoting a report in the *Gazeta de Lisboa* of 29 July 1755

17 See for example TNA/SP/89/50: Edward Hay despatch dated 19 May 1755

18 TNA/SP/89/50: Castres to Sir Thomas Robinson, 15 July 1755

19 Ibid., Castres to Sir Thomas Robinson, 22 September 1755

20 Smith, p. 52

21 APDG, p. 27

22 TNA/SP/89/50: Castres to Sir Thomas Robinson, 17 May 1755

23 MS/Farmer, p. 1, p. 46, p. 5, p. 13

24 Nason, p. 12

25 Ibid., p. 57

26 MS/Goddard (ii)

27 MS/Goddard (i)

28 TNA/SP/89/50: Castres to Sir Thomas Robinson, 20 October 1755

FIVE All Saints' Day

1 Philosophical Transactions of the Royal Society (hereafter PT), Vol. 49 (1755–6), p. 414: letter from Mr Stoqueler read 5 February 1756

2 PT, op. cit., p. 410

3 APDG, p. 107

4 MS/Drumlanrig, 6 November 1755

5 Letter dated 19 November 1755, *Gentleman's Magazine*, Vol. XXV (December 1755), p. 560

6 Braddock account

7 Letter dated 3 November 1755 from a merchant on board Captain Minoch's *Swithington*, *The Boston Gazette*, 12 January 1756

8 MS/Goddard (ii)

9 Fowkes account

10 MS/Drumlanrig, 6 November 1755

11 Farmer, p. 3

12 Braddock account

13 PT, op. cit., pp. 410–13: letter from J. Latham, dated 11 December 1755, read 15 January 1756

SIX A City Laid in Ruins

1 TNA/SP/89/50: Edward Hay dispatch, 19 November 1755

2 MS/Farmer, pp. 14–17

3 MS/Goddard (ii)

4 An anonymous French account referred to 'les rues pavés de corps morts et de mourants'. See Guedes, p. 245

5 Braddock account

6 Nozes, p. 222

7 Quoted in Macaulay, pp. 273–4

8 'Another Gentleman', p. 11

SEVEN Shockwaves

1 PT, Vol. 49 (1755–6), pp. 432–4: letter from Thomas Heberden to his brother dated 1 November 1755, read 8 January 1756

2 MS/Bean

3 PT, op. cit., p. 420: letter from Mr Plummer dated 1 November 1755, read 27 November 1755

4 PT, op. cit., p. 423: letter to the Spanish Consul in London dated 3 November 1755, read 27 November 1755

5 Gazeta de Lisboa, 13 November 1755

6 MS/Agnew, letter from a nephew in Cadiz to his uncle, 25 November 1755

7 Bevis, p. 319

8 A letter to the Western Flying Post printed on 17 November 1755 mentioned 'a very sensible shock' at 9.36 a.m. on 1 November. Quoted by Gould, p. 400

9 PT, op. cit., pp. 389–91: letter from Sir James Colquhoun dated 8 December 1755, read 22 January 1756

10 PT, op. cit., pp. 387–9: letter from Robert Gardener to Dr John Stevenson dated 22 December 1755, read 8 January 1756

11 PT, op. cit., pp. 351–3: letter from John Robertson to Thomas Birch dated 23 November 1755, read 27 November 1755

12 PT, op. cit., pp. 381–4: letter from the Reverend John Harrison to the Rt Reverend Dr Edmund Keene dated 24 December 1755, read 15 January 1756

13 PT, op. cit., pp. 385–6: letter from the Reverend Dr Spencer Cowper to the Rt Hon. William Earl Cowper, read 15 January 1756

14 PT, op. cit., p. 381: letter from Thomas Barber to William Arderon dated 26 January 1756, read 19 February 1756

15 PT, op. cit., pp. 362–3: account of Thomas Birch, read 18 December 1755

16 PT, op. cit., p. 361: letter from Henry Mills to Thomas Birch dated 15 December 1755, read 8 January 1756

17 PT, op. cit., pp. 357–8: letter from Swithin Adee, read 27 November 1755

18 PT, op. cit., pp. 398–402 passim: letter from the Reverend William Bullock, read 11 March 1756

19 PT, op. cit., p. 396: letter from M. De Hondt in The Hague dated 7 November 1755, read 20 November 1755

20 PT, op. cit., p. 437: letter from M. De Valltravers, read 22 January 1756

21 Göttingische Gelehrte Anzeigen, 12 January 1756, quoted in Stuber, Martin, 'Divine Punishment or Object of Research? The Resonance of Earthquakes, Floods, Epidemics and Famine in the Correspondence Network of Albrecht von Haller', Environment and History, Vol. 9, No. 2 (2003), p. 178

22 PT, op. cit., pp. 395–6: letter of Father Joseph Steplin dated 30 January 1756, read 26 February 1756

23 The Public Advertiser, No. 6579, 28 November 1755

24 The Pennsylvania Gazette, 18 December 1755

25 Braddock account

26 Bevis, p. 331

27 Ibid., p. 331 ('benacle' = binnacle)

28 PT, op. cit., p. 430: letter from General Fowke to Rt Hon. Henry Fox, read 4 March 1756

29 Solares and Arroyo, p. 275

EIGHT Fire and Water

1 MS/Chase

2 Braddock account

3 Fowkes account

4 MS/Drumlanrig, 6 November 1755

5 Letter of one of Lord Drumlanrig's servants, dated 8 November, reprinted in The Scots Magazine, Vol. xvii (November 1755), p. 591

6 MS/Goddard (i)

7 MS/Chase

8 Letter dated 19 November 1755, Gentleman's Magazine, Vol. XXV (December 1755), p. 561

9 Braddock account

10 Letter dated 19 November 1755, Gentleman's Magazine, op. cit.

11 Braddock account

12 Letter dated 19 November 1755, Gentleman's Magazine, op. cit.

13 See Pereira, E.J., p. 7

14 PT, Vol. 49 (1755–6), pp. 410–13: letter from

J Latham to his uncle, dated 11 December 1755, read 15 January 1756

15 Letter dated 19 November 1755, *Gentleman's Magazine*, op. cit.

NINE Teletsunami

1 For the latest research in this field see Scheffers, Anja and Kelletat, Dieter, 'Tsunami Relics On The Coastal Landscape West of Lisbon in Portugal', in *Science of Tsunami Hazards*, Vol. 23, No. 1 (2005), pp. 3–16. Evidence has been found by the authors indicating that in certain places on this coast the tidal wave run-up reached as much as 50m above sea level.

2 Bevis, p. 318

3 Sousa, p. 77

4 Ibid., p. 12

5 MS/Agnew: letter from a nephew in Cadiz to his uncle, 25 November 1755

6 Hibbert account: *The Boston Gazette*, 22 December 1755

7 PT, Vol. 49 (1755–6), p. 425: letter from Benjamin Bewick to Joseph Paice dated 4 November 1755, read 18 December 1755

8 PT, op. cit., p. 426: letter from Benjamin Bewick to Joseph Paice dated 4 November 1755, read   18 December 1755

9 PT, op. cit., p. 427: letter from Don Antonio d'Ulloa, read 18 December 1755

10 *Whitehall Evening Post*, 1524, 2 December 1755: letter of 4 November 1755

11 PT, op. cit., p. 433: letter from Dr Tho. Heberden to his brother, read 8 January 1756

12 PT, op. cit., p. 435: letter from Charles Chalmers to his father, dated 1 November 1755, read   8 January 1755

13 PT, op. cit., p. 434: letter from Dr Tho. Heberden to his brother, read 8 January 1756

14 PT, op. cit., p. 429: letter from General Fowke to Rt Hon. Henry Fox, read 4 March 1756

15 PT, op. cit., pp. 373–8: letter from William Borlase, read 18 December 1755

16 PT, op. cit., pp. 391–3: letter from Lewis Nicola, read 22 January 1756

17 PT, op. cit., pp. 668–70: Lt Philip Affleck of the *Advice* man-o'-war to Charles Gray, 3 January 1756.

18 Ibid.

19 See Supplement to *Gentleman's Magazine*, 1755

TEN The Second Aftershock

1 MS/Chase

2 MS/Goddard (ii)

3 MS/Drumlanrig, 8 November 1755

4 Fowkes account

5 MS/Farmer, p. 29

6 Nason, p. 67

7 Pedegache, p. 4

8 Braddock account

9 PT, Vol. 49 (1755–6), pp. 402–7: letter from Richard Wolfall to James Parsons dated 18 November 1755, read 18 December 1755

ELEVEN The First Night

1 Braddock account

2 MS/Chase

3 MS/Drumlanrig, 6 November 1755

4 MS/Chase

5 Fowkes account

6 MS/Chase

TWELVE Horroroso Deserto

1 MS/Drumlanrig, 8 November 1755

2 MS/Chase

3 See Birmingham City Archives: Galton Papers MS3101/C/D/15/5/43, letter from James Farmer to Samuel Galton, 2 December 1755

4 MS/Goddard (i), 7 November 1755

5 Delany, pp. 378–9

6 MS/Drumlanrig, 19 November 1755

7 TNA/SP/89/50: Castres to Sir Thomas Robinson, 6 November 1755

8 Account in Chambers's *Edinburgh Journal*, November 1836, p. 323

9 See letter of David de Purry dated 25 December 1755 in Brandt, Fréderic, *Notice sur la vie de Monsieur le Baron David de Purry* (Neuchâtel, 1826), pp. 59–63 *passim*. Purry and Devisme later held a monopoly on, among other things, the import of brazilwood and Purry became a major benefactor of his home town of Neuchâtel.

10 Braddock account

11 Fowkes account

12 *London Gazette*, No. 9533, 29 November–2 December 1755, p. 1

13 TNA/SP/89/50: Castres to Sir Thomas Robinson, 6 November 1755

14 *Boston Gazette*, 4 May 1756

15 Pereira, Ângelo, p. 17

16 TNA/SP/89/50: Castres to Sir Thomas

Robinson, 6 November 1755
17 Ibid.
18 MS/Hay (ii)
19 MS/Williamson
20 Quoted in Mann, p. 43
21 MS/Goddard (i)
22 MS/Drumlanrig, 6 November 1755
23 Cardoso, Arnaldo Pinto, pp. 21–3
24 MS/Chase
25 Clemente, p. 31
26 Ibid., p. 59

THIRTEEN Laws and Disorder

1 Boxer, 'Some Contemporary Reactions To The Lisbon Earthquake of 1755', p. 4
2 TNA/SP/89/50: Castres to Sir Thomas Robinson, 6 November 1755
3 Gentleman's Magazine, Vol. XXV (December 1755), p. 559
4 MS/Drumlanrig, 8 November 1755
5 MS/Chase
6 Account in Chambers's Edinburgh Journal, November 1836, p. 324
7 TNA/SP/89/50: Hay to Sir Thomas Robinson, 15 November 1755
8 Ibid.
9 Ibid., Castres to Sir Thomas Robinson, 19 November 1755
10 Letter dated 3 November 1755 from a merchant on board Captain Minoch's Swithington, The Boston Gazette, 12 January 1756
11 Kendrick, p. 32
12 TNA/SP/89/50: Castres to Sir Thomas Robinson, 20 November 1755
13 Ibid., Castres to Sir Thomas Robinson, 19 November 1755
14 MS/Hay (ii)
15 Lodge (ed.), The Private Correspondence of Sir Benjamin Keene, p. 437, letter from Keene to Castres, 23 November 1755
16 See PT, Vol. 49 (1755–6), pp. 402–7: letter from Richard Wolfall to James Parsons dated 18 November 1755, read 18 December 1755
17 MS/Drumlanrig, 19 November 1755

FOURTEEN News Spreads

1 Lodge (ed.), The Private Correspondence of Sir Benjamin Keene, p. 434, letter from Keene to Castres, 10 November 1755
2 Ibid., p. 435, letter from Keene to Castres, 20 November 1755

3 Goethe, Johann Wolfgang von, Dichtung und Wahrheit, p. 30, in Trunz, Erich, Goethes Werke, Vol. 10, (Beck, Munich 1981)
4 Whitehall Evening Post 1521, 22–25 November 1755
5 Whitehall Evening Post 1522, 25 November 1755
6 Whitehall Evening Post 1523, 27 November 1755
7 Whitehall Evening Post 1524, 29 November–2 December 1755
8 British Library Manuscript Add. 32860 (Newcastle Papers), f. 428: Benjamin Keene despatch 10 November 1755
9 TNA/SP/89/50: Hay to Sir Thomas Robinson, 15 November 1755
10 The Scots Magazine, Vol. XVI (November 1755), p. 554
11 Delany, pp. 378–9
12 Ibid., pp. 378–9. His father-in-law was the prosperous Lisbon merchant Peter Auriol.
13 Whitehall Evening Post 1524, 29 November–2 December 1755
14 Lewis, W.S. et al (eds), Horace Walpole's Correspondence with Sir Horace Mann (OUP, 1967), Walpole to Mann, 4 December 1755
15 Delany, pp. 378–9
16 Journal of the Reverend Charles Wesley, 1849, entry for 5 April 1750
17 Macaulay, Thomas Babington, Critical and Historical Essays, Vol. II (London, 1907), p. 551
18 TNA/SP/89/50: Fox to Castres, 3 December 1755
19 Baretti, Letter XVI, 29 August 1760
20 TNA/SP/89/50: Fox to Castres, 3 December 1755
21 Delany, p. 380
22 Lewis, op. cit., Walpole to Mann, 4 December 1755
23 Erskine, pp. 189–90.
24 Boston Weekly News, 20 November 1755
25 PT, Vol. 50 (1757–8), 'An Account of the Earthquake Felt in New England, and the Neighbouring Parts of America, on the 18th November 1755'. In a letter to Thomas Birch from Professor Winthrop of Cambridge in New England dated 10 January 1756, pp. 1–18

FIFTEEN Aid and Anxiety

1 MS/Dobson (i)
2 TNA/SP/89/50: Hay to Fox, 11 December 1755
3 Ibid.

4 Lodge (ed.), *The Private Correspondence of Sir Benjamin Keene*, pp. 443–4, letter from Keene to Castres, 19 November 1755

5 Ibid.

6 TNA/SP/89/50, Castres despatches of 24/12 and 30/12

7 Lodge, op. cit., p. 434, letter from Keene to Castres, 10 November 1755

8 PT, Vol. 49 (1755–6), p. 429: letter from General Fowke to Rt Hon. Henry Fox, read 4 March 1756

9 PT, op. cit., p. 437: letter from M. De Valltravers, read 22 January 1756

10 Horace Walpole to George Montagu, 25 November 1755 (Project Gutenberg: *The Letters of Horace Walpole*, letter 162)

11 'MP', pp. 1–2

12 Lodge, op. cit., p. 434, letter from Keene to Castres, 19 December 1755

13 *Notes and Queries*, 28 August 1928, p. 86

14 Smollett, Tobias, *Complete History of England* (Oxford, 1827), pp. 421–2

15 *An Address To The Inhabitants Of Great-Britain; Occasioned By The Late Earthquake at Lisbon*, p. 6

16 Whitefield, *A Letter to The Remaining Disconsolate Inhabitants of Lisbon*, p. 3

17 *An old remedy new reviv'd; or an infallible method to prevent this city from sharing the calamities of Lisbon*, pp. 1–4 passim

18 *Lisbon's Voice to England, particularly to London*, 1755, attributed to Samuel Hayward, Congregational Minister at Silver Street, Cheapside, p. 2, p. 8   and p. 4

19 'MP', p. 2

20 *Lisbon's Voice to England, particularly to London*, p. 2, p. 8 and p. 4

21 Wesley, John, *Serious Thoughts Occasioned by the Late Earthquake at Lisbon* (1755), passim

22 James Bate, *The Practical Use of Public Judgements. A Sermon preached at St Paul's Deptford, Kent, on February 6th, 1756*, p. 4

23 See Kendrick, p. 148

24 See ibid., p. 147

25 Quoted in Macaulay, p. 271

SIXTEEN The Toll

1 *New Universal Magazine*, No. LVIII, Vol. VIII (December 1755), p. 235

2 Lodge (ed.), *The Private Correspondence of Sir Benjamin Keene*, p. 434, letter from Keene to Castres, 19 December 1755

3 For example in Fr Francisco António de S.

Joze, *Canto funebre ou lamentção harmonica na infeliz destruição da famosa cidade de Lisboa* (1756)

4 See, for example, *Destruição de Lisboa e famosa desgraça que padeceo no dia primeira de Novembro de 1755* (Anon, Lisbon, 1756). *Desgraça* can mean misfortune or disgrace.

5 The parish registers of Beato, São João de Praça, Santa Maria Madalena, Martíres, São Julião, São Nicolau and São Paulo all perished according to *A Freguesia de Santa Catarina de Lisboa no 1° quartel do século XVIII* (Instituto Nacional de Estatística, Lisbon, 1959); and the many parishes around the country did not answer the question about the number of deaths.

6 TNA/SP/89/50: Castres despatch, 27 December 1755

7 Oliveira, p. 153

8 Dickens, Charles, article in *Household Words*, 25 December 1858

9 Murray, p. 6

SEVENTEEN
Rain, Ruination and Revolution

1 Cormatin, p. 155

2 Fonseca, p. 122, quoting Montessus de Balore

3 TNA/ADM/51/429, 16 March 1756

4 Nozes, p. 224

5 Tyrawley's 'Considerations upon the affaires of Lisbon in December 1755', British Library Manuscript Add. 26364, f. 140

6 TNA/SP/89/50: Hay to Fox, 14 January and 11 February 1756

7 Edward French to William Wansey, 19 November 1755, quoted in Mann, p. 44

8 Quoted in Mann, p. 35

9 MS/Bean

10 For example João Lúcio de Azevedo in his *O Marquês de Pombal e a sua Época* (Clássica Editora, Lisbon, 1909)

11 Quoted in Pereira, Ângelo

12 Pereira, Álvaro S., p. 15

13 See Cardoso, José Luís, *Pombal, O Terramoto E A Política De Regulação Económica*

14 *New Universal Magazine*, No. LVIII, Vol. VIII (December 1755), extract of letter dated 17 November 1755, p. 234

15 Solares and Arroyo, p. 279

16 Lodge (ed.), *The Private Correspondence of Sir Benjamin Keene*, p. 436, letter from Keene to Castres, 20 November 1755

17 Edward French to William Wansey, 19

November 1755, quoted in Mann, p. 45

18 TNA/SP/89/50: Hay to Fox, 8 May 1756

19 Whitefoord, p. 126

20 Goudar, *passim*

21 TNA/SP/89/50: Castres to Fox, 11 February 1756

22 Ibid., Castres to Fox, 8 May 1756

23 Whitefoord, pp. 126–9

EIGHTEEN **Fasting and Philosophy**

1 Anon, 'A Sermon preached before a congregation on the general fast-day delivered in two parts', pp. 7–8

2 Ibid., p. 11

3 T. Seward, Canon of Lichfield, 'The late dreadful earthquakes no proof of God's particular wrath against the Portuguese', sermon preached at Lichfield, 7 December 1755

4 Richard Terrick, Canon Residential of St Paul's, sermon preached to the House of Commons on   6 February 1756, p. 17

5 Oliveira, Francisco, pp. 9–18 *passim*

6 Shklar, J.N., *The Faces of Injustice* (Yale University Press, 1990), pp. 51–5.

7 Pope, Alexander, *An Essay on Man* (1733–4), l. 294

8 Besterman, p. 12

9 Voltaire to Jean-Robert Tonchin, 24 November 1755 in Besterman, Theodore, *Voltaire's Correspondence* (Publications de l'Institut et Musée Voltaire, Genéva, 1953–65), Vol. XXVIII

10 Voltaire in Besterman, op. cit.

11 Voltaire, p. 97

12 Ibid., p. 99

13 Voltaire to Élie Bertrand, 18 February 1756, in Besterman, op. cit.

14 Voltaire, p. 108

15 Ibid., p. 99

16 Rousseau to Voltaire, 18 August 1756, in Besterman, op. cit.

17 Voltaire to Rousseau, 12 September 1756, in Besterman, op. cit.

18 Voltaire, p.100, translation by Tobias Smollett

NINETEEN **Executions**

1 Hervey, Letter 2, 30 December 1758

2 Letter from The Reverend W. Allen to his friend Mr Thicknesse, High Master of St Paul's, written soon after the earthquake and printed in *Gentleman's Magazine*, Vol. 59

(September 1789), pp. 788–9

3 Hervey, Letter 4, 6 January 1759

4 Hervey, Letter 9, 30 January 1759

5 Hervey, Letter 3, 31 December 1758, and Letter 4, 6 January 1759

6 Hughes, p. 2. *Gentleman's Magazine* suggested that Hughes's account was 'fictitious' (Vol. XXIX, 1759, p. 76), but this can only have been because Hughes was not peddling the official version of events

7 There are excellent discussions about the conspiracy in Dutra, Francis A., 'The Wounding of King José I – Accident or Assassination Attempt?', *Mediterranean Studies*, Vol. 7 (1998), pp. 221–9, and Donovan, Bill M., 'Crime, Policing, and the Absolutist State in Early Modern Lisbon', *Portuguese Studies Review*, Vol. 5, No. 2 (1996–7), pp. 52–71

8 TNA/SP/89/51: Hay to W. Pitt, 13 September 1758

9 Cheke, p. 114

10 Hughes, p. 6

11 MS/Farmer, p. 28

12 Hervey, Letter 4, 6 January 1759

13 MS/Farmer, p. 29

14 MS/Farmer, p. 31

15 *Gentleman's Magazine*, Vol. XXIX (1759), p. 324

TWENTY
The End of Optimism, the Birth of a Science

1 Voltaire, p. 69

2 Ibid., p. xii

3 Ibid., p. 51

4 Ibid., p. 14

5 Ibid., p. 15

6 Ibid., p. 16

7 Besterman, p. 23

8 In 1735 Samuel Johnson had translated Jerónimo Lobo's *Itinerário* as *A Voyage To Abyssinia*

9 Dalrymple, Theodore, 'What Makes Dr Johnson Great', City Journal (Autumn 2006)

10 PT, Vol. 46 (1749–50), pp. 745–6

11 Winthrop, John, *An Account of the earthquake felt in New England, and the neighbouring parts of America*. PT, Vol. 50, Part 1 (1757), pp. 1–18

12 See Clark, p. 352

13 Michell, pp. 37–8; also printed in PT, Vol. 51, Part II (1760), pp. 566–634

14 Michell, pp. 24–5

15 Davison, *Great Earthquakes*, p. 3

TWENTY-ONE
Slow Progress, Slump and a Reign of Terror

1 Baretti, Letters XVI (29 August 1760) – XXXI (15 September 1760) *passim*

2 MS/Pitt (i) *passim*

3 Baretti, Letter XXXI, 15 September 1760

4 PT, Vol. 52 (1761–2), pp. 422–3

5 Ibid., p. 421

6 John Webber to Charles Lyttleton, Dean of Exeter, 2 April 1761, British Library Manuscripts, Stow 754, f. 87

7 Voltaire, p. 124, n. 1

8 MS/Hobart

TWENTY-TWO The End of Pombal

1 Smith, p. 187

2 Twiss, pp. 3–4

3 Cormatin, p. 34

4 Ibid., p. 28

5 Ibid., p. 30

6 Black, 'Portugal in 1775. The Letters of Thomas Pelham', p. 53

7 Blankett/Stephens, p. 57

8 Cormatin, p. 138

9 Boxer, *The Portuguese Seaborne Empire 1415–1825*, p. 366

10 See França, José-Augusto 'Uma Experiência Pombalina', in *Monumentos: revista semestral de edifícios e monumentos* 21 (2004), p. 18

11 Murphy, *Travels in Portugal in the years 1789 and 1790*, p. 159

12 Ibid., pp. 131–2

13 Ibid., p. 146

14 Ibid., p. 147

15 Ibid., p. 151

16 Ibid., pp. 169–70

17 Sequeira, 'A Cidade de D. João V', p. 86

18 Murphy, p. 195

19 Ibid., p. 149

20 Ibid., p. 201

21 Ibid., p. 206

22 Ibid., p. 210

23 Ibid., p. 208

24 Murphy, *A general view of the state of Portugal*, p. 142

25 Murphy, *Travels in Portugal in the years 1789 and 1790*, p. 151

26 Ibid., p. 216

27 Ibid., p. 219

TWENTY-THREE
Memories and Memorials

1 *The Penny Magazine*, June 1842, p. 237. Not every detail was remembered correctly – the author of the article dated the earthquake to 1750.

2 *Illustrated London News*, 30 March 1850, p. 222

3 Timbs, John, *Curiosities of London* (1857)

4 Yates, Edmund, *His Recollections and Experiences* (1885), see chapter on 1847–52

5 *Illustrated London News*, 30 March 1850, p. 222

6 Yates, op. cit., see chapter on 1847–52

7 Murray, John, *Handbook For Travellers In Portugal*, p. 5

8 Murray, John, *Hints to Travellers in Portugal In Search Of The Beautiful and The Grand* (1852), p. 2

9 Murray, p. xxii. Even the well-informed Murray referred in the *Handbook* to the earthquake having taken place on 14 August 1755

10 Murray, p. 4

11 See article by Dickens in *Household Words*, 25 December 1858, pp. 84–9

12 See the feature on Lisbon in *The Penny Magazine*, 22 July 1837, pp. 273–5, and 29 July 1837, pp. 285–6

13 Ibid.

14 Thackeray, William Makepeace, *Notes of a Journey from Cornhill to Grand Cairo, by way of Lisbon, Athens, Constantinople and Jerusalem* (Chapman & Hall, 1846), pp. 10–15 *passim*. Thackeray confused the Palácio da Ajuda and Palácio das Necessidades

15 *The Penny Magazine*, op. cit.

16 Dickens, op. cit.

17 *The Penny Magazine*, op. cit.

18 In 1934, long after the Passeio Público's transformation into the Avenida da Liberdade, a 30-foot-high statue of Pombal on a column 118 feet high was completed looking out imperiously over the Baixa that he had created.

19 Anon, *The Stranger's Guide*, pp. 125, 130

20 *The Penny Magazine*, op. cit.

21 Murray, p. xxxv

22 *The Penny Magazine*, op. cit.

23 Owen, Hugh, *Here and There in Portugal* (London, 1856), pp. 68–71 *passim*

24 Thackeray, op. cit., p. 11

25 *The Penny Magazine*, op. cit.

Bibliography

BOOKS AND ARTICLES

'Amador Patricio de Lisboa' (pseud. Padre Francisco José Freire), *Memorias das Principaes Providencias que se derão no Terremoto, que Padeceo a Côrte de Lisboa no anno de 1755* (Lisbon, 1758)

Anon, *Description de la ville de Lisbonne* (Paris, 1730)

Anon, *Destruição de Lisboa e famosa desgraça que padeceo no dia primeira de Novembro de 1755* (Lisbon, 1756)

Anon, *Explication de l'estampe de Lisbonne avec une description succincte des curiosités et événements mémorables de cette ville* (c. 1735)

Anon, *A Genuine Account Of The Execution Of The Conspirators At Lisbon on January 13th 1759* (London, 1759)

Anon, *A Picture of Lisbon by a gentleman many years resident at Lisbon* (London, 1809)

Anon, *The Stranger's Guide In Lisbon and its Environs* (Lisbon, 1848)

'Another Gentleman', *Two very circumstantial accounts of the late dreadful earthquake at Lisbon: giving a more particular relation of that event than any hitherto publish'd. The first drawn up by Mr Farmer, a merchant, of undoubted veracity . . . the second by another gentleman* (Exeter, 1755)

APDG, *Sketches of Portuguese Life, Manners, Costume, and Character* (London, 1826)

Araújo, Ana Cristina, 'The Lisbon Earthquake of 1755 – Public Distress and Political Propaganda', *e-JPH*, Vol. 4, No. 1 (Summer 2006)

Araújo, Ana Cristina, *O Terramoto De 1755: Lisboa E A Europa* (CTT Correios de Portugal, Lisbon, 2005)

Araújo, Ana Cristina; Cardoso, José Luís; Monteiro, Nuno Gonçalo; Rossa, Walter and Serrão, José Vicente, *O Terramoto De 1755: Impactos Históricos* (Livros Horizonte, Lisbon, 2007)

Baptista, M.A.; Miranda, J.M. and Luis, J.F., 'In Search of the 31 March Earthquake and Tsunami Source', *The Bulletin of the Seismological Society of America*, Vol. 96, No. 2 (April 2006), pp. 713–21

Baptista, M.A. et al., 'The 1755 Lisbon Tsunami: evaluation of the Tsunami Parameters', *Journal of Geodynamics*, Vol. 25, No. 2 (1998), pp. 143–57

Baretti, Giuseppe, *A Journey From London To Genoa*, (London, 1770)

Battestin, Martin and Probyn, Clive (eds), *The Correspondence of Henry and Sarah Fielding*, (Clarendon Press, 1993)

Belo, André, 'Between History and Periodicity: Printed and Hand-Written News in 18th-Century Portugal', *e-JPH*, Vol. 2, No. 2 (Winter 2004)

Belo, André, 'A Gazeta de Lisboa e o terramoto de 1755: a margem do não escrito', *Análise Social*, No. 151–2, Vol. XXXIV (Winter 2000), pp. 619–36

Besterman, Theodore, 'Voltaire et le désastre de Lisbonne: ou, La mort de l'optimisme', *Studies on Voltaire and the Eighteenth Century*, Vol. 2 (1956), pp. 7–24

Bethencourt, Francisco and Curto, Diogo Ramada (eds), *Portuguese Oceanic Expansion, 1400–1800* (CUP, 2007)

Bevis, John, *The History and Philosophy of Earthquakes, from the Remotest to the Present Times* (London, 1757)

Birmingham, David, *A Concise History of Portugal* (CUP, 2003)

Black, Jeremy, 'Anglo-Portuguese Relations in the Eighteenth Century: A Reassessment', *The British Historical Society of Portugal Fourteenth Annual Report* (1987), pp. 125–42

Black, Jeremy, 'Lisbon in 1730: The Account of a British Traveller', *Bulletin of the British Society for Eighteenth Century Studies*, Nos. 7–8 (Spring/Summer 1985), pp. 11–14

Black, Jeremy, 'Portugal in 1730 by the Reverend John Swinton', *The British Historical Society of Portugal Thirteenth Annual Report* (1986), pp. 65–87

Black, Jeremy, 'Portugal in 1775. The Letters of Thomas Pelham', *The British Historical Society of Portugal Fourteenth Annual Report* (1987), pp. 49–56

Blankett, John (also attrib. Stephens, Philadelphia), *Letters from Portugal, on the late and present state of that kingdom* (London, 1777)

Boiça, Joaquim and Barros, Maria de Fátima Rombouts de, *1755: A Memória das Palavras* (Edição da Câmara de Oeiras, 2005)

Boxer, C.R., 'Brazilian Gold and British Traders in the First Half of the Eighteenth Century', *Hispanic American Historical Review*, Vol. 49, No. 3 (August 1969), pp. 454–72

Boxer, C.R., 'Lord Tyrawley in Lisbon: An Anglo-Irish Protestant at the Portuguese Court 1728–41', *History Today*, Vol. 20 (November 1970), pp. 791–8

Boxer, C.R., *The Portuguese Seaborne Empire 1415–1825* (Hutchinson, 1977)

Boxer, C.R., 'Some Contemporary Reactions to the Lisbon Earthquake of 1755', *Separata da Faculdade de Letras, Universidade de Lisboa*, Vol. XXII, 2nd Series, No. 2 (1956)

Braddock, A., 'Letter to Revd. Dr. George Sandby dated 13th November 1755', in Davy, Charles, *Letters addressed chiefly to a young gentleman upon subjects of literature*, Vol. II (London, 1787), pp. 12–60

Braun, Theodore E.D., and Radner, John B. (eds), *The Lisbon Earthquake of 1755: Representations and Reactions* (The Voltaire Foundation, Oxford, 2005)

Brockwell, Charles, *The Natural and Political History of Portugal* (London, 1726)

Brown, Bahngrell W., 'The Quake That Shook Christendom – Lisbon 1755', *The Southern Quarterly*, Vol. VII (July 1969), No. 4, pp. 425–31

Buescu, Helena Carvalhão et al (eds), *1755: Catástrofe, Memória e Arte*, ACT 14, (Centro de Estudos Comparatistas, Edições Colibri, Lisbon, 2006)

Buescu, Helena Carvalhão and Cordeiro, Gonçalo (eds), *O Grande Terramoto De Lisboa: Ficar Diferente* (Gradiva, Lisboa, 2005)

Cardoso, Arnaldo Pinto (ed.), *O Terrível Terramoto Da Cidade Que Foi Lisboa: Correspondência do Núncio Filippo Acciaiuoli* (Alêtheia Editores, Lisboa, 2005)

Cardoso, José Luís, *Pombal, O Terramoto E A Política De Regulação Económica*, in Araújo et al., pp. 165–81

Carozzi, Marguerite, 'Reaction of the British Colonies In America To The 1755 Lisbon Earthquake', *Earth Sciences History*, Vol. 2, Part 1 (1983), pp. 17–27

Castilho, Julio de, *A Ribeira de Lisboa* (Câmara Municipal de Lisboa, Lisbon, 1940–44)

Castinel, G., 'Le Désastre de Lisbonne', *Revue du dix-huitième siècle*, Année 1, No. 4 (1913), pp. 396–409 and Année 2, No. 1 (1914), pp. 72–92

Castro, João Baptista de, *Mappa de Portugal antigo e moderno* (Lisbon, 1763)

Chaves, Castelo Branco, *O Portugal de D João V visto por três forasteiros* (Biblioteca Nacional, Lisbon, 1983)

Cheke, Marcus, *Dictator of Portugal: A life of the Marquis of Pombal 1699–1782* (Sidgwick & Jackson, 1938)

Chester, D.K., 'The 1755 Lisbon Earthquake', *Progress in Physical Geography*, Vol. 25, No. 3 (2001), pp. 363–83

'Citizen', *An old remedy new reviv'd: or, an infallible method to prevent this city from sharing in the calamities of Lisbon* (London, 1755)

Clark, Charles Edwin, 'Science, Reason, And

An Angry God: The Literature Of An Earthquake', *The New England Quarterly*, Vol. 38, No. 3 (September 1965), pp. 340–62

Clemente, D. Manuel (preface), *Memórias De Uma Cidade Destruída: Testemunhos Das Igrejas Da Baixa-Chiado* (Alêtheia Editores, Lisbon, 2005)

Conceição, Fr Claudio da, *Gabinete Historico*, Vol. XIII (Lisbon, 1829)

Cormatin, Pierre Desoteux de, *Travels of the Duke de Châtelet in Portugal* (London, 1809)

'Costigan, Arthur' (pseud. Ferrier, James), *Sketches of Society and Manners in Portugal*, Vol. II (London 1787)

Courtils, Charles-Christian, Chevalier des (Aman, Jacques ed.), 'Une description de Lisbonne en Juin de 1755, *Bulletin des Études Portugaises*, L'Institut Français au Portugal, Vol. XXVI (1965), pp. 145–80

Davison, Charles, *The Founders of Seismology* (CUP, 1927)

Davison, Charles, *Great Earthquakes* (Thomas Murby, 1936)

Delaforce, Angela, *Art and Patronage in Eighteenth-Century Portugal* (CUP, 2002)

Delaforce, Angela, 'Paul Crespin's Silver-Gilt Bath for the King of Portugal', *The Burlington Magazine*, Vol. 139, No. 1126 (January 1997), pp. 38–40

Delany, Mary, *The Autobiography and Correspondence of Mary Granville, Mrs Delany*, Vol. III (Richard Bentley, 1862)

Donovan, Bill M., 'Crime, Policing, and the Absolutist State in Early Modern Lisbon', *Portuguese Studies Review*, Vol. 5, No. 2 (1996–7), pp. 52–71

Dumouriez, Charles-François, *État présent du royaume de Portugal* (Lausanne, 1775)

Dumouriez, Charles-François, *An Account of Portugal As It Appeared in 1766 to Dumouriez, since a celebrated general in the French army* (London, 1797)

Dutra, Francis A., 'The Wounding of King José I – Accident or Assassination Attempt?', *Mediterranean Studies*, Vol. 7 (1998), pp. 221–9

Dynes, Russell, 'The Dialogue between Voltaire and Rousseau on the Lisbon earthquake: The Emergence of a Social Science View', *International Journal of Mass Emergencies and Disasters*, Vol. 18, No. 1 (March 2000), pp. 97–115

Dynes, Russell, 'The Lisbon Earthquake of 1755: the first modern disaster', in Braun and Radner, pp. 34–49

Erskine, David (ed.), *Augustus Hervey's Journal* (Chatham Publishing, 2002)

Estorninho, Carlos, 'O Terramoto de 1755 e a sua repercussão nas relações Luso-Britânicas', *Separata da Faculdade de Letras, Universidade de Lisboa*, Vol. XXII, 2nd Series, No. 1 (1956)

Farmer, Benjamin, *Two very circumstantial accounts of the late dreadful earthquake at Lisbon: giving a more particular relation of that event than any hitherto publish'd. The first drawn up by Mr Farmer, a merchant, of undoubted veracity . . . the second by another gentleman* (Exeter, 1755)

Ferro, João Pedro, *A População Portuguesa no Final do Antigo Regime (1750–1815)* (Editorial Presença, Lisbon, 1995)

Fielding, Henry (ed. Keymer, Tom), *The Journal of a Voyage to Lisbon* (Penguin, 1996)

Figueiredo, António Pereira de, *Diário dos Sucessos de Lisboa, desde o Terramoto até o Extermínio dos Jezuítas* (Lisbon, 1761)

Figueiredo, António Pereira de, *A narrative of the earthquake and fire of Lisbon* (London, 1756)

Fisher, H.E.S., 'Anglo-Portuguese Trade', *Economic History Review*, Vol. 16, No. 2 (1963), pp. 219–33

Fisher, H.E.S., *The Portugal Trade: A Study of Anglo-Portuguese Commerce, 1700–1770* (Methuen, 1971)

Fisher, Stephen *Lisbon As A Port Town* (Exeter Maritime Studies No. 2, 1988)

Fonseca, João Duarte, *1755: O terramoto de Lisboa* (Argumentum, Lisbon, 2005)

Fowkes, Lawrence, *A Genuine Letter to Mr Joseph Fowkes, from his brother near Lisbon, in which is given a very minute and striking description of the late earthquake* (London, 1755)

França, José-Augusto, *Une Ville des Lumières: La Lisbonne de Pombal* (Fondation Calouste Gulbenkian, Paris, 1988)

Francis, A.D., *Portugal 1715–1808: Joanine, Pombaline and Rococo Portugal As Seen By British Diplomats and Traders* (Tamesis Books, 1985)

Goudar, Ange, *Relation historique du tremblement de terre survenu à Lisbonne le premier Novembre 1755* (The Hague, 1756)

Gould, Peter, 'Lisbon 1755: Enlightenment,

Catastrophe, and Communication', in Livingstone, David N. and Withers, Charles W.J. (eds), *Geography and Enlightenment* (The University of Chicago Press, 1999), pp. 399–411

Grey, Zachary, *A farther account of memorable earthquakes to the present year 1756 wherein is inserted a short and faithful relation of the late dreadful calamity at Lisbon. By a Gentleman of the University of Cambridge* (Cambridge, 1756)

Grey, Zachary ('Ingenious Gentleman'), *The General Theory and Phaenomena of Earthquakes and Volcanoes* (London, 1756)

Guedes, Fernando, *O Livro E A Leitura* (Editorial Verbo, Lisbon, 1987)

D'Haen, Theo, 'On How Not to be Lisbon if you want to be modern – Dutch reactions to the Lisbon earthquake', *European Review*, Vol. 14, No. 3 (2006), pp. 351–8

Hanson, Carl A., *Economy and Society in Baroque Portugal, 1668–1703* (Macmillan, 1981)

Hayward, Samuel (attrib.), *Lisbon's voice to England, particularly London* (London, 1755)

Henriques, Paolo, *Lisbonne avant le tremblement de terre de 1755* (Chandeigne-gotica, Paris, 2004)

Hervey, Christopher, *Letters from Portugal, Spain, Italy and Germany, in the years 1759, 1760, and 1761* (London, 1785)

Hufton, Olwen, *Europe: Privilege and Protest 1730–1789* (Blackwell, 2000)

Hughes, Joseph, *An authentick letter from Mr Hughes, a gentleman residing at Lisbon, to his friends in London; containing several curious and interesting particulars in relation to the late conspiracy against the King of Portugal* (London, 1759)

Ingram, Robert G., 'The trembling Earth is God's Herald: earthquakes, religion and public life in Britain during the 1750s', in Braun and Radner (eds), pp. 97–115

Justo, J.L. and Salwa, C., 'The 1531 Lisbon Earthquake', *Bulletin of the Seismological Society of America*, Vol. 88, No. 2 (April 1988), pp. 319–28

Kendrick, T.D., *The Lisbon Earthquake* (Methuen, 1955)

Kent, Henry, *Kent's Directory for the year 1754* (London, 1754)

Labourdette, Jean-François, *La Nation Française à Lisbonne de 1669 à 1790 entre Colbertisme et Liberalisme* (Fondation Calouste Gulbenkian, Paris, 1988)

Leake, John, *A Dissertation on the Properties and Efficacy of the Lisbon Diet-Drink* (London, 1757)

Levret, A., 'The effects of the November 1, 1755 "Lisbon" earthquake in Morocco', *Tectonophysics*, Vol. 193 (1991), pp. 83–94

Lima, Durval R. Pires de, *O Terremoto de 1755 e A Freguesia de Sta Isabel de Lisboa* (Imprensa Lucas, Lisbon, 1930)

Lodge, Richard, 'The English Factory At Lisbon: Some Chapters In Its History', *Transactions Of The Royal Historical Society*, 4th Series, Vol. XVI (1932), pp. 211–42

Lodge, Richard (ed.), *The Private Correspondence of Sir Benjamin Keene, KB* (CUP, 1933)

Loupès, Philippe, '*Castigo de Dios*, le tremblement de terre de 1755 dans les publications espagnoles de circonstance', in *Lumières*, No. 6 (2005), pp. 77–93

Lousada, Maria Alexandre, and Henriques, Eduardo Brito, *Viver Nos Escombros: Lisboa Durante A Reconstrução*, in Araújo et al, pp. 183–97

Lüsebrink, Hans-Jürgen, 'Le tremblement de terre de Lisbonne dans les périodiques français et allemands du XVIIIe siècle', in Duranton and Rétat (eds), *Gazettes et information politique sous l'Ancien Régime* (Centre d'Études du XVIIIe siècle, Publications de l'Université de Saint-Étienne, 1999)

Macaulay, Rose, *They Went to Lisbon* (Jonathan Cape, 1946)

Macedo, Joaquim Antonio de, *A Guide To Lisbon and its environs, including Cintra and Mafra* (London, 1874)

Macedo, Luís, Pastor de, *Lisboa De Lés-a-Lés* (Publicações Culturais da Câmara Municipal de Lisboa, 1960)

Macedo, Luís, Pastor de, *A Rua das Pedras Negras* (Lisbon, 1931)

Macedo, Luís, Pastor de, *O terremoto de 1755 na Freguesia da Madalena* (Edição da Solução Editora, Lisbon, n.d.)

Madureira, Nuno, *Cidade: espaço e quotidiano (Lisboa 1740–1830)* (Livros Horizonte, Lisbon, 1992)

Mann, Julia De L (ed.), *Documents Illustrating the Wiltshire Textile Trades in the Eighteenth*

Century (Wiltshire Archaeological and Natural History Society, 1964)

Marques, José, 'The Paths of Providence: Voltaire and Rousseau on the Lisbon Earthquake', *Cadernos de História e Filosofia da Ciência*, Série 3, Vol. 15, No. 1 (January–June 2005), pp. 33–57

Matos, A. and Portugal, F., *Lisboa em 1758: Memórias Paroquiais de Lisboa* (Coimbra Editora, 1974)

Maxwell, Kenneth, *Conflicts and Conspiracies: Brazil and Portugal, 1750–1808* (Routledge, 2004)

Maxwell, Kenneth, *Naked Tropics* (Routledge, 2003)

Maxwell, Kenneth, 'Pombal and the Nationalization of the Luso-Brazilian Economy', *Hispanic American Historical Review*, Vol. 48, No. 4 (November 1968), pp. 608–31

Maxwell, Kenneth, *Pombal: Paradox of the Enlightenment* (CUP, 1995)

Mendonça, Joachim José Moreira de, *História Universal dos Terremotos* (Lisbon, 1758)

Mercator, *Letters on Portugal and its Commerce* (London, 1754)

Merveilleux, Charles Frédéric de, *Mémoires Instructifs pour un voyageur dans les divers états de l'Europe* (Amsterdam, 1738)

Michell, John, *Conjectures concerning the cause and observations of the phaenomena of earthquakes: particularly of that great earthquake of the first of November, 1755, which proved so fatal to the city of Lisbon* (London, 1760)

'MP', *Reflections Physical and Moral upon the various and numerous uncommon phenomena in the air, water or earth which have happened at Lisbon to the present time: letters from an MP to his friend in the country* (London, 1756)

Mullin, John R., 'The Reconstruction of Lisbon following the earthquake of 1755: a study in despotic planning', *Planning Perspectives*, Vol. 7 (1992), pp. 157–79

Murphy, James, *A general view of the state of Portugal* (London, 1798)

Murphy, James, *Travels in Portugal in the years 1789 and 1790* (London, 1795)

Murray, John, *Murray's Handbook For Travellers In Portugal* (London, 1856)

Murteira, Helena, *Lisboa da Restauração Às Luzes* (Editorial Presença, Lisbon, 1999)

Nason, Elias, *Sir Charles Henry Frankland, Baronet: or, Boston in the Colonial Times* (Albany, New York, 1865)

Nozes, Judite (ed.), *The Lisbon earthquake of 1755: some British eye-witness accounts* (The British Historical Society of Portugal/Lisóptima, Lisbon, 1990)

Nugent, Thomas, *The Grand Tour*, Vol. IV (London, 1749)

Oliveira, Eduardo Freire de, *Elementos para a história do municipio de Lisboa*, Vol. XVI (Typographia Universal, Lisbon, 1908)

Oliveira, Francisco Xavier de, *A Pathetic Discourse on the present Calamities of Portugal* (London, 1756)

Pedegache, Miguel Tibério, *Nova e Fiel Relação do Terremoto, que experimentou Lisboa, e todo Portugal no 1° de Novembro de 1755* (Lisbon, 1756)

Pedreira, Jorge, 'Costs and Financial Trends in the Portuguese Empire, 1415–1822', in Bethencourt and Curto, pp. 49–86

Pedreira, Jorge, 'From Growth to Collapse: Portugal, Brazil, and the Breakdown of the Old Colonial System (1760–1830)', *Hispanic American Historical Review*, Vol. 80, No. 4 (2000), pp. 840–64

Penn, Richard; Wild, Stanley and Mascarenhas, Jorge, 'The Pombaline Quarter of Lisbon: An Eighteenth Century Example Of Prefabrication and Dimensional Coordination', *Construction History*, Vol. 11 (1995), pp. 3–17

Pereira, Álvaro S., *The opportunity of a Disaster: The Economic Impact of the 1755 Lisbon earthquake*, Centre for Historical Economics and Related Research at York, Discussion Paper 03/2006

Pereira, Ângelo (ed.), *O Terramoto de 1755: Narrativa De Uma Testemunha Ocular* (Livraria Ferio, Lisbon, 1953)

Pereira, E.J., *The great earthquake of Lisbon*, in *Transactions of the Seismological Society of Japan*, Vol. 12 (1888), pp. 5–19

Pereira, José Fernandes et al., *Lisbon In The Age of Dom João V* (Instituto Portugues de Museus, Lisbon, 1994)

Poirier, Jean-Paul, *Le Tremblement de Terre de Lisbonne* (Odile Jacob, Paris, 2005)

Portal, Manuel, *História da ruina da cidade de Lisboa* (Lisbon, 1756)

Quenet, Grégory, *Les Tremblements de Terre aux*

XVIIe et XVIIIe Siècles: La Naissance d'un Risque (Champ Vallon, Seysel, 2005)

Reeves, Robert K., *The Lisbon Earthquake of 1755: Confrontation Between The Church And The Enlightenment In Eighteenth Century Portugal*, http://nisee.berkeley.edu/elibrary

Reid, Harry Fielding, 'The Lisbon earthquake of November 1, 1755', *Bulletin of the Seismological Society of America*, Vol. IV, No. 2 (June 1914), pp. 53–80

Rhys, Udal ap, *An Account of the Most Remarkable Places and Curiosities in Spain and Portugal* (London, 1749)

Rodrigues, Teresa, *A Vida Em Lisboa do Século XVI Aos Nossas Dias* (Edicões Cosmos, Lisbon, 1997)

Rossa, Walter, *Beyond Baixa: Signs of Urban Planning in Eighteenth Century Lisbon* (IPPAR, Lisbon, 1998)

Russell-Wood, A.J.R., *The Portuguese Empire, 1415–1808* (The John Hopkins University Press, 1998)

'Scots Gentleman', 'A short description of Lisbon, taken upon the spot, in the year 1745, by a Scots gentleman', *The Scots Magazine*, Vol. xvii (November 1755), pp. 560–3

Sequeira, Gustavo de Matos, 'A Cidade de D. João V', in *D. João V: conferêrencias e estudos comemorativos do segundo centenário da sua morte, 1750–1950* (Câmara Municipal de Lisboa, 1952)

Sequeira, Gustavo de Matos, *Depois do terremoto* (Academia das Sciências de Lisboa, 1916–34)

Serrão, Joel; Marques, A.H. de Oliveira and Meneses, Avelino de Freitas de, *Nova História de Portugal*, Vol. 7 (Editorial Presença, Lisbon, 2001)

Serrão, José Vicente, *Os Impactos Econónomicos Do Terramoto*, in Araújo et al., pp. 141–63

Shaw, L.M.E., *The Anglo-Portuguese Alliance and the English Merchants in Portugal, 1654–1810* (Ashgate, 1998)

Silva, Augusto Vieira da, *Dispersos* (Câmara Municipal de Lisboa, 1954–1960)

Smith, John Athelstane (Conde de Carnota), *Memoirs of the Marquis de Pombal* (London, 1871)

Solares, J.M. Martínez and Arroyo, A. López, 'The great historical 1755 earthquake: effects and damage in Spain', *Journal of Seismology*, Vol. 8 (2004), pp. 275–94

Sousa, Francisco Luiz Pereira de, *O terramoto de 1 de Novembre de 1755 em Portugal e um estudo demográfico* (Serviços Geológicos, Lisbon,1919)

Subtil, José, *O Terramoto Político (1755–1759)* (Universidade Autónoma de Lisboa, 2006)

Sutherland, L.S., 'The Accounts of an Eighteenth-Century Merchant: The Portuguese Ventures of William Braund', *Economic History Review*, Vol. 3, No. 3 (April 1932) pp. 367–87

Tavares, Rui, *O Pequeno Livro Do Grande Terramoto* (Tinta-da-china, Lisbon, 2005)

Twiss, Richard, *Voyages Through Portugal and Spain in 1772 and 1773* (London, 1775)

Vaughan, H.S. (ed.), *The Voyages and Cruises of Commodore Walker* (Cassell, 1928)

Villiers, John, 'Singers, Sailors, Watches and Wigs: Foreign Influences In Portugal In The Reign Of D. João V', *The British Historical Society of Portugal Fourteenth Annual Report* (1987), pp. 57–77

Voltaire (transl. and ed. Cuffe, Theo; introduction by Wood, Michael), *Candide, or Optimism* (Penguin Classics, 2005)

Walford, A.R., *The British Factory in Lisbon* (Instituto Británico em Portugal, Lisbon, 1940)

Whitefield, George, *A brief account of some Lent and other extraordinary processions and ecclesiastical entertainments seen last year at Lisbon* (London, 1755)

Whitefield, George, *A Letter To The Remaining Disconsolate Inhabitants of Lisbon* (London, 1755)

Whitefoord, Charles, *The Whitefoord Papers. Being the correspondence and other manuscripts of Colonel Charles Whitefoord and Caleb Whitefoord from 1739 to 1810* (Clarendon Press, 1898)

Young, George, *Portugal Old and Young* (Clarendon Press, 1917)

NEWSPAPERS AND JOURNALS

Gazeta de Lisboa

The Gentleman's Magazine

Household Words

Illustrated London News

The London Gazette

New Universal Magazine

The Penny Magazine

The Scots Magazine

Whitehall Evening Post

THESIS

Villiers, John, 'Portuguese Society in the Reigns of Pedro II and João V, 1680–1750', PhD thesis number 4441, Cambridge University, 1962

OTHER

TNA

The National Archives of the United Kingdom, Document Series SP/89 (State Papers Foreign, Portugal) and ADM (Admiralty)

PT

Philosophical Transactions of the Royal Society of London

MANUSCRIPTS (MS)

Agnew, Major-General Patrick
Family papers of the Agnew and Stuart-Menteath (Mentieth) families, British Library (India Office Records) Private Papers: Mss Eur E313/12

Bean, Thomas
Letter from Captain Bean on board the *Bean Blossome* at Faro, 5 December 1755, East Sussex Record Office, Archive of Drake and Lee ref SAS-DM/281

Chase, Thomas
Letter to his mother, Centre for Kentish Studies, Gordon Ward Collection U442 and British Library Add. 38510 ff. 7–14 'Narrative of his escape from the earthquake at Lisbon'

Devisme, Gerard
Account of 4 November 1755, British Library Add. 32860 f.354

Dobson, John
(i) Letter of John Dobson to Sir John Mordaunt 15 December 1755, Warwickshire County Record Office, CR1368/Vol. V item16

(ii) Letter of John Dobson to Mrs Philippa Hayes, housekeeper to George Lucy at Charlecote n.d., Warwickshire County Record Office, L6/1481

(iii) Letter from John Dobson to his uncle Sir Charles Mordaunt 25 March 1756, Warwickshire County Record Office, CR1368/Vol. V item16

With thanks to the Trustees of the Sir Richard Hamilton Will Trust

Drumlanrig, Lord (Charles Douglas)
Letters to his parents, the Duke and Duchess of Queensbury, 6 November 1755, 8 November 1755 and 19 November 1755, Gloucestershire Archives, D2700.W/4 (by kind permission of Duke of Beaufort)

Farmer, Benjamin
'Some account of Timothy Quidnunc, the author, by the Editor' *c.*1790, private collection

Farmer, James
Letter to Samuel Galton 2 December 1755, Galton Papers, Birmingham City Archives, MS3101/C/D/15/5/43

Goddard, Richard
(i) Letter dated 7 November 1755 from Richard Goddard to Thomas Goddard reporting the former's safety after an earthquake in Lisbon, Wiltshire and Swindon Archives (WSA): 1461/2732

(ii) Letter dated 22 October 1755 from Richard Goddard to Thomas Goddard, and letter dated 9 November 1755 from Richard Goddard to a friend, British Library Add. 69847 A-M item F

Hay, Hon. Edward
(i) Letter dated 4 November 1755 to Bishop of St Asaph, British Library Add. 32860 f.352

(ii) Letter dated 14 November to Lord Dupplin, British Library Eg. 3482 f.145

Hobart, Henry
'Journal of tours by Henry Hobart in Portugal and Spain', 20 June–9 September 1767, 31 May – 31 October 1768, and 28 March–27 July 1769, Norfolk Record Office, The Colman Manuscript Collection, Papers of the Reverend James Bulwer, COL/13/27

Jacomb, Thomas
Account of the Earthquake at Lisbon, British Library Add. 40015 f.39

Pitt, Thomas
i) 'Observations in a Tour to Portugal and Spain in 1760 by John Earl of Strathmore and Thomas Pitt Esq.', British Library Add. 5845, Vol. XLIV 'Mr Cole's collections, the contents of which are miscellaneous' ff.111–147

ii) Letter to Dean of Exeter 24 March 1760, British Library Stow 754, ff.48–9

Williamson, Reverend John
Letter of 20 November 1755 to Andrew Millar, British Library Add. 4326B f.214

PICTURE CREDITS

Index